ENLIGHTENED VAG

Buddha Shakyamuni

Guru Padmasambhava

Longchen Rabjam
(Longchenpa, 1308–1364)

Jigme Lingpa
(1729–1798)

Statue of Patrul Rinpoche, said to bear an accurate resemblance, made by his close disciples Önpo Tenga and Mura Tulku. About a foot high, it was placed as a relic inside another statue at Gemang Monastery and is therefore no longer visible. (Photo by Khenpo Dönnyi, ca. 1997)

Enlightened Vagabond

The Life and Teachings of Patrul Rinpoche

Tales of wisdom and compassion passed on by

Dilgo Khyentse Rinpoche · Dodrup Tenpai Nyima
Garchen Rinpoche · Khenpo Jampel Dorje
Khenpo Könchog Mönlam · Khenpo Kunpel · Khenpo Palga
Khenpo Ngawang Palzang · Khenpo Pema Wangyal
Khenpo Shönri · Khenpo Tsering Gonpo
Kunu Rinpoche Tendzin Gyaltsen · Nyoshul Khen Rinpoche
Nyoshul Lungtok Tenpai Nyima · Trogawa Rinpoche
Tsoknyi Rinpoche · Tulku Orgyen Tobgyal
Tulku Pema Wangyal · Tulku Thondup
Tulku Urgyen Chemchog · Tulku Urgyen Rinpoche
Yantang Rinpoche

Collected and translated from the Tibetan by
MATTHIEU RICARD

Edited by
CONSTANCE WILKINSON

Shambhala
BOULDER
2017

Shambhala Publications, Inc.
4720 Walnut Street
Boulder, Colorado 80301
www.shambhala.com

9 8 7 6 5 4 3 2 1

FIRST EDITION
Printed in the United States of America

♾ This edition is printed on acid-free paper that meets the American National Standards Institute z39.48 Standard.
♻ This book was printed on 30% post-consumer recycled paper.
For more information please visit www.shambhala.com.

Distributed in the United States by Penguin Random House LLC and in Canada by Random House of Canada Ltd

Designed by Michael Russem

LIBRARY OF CONGRESS CATALOGING-IN-PUBLICATION DATA
Names: Ricard, Matthieu. | Wilkinson, Constance, editor.
Title: Enlightened vagabond: the life and teachings of Patrul Rinpoche / collected and translated from the Tibetan by Matthieu Ricard; edited by Constance Wilkinson.
Description: First edition. | Boulder, Colorado: Shambhala, 2017. |
Includes bibliographical references and index.
Identifiers: LCCN 2016036699 | ISBN 9781611803303 (paperback)
Subjects: LCSH: O-rgyan-'jigs-med-chos-kyi-dbang-po, Dpal-sprul, 1808–1887. |
Rnying-ma-pa lamas—China—Tibet Autonomous Region—Biography. |
BISAC: RELIGION / Buddhism / Tibetan. | BIOGRAPHY & AUTOBIOGRAPHY / Religious.
Classification: LCC BQ7950.O767 E55 2017 | DDC 294.3/923092 [B]—dc23
LC record available at https://lccn.loc.gov/2016036699

CONTENTS

LIST OF ILLUSTRATIONS

THE DALAI LAMA

FOREWORD

Patrul Rinpoche, Orgyen Jigme Chökyi Wangpo, was one of the most influential Tibetan masters of the nineteenth century, renowned for the simplicity of his way of life, his dedication to spiritual practice, and his nonsectarian approach to all four schools of Tibetan Buddhism. Because he hailed from the region of Dzachukha in Kham, he was known as Dza Patrul Rinpoche. Emulating the homeless life of the Buddha and his followers, Dza Patrul lived the life of a wandering yogi with no settled abode and practiced in solitude.

He is particularly renowned for his putting into practice the instructions contained in Shantideva's *Way of the Bodhisattva* (*Bodhicharyavatara*), which he also taught extensively. Legend has it that whenever he taught this text, *serchen* flowers would bloom in the vicinity with many more petals than usual. These came to be known as "*Bodhicharyavatara* flowers," while Dza Patrul Rinpoche was known as the "*Bodhicharyavatara* Lama."

Loved for his humility and respected for his vast and profound knowledge, as well as his great yogic realization, he attracted disciples from all four schools of Tibetan Buddhism. Although there is no extensive written biography of Dza Patrul Rinpoche extant, his legacy lives on in tales that are told about him. Ven. Matthieu Ricard has compiled many of these in this book and so made them available to a wider readership. I commend him for the hard work he has put into this.

Traditionally, biographies of eminent spiritual masters are not just stories for the purpose of entertainment. They serve as an inspiration for those who come after to learn from. I pray that this new book about Dza Patrul Rinpoche will long fulfill this worthy purpose.

February 18, 2017

FOREWORD

Alak Zenkar Tudeng Nima

O you who shine with the light of blessings, endless, inexhaustible,
Bright dazzling orbs, like sun and moon, of knowledge and of love,
King of the Shakyas, mighty sage, and you the Guru, Lotus Born,
And you the Awareness-Holding Teachers of the threefold lineage,
Grant excellence and virtue!

The lord of the secret teachings of the tradition of the Old Translation, the mighty sovereign of learned and accomplished beings, whose name I scarcely dare to say—the supreme refuge and vajradhara Rabsel Dawa, Dilgo Khyentse Rinpoche, had as his attendant the Shakya Bhikshu Konchog Tendzin, better known as Matthieu Ricard, a person gifted with deep respect for the supreme qualities of holy beings. With great and persevering exertion, Matthieu has gathered, arranged, and translated the narratives about the Life and Perfect Liberation of the lord of erudition and realization, Dza Palge Tulku, Orgyen Jigme Chökyi Wangpo [Patrul Rinpoche], who was none other than the bodhisattva Shantideva, come again in human form in this degenerate age. In collaboration with the outstanding editor Constance Wilkinson (Dawa Chötso), he prepared this book for Shambhala Publications. I rejoice from the depth of my heart and from the marrow of my bones that, thanks to their endeavor, this volume is now available to English readers.

Indeed, the biographies of Patrul Rinpoche composed by Dodrup Tenpai Nyima and Khenpo Kunzang Palden have been used as a basis on which to place anecdotes passed down from Nyoshul Lungtok Tenpai Nyima (as recorded in Khenpo Ngawang Palzang's autobiography), from the biographies of Adzom Drukpa and Do Khyentse Yeshe Dorje, and from many oral accounts supplied by eighteen sublime masters, including that lord of refuge Dilgo Khyentse Rinpoche, Domang Yantang Rinpoche, Garchen Rinpoche, Khenpo Jampel Dorje, Khenpo Könchog Mönlam, Khenpo

Palga, Khenpo Pema Wangyal, Khenpo Shönri, Khenpo Tsering Gonpo, Kunu Lama Rinpoche Tendzin Gyaltsen, Nyoshul Khen Rinpoche, Trogawa Rinpoche, Tsoknyi Rinpoche, Tulku Orgyen Tobgyal, Tulku Pema Wangyal, Tulku Thondup, Tulku Urgyen Chemchog, and Tulku Urgyen Rinpoche.

This is indeed a wonderful achievement, the great benefits of which will shed the light of virtue and excellence in our time. Day after day, the bees of my praises will continue to hum melodiously among these delightful flowers, which will never close their petals.

The radiance of this perfect deed
Destroys the dark of suffering!
The stream of nectar, the transmitted lineage
Arising from this gathering of sublime beings,
Falls gently from the radiant moon of perfect liberation
And foretells a glorious spring—
The fully blossomed lilies of the Buddha's teaching.
May the kindliness of Konchog Tendzin,
Aid and instrument of the enlightened work
Of Brilliant Moon of Knowledge and of Love [Khyentse Rabsel Dawa],
Extend to the extremities of space.
May this deed done for others' sake
Now cover all the surface of the earth!

This was written with joy, admiration, and homage, on the 20th of December 2016, in the Tibetan year of the Fire Monkey, in a place not far from the American city of New York, by the humble servant Tudeng Nima [Alak Zenkar], *who offers it on the petals of his ten fingers held above his head.*

FOREWORD

Jigme Khyentse

Reading this book reminded me of the stories I used to hear as a child from my father, Kangyur Rinpoche, about his teachers, such as Jedrung Rinpoche. I heard similar stories from Kyabje Khyentse Rinpoche during the precious time I spent with him, and also from Nyoshul Khen Rinpoche when I was young. This book really brought these stories back to life for me. There is a little bit of Patrul Rinpoche in all my teachers. There is some of his uncompromising integrity in all of them.

I have known Matthieu since I was a child in Darjeeling when he first met my father, Kangyur Rinpoche. Later, during the time we spent together in the presence of Kyabje Dilgo Khyentse Rinpoche, I remember him relentlessly gathering stories with a tape recorder. Some of the stories he sought were from nomadic teachers from far East Tibet whose accents were difficult to understand, even for Tibetans.

Through such efforts, he has collated these precious stories in order for people to gain some sense of what Patrul Rinpoche was really like. Even though we know of Patrul Rinpoche through *The Words of My Perfect Teacher*, these stories enable us to take a more in-depth look at this extraordinary master. In a way, Matthieu's own history—that of a biologist from Paris who met Kangyur Rinpoche and then left his ordinary life behind to devote himself to following the same path illuminated in the stories he has gathered—is very much in keeping with the spirit of Patrul Rinpoche's life.

Patrul Rinpoche is both a reference and an inspiration. I often wonder, "What would Patrul Rinpoche do in this situation?" or "What would he think?" Even though he is not alive, he is still able to make us feel uncomfortable and to cut through the hypocrisy or insecurities that we have as students. This can transform our lives. Even if we try to ignore this uncomfortableness, his compassionate activity continues to haunt us in spite of our thick-skinned ignorance. I also feel that this book is invaluable for those who are studying

Kangyur Rinpoche

Patrul Rinpoche's writings such as *The Words of My Perfect Teacher*. It will give us a greater understanding of what he is transmitting.

Not every biography embodies the true meaning of "biography" in Tibetan, which is *namthar*, or complete liberation. I feel that this biography does, in the sense that, as we read it, it can liberate us from our confusion.

PREFACE

The stories in this book are based on both oral and written sources. In the 1970s, I began to write down the stories of Patrul Rinpoche (1808–1887) that I'd heard from my teachers, and also began reading some of Patrul Rinpoche's spiritual advice in Tibetan and translating them into English

The primary written sources for Patrul Rinpoche's life are two short traditional biographies (*namthar*) written by his own disciples. The first, *Dewdrop of Amrita*, written by Dodrup Tenpai Nyima, the 3rd Dodrupchen Rinpoche, describes the main events of Patrul Rinpoche's life as well as the places where he studied, taught, and practiced. It also contains a few anecdotes and offers a lively portrait of Patrul Rinpoche's unique qualities of being. The second biography, *Elixir of Faith*, written by Gegong Khenpo Kunzang Palden (better known as Khenpo Kunpel), is an elaboration of the prayer written by Jamyang Khyentse Wangpo to commemorate the main events of Patrul's life. This later biography incorporates most of Dodrup Tenpai Nyima's work, supplemented with information from other sources, especially the diaries of Sönam Tsering, the humble and devoted attendant from Amdo who served Patrul Rinpoche during most of the last part of the great sage's life.[1]

Despite the lack of a detailed written hagiography, a rich oral tradition recounting Patrul Rinpoche's life and teachings remains very much alive. Recent contemporary teachers have continued this tradition, such as Kyabje Dilgo Khyentse Rinpoche (who met Patrul's direct students, such as Lama Mipham, Khenpo Kunpel, Khenpo Shenga of Dzogchen, Jigme Gyalwai Nyugu's *tulku* Trama Tulku Kunzang Dechen, among others), Khenpo Pema Wangyal of Gemang, also a student of Khenpo Kunpel and Nyoshul Khen Rinpoche, just to cite a few. Other anecdotes come down to us from Patrul's heart-disciple Nyoshul Lungtok to his own student Khenpo Ngakchung (Khenpo Ngawang Palzang), and on to later disciples, very few of whom are still alive.[2] Through the family line of the great *tertön* Chokgyur Dechen Lingpa, whose three children were all direct disciples of Patrul, we have first-person accounts of events they themselves witnessed.

A wider local oral tradition provides other anecdotes, as stories of Patrul are widely venerated and continue to be extremely popular throughout Kham, Golok, and other regions of Tibet.

Please see the section "About the Contributors" for brief biographies of the sources listed on the title page.

As the contemporary master Nyoshul Khen Rinpoche told us, although one cannot confirm each and every detail in each and every story, all of these precious stories will certainly be lost unless preserved. Today, when I hear these stories retold by the younger generation in Kham or elsewhere, many of the accounts have already been diminished, losing both detail and substance. Therefore, the main intention here is not to offer exhaustive translations from the written biographies, but rather to use biographical material as a framework upon which to preserve the oral tradition.

I tried my best to arrange the stories in chronological order. For this I used the details available in the story: first, the approximate age of Patrul Rinpoche, whenever it could be guessed; second, the locations given in the stories. Some of these locations are quite far away from the Dzachukha region (where Patrul Rinpoche was born, spent a great part of his life, and passed away), and in many cases it is roughly known, according to written sources (biographies of Patrul and of other masters), at which time of his life he visited them. Knowing the areas, we also tried to figure out the routes that Patrul Rinpoche might have followed when going from one place to the other. In addition, the other teachers and students who are mentioned in the stories were a guide to the chronological order, since the dates of most of them are known and some chronological details are also found in the available biographies of these teachers.

This collection also includes some of the gems of spiritual advice found in Patrul Rinpoche's own writings (in the table of contents, these are indicated by small ornamental guillemets; in the text, they have italicized titles with small guillemets). Most of these selections are either pieces of advice given to students or spontaneous expressions of realization called vajra songs, drawn from Patrul Rinpoche's collected works.[3] These colorful, often lyrically beautiful compositions display Patrul's unique teaching style, combining uncompromising toughness with ironic humor, profound simplicity with deep understanding rooted in personal practice, and extraordinary compassion for all beings.

In the 1980s, I shared a preliminary manuscript of my translations with several friends, and a few of the stories later found their way into print. More recently, I included several stories that I heard from Nyoshul Khen Rinpoche in slightly different versions in *On the Path to Enlightenment: Heart Advice from the Great Tibetan Masters* (Boston: Shambhala Publications, 2013). The majority of the stories I collected appear here for the first time.

To add to the picture of Patrul's life and times, the book provides a series of short biographies of masters and disciples of Patrul Rinpoche as well as several important earlier figures who played an influential role in Patrul Rinpoche's life. Photographs, a lineage chart and a Patrul family tree, and a map of eastern Tibet are also included to enhance this portrait of the Enlightened Vagabond, to offer the reader a history of Patrul Rinpoche that is as complete as we have been able to make it.

Jamyang Khyentse Wangpo
(1820–1892)

Jamgön Kongtrul Lodrö Thaye
(1813–1899)

Chokgyur Dechen Lingpa (1829–1870),
with his hand- and footprints

Dilgo Khyentse Rinpoche
(1975)

Khenpo Ngawang Palzang,
also known as Khenpo Ngakchung
(1930s; Shechen Archives)

Tulku Urgyen Chemchog
(1988)

Nyoshul Khen Rinpoche
(1975)

Kunu Rinpoche Tendzin Gyaltsen
(1971)

Tulku Urgyen Rinpoche
(1989)

Khenpo Pema Wangyal
(2016)

Khenpo Shönri
(2002)

Khenpo Palga
(2016)

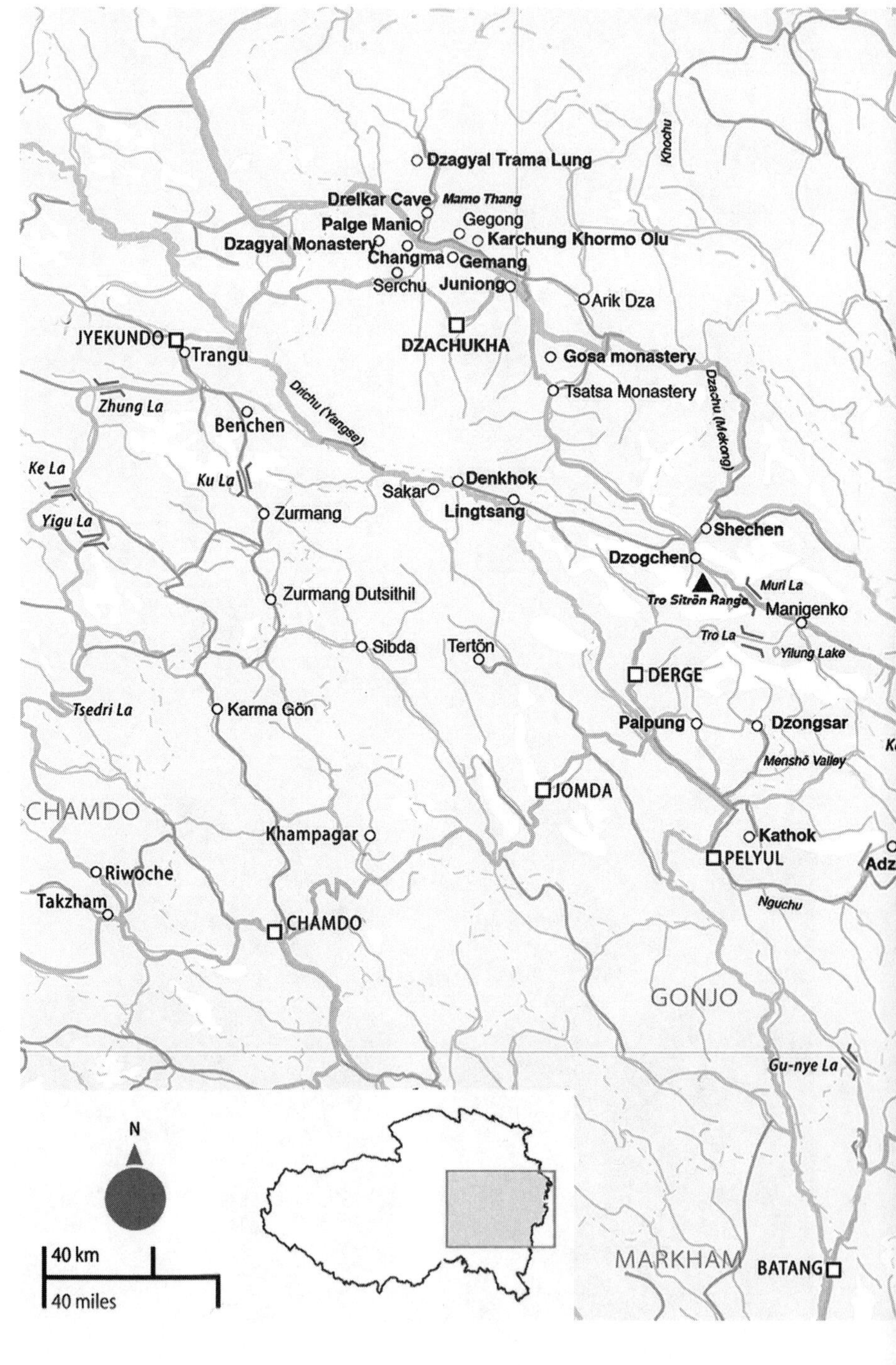

Dzagyal Trama Lung
Khochu
Drelkar Cave
Mamo Thang
Palge Mani
Gegong
Dzagyal Monastery
Karchung Khormo Olu
Changma
Gemang
Serchu
Juniong
Arik Dza
JYEKUNDO
DZACHUKHA
Trangu
Gosa monastery
Dzachu (Mekong)
Tsatsa Monastery
Zhung La
Drichu (Yangse)
Benchen
Ke La
Ku La
Sakar
Denkhok
Lingtsang
Zurmang
Yigu La
Shechen
Dzogchen
Muri La
Tro Sitrön Range
Manigenko
Zurmang Dutsithil
Tro La
Sibda
Tertön
Yilung Lake
DERGE
Tsedri La
Karma Gön
Palpung
Dzongsar
Menshö Valley
JOMDA
CHAMDO
Khampagar
Kathok
PELYUL
Riwoche
Takzham
CHAMDO
Nguchu
GONJO
Gu-nye La
N
40 km
40 miles
MARKHAM
BATANG

Nyenpo Yurtse
NGAWA
PADMA
EWA
GOLOK
Dodrupchen Monastery
Ari Forest
Shukchen Tago
Do River
SERTA
DZAMTHANG
Yarlung Pemakö
Larung Gar
BARKHAM
Trakar La
KHAM
RABDEN
KANDZE
Dzachu (Mekong)
TRANGO
GYALMO RONG
Zhechu
TAWU
RONGMI
NYAKRONG
Nedreheka La
Tromgo
Tsopu
Zhechu
Lauthang
Zara Lhatse
MINYAK
Ngul River
Dzachu (Mekong)
Lhagang
Gye La
DARTSEDO
CHAKZAMKA
Erhlan Shan
Li River
LITANG
Getse
Kabzhi La
Minyak Gangkar

INTRODUCTION

Patrul Rinpoche, Orgyen Jigme Chökyi Wangpo (1808–1887), a wandering practitioner in the ancient tradition of vagabond renunciants, became one of the most revered spiritual teachers in Tibetan history, widely renowned as a scholar and author, while at the same time living a life of utmost simplicity. A strong advocate of the joys of solitude, he always stressed the futility of worldly pursuits and ambitions. The memory of his life's example is still very much alive today, offering an ever-fresh source of inspiration for practitioners of Tibetan Buddhism.

An exemplary upholder of the purest Buddhist ideals of renunciation, wisdom, and compassion, Patrul Rinpoche spent most of his life roaming the mountains and living in caves, forests, and remote hermitages. When he left one place, he left with no particular destination; when he stayed somewhere, he had no fixed plans. In the wilderness, his favored meditation was the practice of cultivating *bodhichitta*—the wish to relieve all sentient beings from suffering and bring them to the ultimate freedom of enlightenment.

In youth Patrul studied with the foremost teachers of the time. With his remarkable memory, he learned most of the oral teachings he heard by heart, thus becoming able to elucidate the most complex aspects of Buddhist philosophy without referring to a single page of text, not even when he taught for months at a time.

Utterly uninterested in ordinary affairs, Patrul naturally abandoned the eight worldly concerns, which consist of everyone's ordinary hopes and fears—hoping for gain and fearing loss; hoping for pleasure and fearing pain; hoping for praise and fearing blame; hoping for fame and fearing disgrace.

Patrul generally refused to accept the offerings that are often made to a teacher or a respected religious figure according to tradition. Presented with valuable gifts such as gold and silver, he would leave them on the ground, abandoning them as easily as one abandons spit in the dust. In old age, however, he began to accept some offerings that he gave to beggars or used for making statues, building *mani* walls (amazing walls of sometimes hundreds of thousands of stones carved with the mani mantra, *Om mani padme hung*), making butter-lamp offerings, and engaging in other meritorious activities.

At the time of his death in his late seventies, Patrul Rinpoche's few personal possessions were much the same as they had been when he first set out as a renunciant: two texts—*The Way of the Bodhisattva* and *The Root Verses on the Middle Way*—a begging bowl, a red wool pouch holding his yellow monk's shawl, a prayer wheel, his walking stick, and a little metal pot for boiling tea.[4]

Patrul Rinpoche is remembered today by illustrious contemporary masters as a contemplative and scholar who, through his practice, achieved the highest realization of ultimate reality. Dilgo Khyentse Rinpoche affirmed that Patrul was unsurpassed in his realization of the view, meditation, and conduct of Dzogchen. His Holiness the 14th Dalai Lama often praises Patrul Rinpoche's teachings on bodhichitta, which he himself practices and transmits.

While in retreat at remote places, Patrul wrote profound original treatises, most of which have survived.[5] He spontaneously composed many poems and pieces of spiritual advice; many of these vanished into the hands of the individuals for whom they were written.

His best-known work, composed in a cave above Dzogchen Monastery, is *The Words of My Perfect Teacher*. Composed in a blend of classical and colorful colloquial Tibetan, it is one of the most widely read teaching instructions on the preliminary practices of the Nyingma school. Revered by all four schools of Tibetan Buddhism, it has been translated into many languages.

Patrul Rinpoche collected and wrote down in essentialized form the pith instructions of his own masters on Great Perfection (Dzogchen) meditations, as, for instance, in his famous commentary on *Three Sentences That Strike the Vital Point*[6] by Garab Dorje.

Patrul Rinpoche knew almost by heart the famed *Seven Treasuries*[7] and other works of the fourteenth-century Tibetan master Gyalwa Longchen Rabjam, also known as Kunkhyen (Omniscient) Longchenpa, whom he considered the ultimate authority on the Buddhist path. Yet Patrul was beyond any need to display his immense knowledge and realization, and he taught in a manner that was immediately accessible to even the most simple-minded listeners, imparting teachings that pointed directly to the very heart of spiritual life. Patrul Rinpoche taught followers of all schools, without partiality.

Like his contemporaries Jamgön Kongtrul Lodrö Thaye, Jamyang Khyentse Wangpo, and Lama Mipham Rinpoche, he played a major role in the development of the nonsectarian Rime movement that flourished in the nineteenth century, contributing to the revival of Tibetan Buddhism at a time when many rare lineages and practices had been on the verge of extinction.

Patrul Rinpoche's rugged lifestyle was in sharp contrast to the ecclesiastic pomp and ceremony often found in large monasteries, a striking reminder to everyone high and low of the humility and simplicity at the heart of Lord Buddha's teachings. Living as an ordinary person and a mendicant, he was nevertheless revered by all, from simple nomads to the greatest masters of his times. His unyielding emphasis on actual contemplative practice, impeccable conduct, and unstinting compassion in action has set a high spiritual standard for Buddhists of all schools and traditions.

The two short written biographies offer a general account of the great master's life, along with glowing praise for his matchless achievements, and include a few inspiring anecdotes. But we would indeed like to know more about the life of such an extraordinary being. I feel therefore very fortunate to have been able to collect, over more than thirty years, a large number of oral stories that were recounted with great love and enthusiasm by the spiritual heirs of Patrul Rinpoche's lineage, some of whom actually met Patrul Rinpoche's direct disciples. In a culture in which oral transmission still plays an important role, Tibetans are known for their ability to retain and retell stories in great detail. When hearing them, one often has the feeling of witnessing the events as they took place. They provide vivid glimpses into the ways of a highly realized being as he interacts with people, conveys the Buddhist teachings both formally and informally, and lives his everyday life, which is both astonishing and humble, often quite humorous, and the perfect illustration of inner freedom.

A white stone marks the place where Patrul Rinpoche was born in a nomad tent in Karchung Khormo Olu, Kham. (2016)

ENLIGHTENED VAGABOND

Beginnings

Patrul Rinpoche was born in the Male Earth Dragon Year (1808), at Karchung Khormo Olu, in the Dzachukha region of Kham.[8] Located near the northernmost of the six ranges of Kham, Dzachukha is the remote high-altitude grassland along the Dza River, the faraway source of the Mekong.[9]

The air there is thin, the sky horizon vast and bright. The region features wide plains curling between rolling hills that later rise up into glaciered snow mountains.

There are few farmers in Dzachukha, as only a handful of crops can survive the harsh, short-summered climate. Most who dwell on the high-altitude pastures are nomadic herders whose livelihood has depended for thousands of years on raising horses, yak, and sheep.

With no permanent abode beyond their yak-hair tents, these pastoral nomads are constantly on the move, changing locations two to four times a year, driving their precious livestock from one high grassland to another, moving according to the seasons, in search of the best pasturage for grazing.

At the time of Patrul's birth, the Chögyal (King) of Derge ruled Dzachukha. Patrul's father's family belonged to the Upper Getse branch of the celestially descended Mukpo Dong[10] clan that had provided thirty-five hereditary ministers to the Kings of Derge. Patrul's father was called Gyaltok Lhawang; his mother was Drolma, daughter of the Je-Ngö family of Dromza. They lived in a prosperous nomadic community at Dru Karchung Khohor, also known as Khormo Olu, in Upper Getse, in Dzachukha.

He thus spent his early years in the peaceful, vast, and open landscape of the high-altitude plateaus and rolling hills surrounding the upper course of the Mekong River, blanketed with a myriad of flowers in the height of summer and parched by frost in the harsh winters. These are places where the outer landscapes are naturally conducive to an expansive inner life and contemplative practice.

The Palge Lineage

The name Patrul (the "incarnation of Pal") comes from the name of the Palge lineage. The first Palge Lama was Samten Phuntsok. Manjushri was his tutelary deity (*yidam*), and he had recited *Chanting the Names of Manjushri*[11] more than a hundred thousand times.

The story is told that once, when Palge Samten Phuntsok was on the way to visit Upper Dromza, he stopped in a place called Mamo Thang, the Plain of the Mamos,[12] to rest his mule. There he had a vision in which he heard the spontaneous sound of the mani mantra pervading the whole area. In accordance with this auspicious omen, Samten Phuntsok chose Mamo Thang as the site for his residence, known as the Palge Labrang,[13] also known as Palge Samten Ling.

A great geomancer named Detö Pönmo had come to Mamo Thang years before. She, too, had been struck by the auspicious geography of this wide floodplain, and wrote:

East: sun and moon, like offerings of light;
South: a sweet-smelling forest, like an offering of incense;
West: snow mountains, like an offering of tormas;
South: the cooling Dza River, like an offering of water.

She predicted that building a sacred monument in Mamo Thang would bring great benefit to sentient beings. Accordingly, Palge Samten Phuntsok erected a mani wall.

The wall was made of more than one hundred thousand flat stones, each engraved with the mantra *Om mani padme hung*[14] and various mantras, sacred texts, and sacred images, carved by hand. This huge wall of mani stones towered higher than a man's head and was twice as wide; eventually it extended for nearly a mile. The wall was dedicated to the benefit of all sentient beings—anyone who saw it, touched it, circumambulated it, kept it in mind, or even merely heard of its existence. After the death of Palge Samten Phuntsok, a stupa with white designs containing his relics was built along the Palge Mani Wall.[15]

The next Palge tulku was found in the Ralo family of the Gya tribe, and became known as Palge Umdze. Recognized by the 3rd Dzogchen Rinpoche, Ngedön Tendzin Zangpo, he manifested wondrous qualities from an early age, declaring as a child, "I'm the one who built the hundred-thousand-mani wall!" Palge Umdze enlarged the wall as an adult.

Once, while he was giving teachings to a crowd of people in Upper Dromza, his ceremonial hat fell off his head and into the lap of a local girl, Drolma—whereupon he said, "My next rebirth will be as her son."

When he was twenty-five, Palge Umdze decided to go to Lhasa. The night before he was to leave, he visited the Gya Kathok family. After he left them, the family found some ritual objects that he had left behind. When the family tried to return them to him, the tulku refused, saying, "I won't be needing those for the time being."

He set out for Lhasa and suddenly fell ill shortly after arriving. He died near the hermitage of Götsang. At the place where his body was cremated, even though it was the dead of winter, flowers burst into bloom. The local people built a stupa to contain the relics of this unusual young lama from Kham.

Advice was sought from Taklung Matrul Rinpoche,[16] a lama renowned for his clairvoyance, as to where the Palge Tulku would take rebirth. The lama gave clear indications for finding the tulku.

The epithet "Palge Tulku" can be abbreviated as Paltrul or Patrul (*trulku* is an alternative way of phoneticizing *tulku*). Thus, the Palge Tulku would become known as Dza Patrul Rinpoche, or Patrul from Dzachukha.

View of the Dzachukha region, where Patrul Rinpoche was born. (2006)

Infant Patrul

On the day Patrul was born, his mother reported that the family's tent dwelling became filled with white light.

The newborn infant began to speak at once. At first, he said just a few short syllables—*a, o, om.* By the next night, he was heard murmuring, "*Om mani padme hung,*"[17] the six-syllable mantra of Avalokiteshvara, who embodies the compassionate aspect of enlightenment. Every day, the mantra became more and more distinct, until after five days, his mantra recitation was perfectly clear. The six syllables of the mani mantra were visible on his wrist; on his tongue was a red syllable *dhi,* the seed syllable of Manjushri, the wisdom aspect of enlightenment.

His mother noticed all these signs but kept them to herself, not even telling her husband. She did not want people teasing and saying sarcastic things like "Oh, the son of a well-born mother *always* turns out to be a tulku!" If her son *were* indeed a high incarnation, she did not want any obstacles to arise for him through his having been recognized prematurely.

However, soon, the infant's exceptional qualities became evident to all. He was recognized as a tulku by Dola Jigme Kalzang, a great master of the Longchen Nyingthig teachings, the "Heart Essence of the Great Expanse." Dola Jigme reported his discovery to his teacher Jigme Trinley Özer, the 1st Dodrupchen.

Confirming the choice, he said, "You were right to recognize this child as the tulku of the Palge Lama. He will be known as Orgyen Jigme Chökyi Wangpo (Fearless Lord of Dharma from Orgyen).[18] Through my prayers, I will entrust to him the entire Longchen Nyingthig lineage."

Not long afterwards, a group of important monks and lamas arrived at the home of Patrul's parents to pay their respects to the newly recognized tulku, headed by the *umdze,* a senior monk. Just as they came in, Patrul's mother was taking the infant to her breast. Patrul, however, did not nurse, but turned away from his mother. Looking directly at the senior monk, the child said, "Uncle,[19] are you all right? You've gotten *old*!"

Patrul's Root Guru

The nephew of the prior Palge Lama, Önpo Könchog, was in charge of the Palge estates as treasurer-administrator. He brought the young tulku to the

A thangka of Jigme Gyalwai Nyugu that Patrul Rinpoche always kept with him. Preserved at Khormo Olu, Kham, with other relics of Patrul Rinpoche. (2016)

Palge Labrang, the large stone mansion that Palge Samten Phuntsok had built and that now served as the main residence of the Palge tulkus. At his enthronement ceremony, Patrul first met Jigme Gyalwai Nyugu, the highly accomplished practitioner who would become his root guru.[20]

Jigme Gyalwai Nyugu, the heart-disciple of Jigme Lingpa, had spent many years in solitary retreat on a windswept mountainside of Dzagyal Trama Lung, Valley of Dry Twigs.[21]

For his retreat, this master did not take shelter in cave or a retreat hut but lived out in the open, below a natural overhang or in a shallow hollow in the ground. Taking his nourishment from wild plants and roots, he was the very model of a determined ascetic, having simplified his life down to bare essentials. Gyalwai Nyugu made a vow to remain where he was until he had achieved realization.

Jigme Gyalwai Nyugu often came to the Palge Labrang to teach Patrul, beginning when the tulku was very young. He confided to his old disciple Umdze Sangye Palzang, "When I come to Upper Dza, it's only for the sake of the Palge Tulku."

Little Monk

As a youth, Patrul traveled through Golok, a wild nomad area north of Dzachukha, in the company of his teacher, Jigme Gyalwai Nyugu, and his teacher's teacher, the 1st Dodrupchen, Jigme Trinley Özer. Ahead of them they saw a large nomad encampment and decided to approach.

A young man was standing at the entrance of a large black yak-hair tent. He asked the lamas, "Where have you just come from?"

"We've come from Dokhok," they answered.

"Can you perform rituals for the dead? My mother died a few days ago. We've already sent for a lama, but it will be a long time before he arrives. The nearest lama lives three days' journey away."

"Yes," they replied, "we can do it."

The three visitors were invited into the tent and were given seats on nice white wool felt carpets. A formal request was then made, with the presentation of ceremonial white silk scarves, that they perform rituals and prayers to benefit the recently deceased mother of the family.

The two older lamas, Dodrup Jigme Trinley Özer and Jigme Gyalwai

Nyugu, were offered tea. They both remained inside the tent doing preliminary prayers. Young Patrul went outside and busied himself making tormas and preparing offerings for the main ritual, *phowa,* the transference of consciousness to a buddhafield, a pure land where enlightenment will ultimately be attained.

While Patrul was working, the daughter of the family kept interrupting his work, asking that he *please* give her a hand to start the fire, *please* keep a sharp watch over the boiling milk, and so on. Each time, she addressed Patrul in a casual way, calling him *benchung,* "little monk."

After a while, everything was ready. The three lamas performed the ritual for the dead known as Spontaneous Liberation from Suffering, an Avalokiteshvara practice, or *sadhana,* from Jigme Lingpa's Longchen Nyingthig cycle.

The three lamas stayed on and spent the night. The next morning, as they were getting ready to leave, the father of the household begged them, "Please stay with us longer! At best, stay for three years. If not, stay for three months. At least, stay for three more days!"

"No, we can't stay. We must go on," the lamas replied.

"Well, at least, please let us know your names," asked the father.

"In all honesty," replied the young Patrul, "these two are very great lamas. The one with white hair is Jigme Trinley Özer. The gray-haired one is Jigme Gyalwai Nyugu."

The man was astonished; he had indeed heard of these two famous lamas.

"And who might you be?" the father asked Patrul.

"Oh, I'm Abu Ullo," Patrul answered, casually referring to himself by a family nickname. "Just a kid!"

The nomad family was overwhelmed with devotion and asked for the lamas' blessings. As the three lamas were leaving, the son offered each of them a fine horse with full riding gear. Wealthy nomads often gave just such valuable offerings to lamas, in gratitude for their having performed rituals for the dead.

"Please keep your horses," the lamas said. "We have no need of lavish offerings. Even if you offered us pure gold, we would not accept it. Some tea leaves and *tsampa* would be welcome, though, since we have none."

This was done. When the three lamas set off, the whole nomad family came along with them as escorts and accompanied them for a day's walk along the way, such was the respect they felt.

Patrul Takes On a Powerful Adversary

Patrul was an endearing child of robust constitution, natural gentleness, and sharp intelligence, someone who quickly earned affection and praise from all sides. He was full of loving-kindness and compassion. He never harmed others and would not tolerate others doing harm. Seeing sheep being led off to slaughter, he would burst into tears and refuse to eat or drink for some time.

First known for his compassion, as he matured, he became known for his eloquence: he was able to persuade people to stop hunting foxes and killing other wild animals.

Eventually, he also became known for his courage. For example, Palge treasurer-administrator Önpo Könchog became embroiled in a bitter legal dispute; the case had to be heard by the official representative of the King of Derge.

The opposition was led by a powerful Dzachukha official, Bunshul Thuthop Namgyal. By repeatedly defeating his oral arguments, Patrul demonstrated his exceptional skill in debate and succeeded in winning the case for Önpo Könchog. After this remarkable and completely unexpected victory, Önpo Könchog was heard to say, "Whether or not that young man is the real Palge Tulku, he sure has guts!"

From Jigme Gyalwai Nyugu, Patrul received teachings on the preliminary practices of Rigdzin Jigme Lingpa's Longchen Nyingthig lineage. He received these teachings from his root guru on at least twenty-five different occasions. Patrul accomplished the practices thoroughly, in addition to completing many other meditation practices and recitations of the Vajrayana.

Jigme Gyalwai Nyugu taught Patrul yogic practices involving the subtle channels and energies according to the Longchen Nyingthig tradition. He also gave him the oral instructions and personal guidance on the essential practices of Dzogchen, the Great Perfection. He bestowed upon Patrul numerous empowerments from the uninterrupted continuous transmission of the Kahma, the major texts of the ancient Nyingma tradition.[22]

The Palge Tulku Goes His Own Way

When Patrul was about twenty, the powerful treasurer-administrator of the Palge Labrang, Önpo Könchog, passed away. After his death, Patrul made the decision to renounce all worldly affairs so that he could devote himself entirely to practicing the dharma.[23]

Patrul closed his official residence and settled all the financial affairs of the Palge Labrang estate. He renounced all the material wealth and properties due to him as the recognized incarnation of the prior Palge tulkus. Like his teacher, Jigme Gyalwai Nyugu, Patrul chose to simplify his life in order to reach his spiritual goal, realization for the sake of all beings.

Unlike his teacher, who had vowed to remain practicing in one place until enlightenment, Patrul chose to become a wandering practitioner following the tradition of vagabond renunciants, without any permanent abode, not unlike the pastoral nomads among whom he had been raised.

Perhaps reflecting his decision to abandon the high social position, property, possessions, and comfortable life of a recognized incarnation, Patrul would later write:

When you're eminent, it's bad.
When you're reviled, it's good.
When your position is lofty, vanity and envy flourish.
When your position is lowly, you're at ease and your practice can flourish.
The lowest seat is the abode of great masters of the past.

When you've got wealth, it's bad.
When you've got next to nothing, it's good.
When you've got wealth, increasing it and preserving it are a nuisance.

When you've got next to nothing, you'll progress in practice.
If you've got just the bare necessities, it's the perfect dharma life.[24]

There had been predictions that Patrul would become a *tertön,* a revealer of spiritual treasures (*terma*), and that, accordingly, he should live as a married yogi rather than as a celibate monk, since tertöns usually need to associate with a spiritual consort in order to gather all the auspicious connections needed to rediscover the termas they have been entrusted with by Guru Padmasambhava.[25]

However, Patrul was not inclined to marry, and strictly adhered to the monastic vow of celibacy.

So as not to disrupt any auspicious connections and thereby risk shortening his life span, he took the 33 vows of a novice monk (*getsul*) rather than the 253 vows of a fully ordained monk (*gelong*). Patrul received the *getsul* ordination from Khenpo Sherab Zangpo of Dzogchen Monastery and was given the monastic name Jigme Gewai Jungne (Fearless Source of Virtue).

Not to countermand the prediction that he should be a yogi, he chose to dress as a layman, not a monk, though in all other respects Patrul maintained monastic discipline purely and completely. He observed the monastic practices of begging for food each morning, not eating after midday, and not keeping more food than necessary for his immediate use.

Dressed either in a thick white felt coat, or *chuba,* or in the sheepskin garment worn in winter, Patrul set out on his own. He took with him no possessions beyond his begging bowl, teapot, and a copy of *The Way of the Bodhisattva* (*Bodhicharyavatara*)[26] by Shantideva. He always made his way on foot, forgoing horseback. Sometimes he traveled in the company of others and sometimes he traveled alone. He lived in accordance with the wisdom of masters:

> Wherever you've stayed, leave nothing behind but the trace of your seat.
> Wherever you've walked, leave nothing behind but your footprints.
> Once you've put on your shoes, let there be nothing else left.

Now living in an absence of ordinary commitments, Patrul had set himself free; without agenda, his life became spontaneous and complete. He was able to stay in one place as long as he wished and no longer. When he felt it was time to move on, he could just get up and go, without giving it a second thought.

From that instant of bold decision until his last breath, Patrul remained a vagabond renunciant, devoting his entire life to the dharma.

After leaving Palge Samten Ling, Patrul stayed in the area around Dzogchen Monastery, where he received extensive teachings from the abbot of Dzogchen Monastery, Mingyur Namkhai Dorje, and from Gyalse Shenphen Thaye.[27]

During that period, to complete his education, Patrul also went to Shechen Monastery, one of the six main monasteries of the Nyingma tradition in Tibet.[28] Located between Nangdo and Dzogchen monasteries, it was founded in 1695 by Shechen Rabjam Tenpai Gyaltsen. There Patrul studied the Tripitaka, the three collections of the Buddha's teachings; *Thirteen Great Treatises,*[29] and the works of Kunkhyen Longchen Rabjam and Rigdzin Jigme Lingpa; as well as the major writings of all the Tibetan Buddhist traditions.

Shinje Druphuk, known as the Yamantaka Cave, where Patrul Rinpoche wrote *The Words of My Perfect Teacher.* The monk at the door of the cave has been living there since 2009. (2016)

Patrul the Scholar

While Patrul was at the Shechen Philosophical College, or *shedra,* to continue his education with Shechen Öntrul Thuthop Namgyal, among his fellow students were two illustrious young tulkus, Jamyang Khyentse Wangpo and Jamgön Kongtrul Lodrö Thaye.

Now, Khyentse Wangpo's provisions were always more than sufficient for his needs, since his aristocratic father came from a wealthy and powerful family. Jamgön Kongtrul always had plenty, since his family was fairly well off and lived nearby. Patrul, however, for some unknown reason, frequently ran out of food. It was his habit to polish off the leftover scraps on the plates of his fellow scholars. After he was done eating, Patrul enjoyed a nice nap. Whenever he did this, Khyentse and Kongtrul used to give him a hard time, telling Patrul he ought to be *studying*, not snoring!

"What's the matter with you? You just wolf down our food and go to sleep!" they'd complain. "What's that got to do with studying?"

"If I can recite what our teacher said, isn't that good enough?" asked Patrul.

"Of course! But to do that, you need to study, don't you?"

Patrul shook his head. "I've got nothing to worry about. All I have to do is repeat what I've heard in class."

And so it went. Kongtrul and Khyentse diligently studied every day after classes, while Patrul diligently gobbled up their leftovers and took his daily nap.

Once, after teachings were done, the three students returned to their monastic cells as usual. Patrul was eating tsampa, a traditional snack made by mixing roasted barley flour with tea and butter. When he finished, he covered his head with his shawl, leaned back, and was just about to doze off when his friends suddenly interrupted him.

Jamgön Kongtrul nudged Patrul, saying, "Wake up, friend. We need you to explain a few things to us!"

Removing the shawl from his head, Patrul replied, "What would you like me to explain?"

"Won't you tell us what we were taught today?" said Jamgön Kongtrul. "We can't remember." He and Khyentse exchanged mischievous glances; they were sure they'd find Patrul at a loss.

Patrul replied enthusiastically, "Sure!"

To the amazement of both of his fellow students, Patrul proceeded to repeat virtually word for word the entirety of the text and commentary that had been spoken aloud just that morning by Shechen Öntrul. Like a replica made from a mold, it was exact.

Kongtrul and Khyentse had to acknowledge that Patrul—like the famed Rongzom Mahapandita[30]—had the ability to commit the teachings to memory merely by hearing them once.

PATRUL SPENT SOME YEARS in the wilderness of Rudam above Dzogchen Monastery. He was staying at the Shinje Cave, also known as the Yamantaka Cave, when he composed his famous work *The Words of My Perfect Teacher* (Kunzang Lamai Shelung), a guide to the preliminary practices of the Longchen Nyingthig cycle.

When he stayed at the cave known as Long-Life Cave,[31] high on a steep slope opposite Yamantaka Cave, it is said that his realization of the Great Perfection became as vast as the sky.

Do Khyentse Takes Patrul by Surprise

Patrul felt deep devotion toward the wild yogi Do Khyentse Yeshe Dorje, a realized practitioner and great *siddha* known for his spontaneous and unpredictable behavior. Do Khyentse was recognized as the incarnation of Jigme Lingpa.[32]

Once, Do Khyentse decided to travel to Patrul's home province of Dzachukha. He set out on foot and, miraculously, arrived in record time! Yet he insisted that he'd only left that same morning—on a journey that normally takes two weeks on horseback.

Patrul had been staying in the area of caves and hermitages above Dzogchen Monastery. When Patrul heard the news of Do Khyentse's arrival, he instantly set off to find him. He went into town and found his teacher sitting outside Dzogchen village.

As Patrul came into view, Do Khyentse called out, "Hey, Patrul! If you're so brave, why don't you come over here?"

As he drew closer, Patrul realized that Do Khyentse must have been drinking—his breath stank of *chang,* the potent Tibetan brew made from fermented barley. Remembering the Buddha's teachings on the harmful effects of alcohol, Patrul began to wonder: "So, even a great master can get dead drunk and behave boorishly?"

At that very moment, Do Khyentse grabbed Patrul, threw him violently to the ground, and started dragging him along by his hair. Then Do Khyentse loosened his grip and roughly flung Patrul away.

Do Khyentse glared at him fiercely. "*Pah!*" he cried, spitting in Patrul's face. "You old dog—your head is still stuffed full of concepts!"

In Tibetan culture, to call someone "Old Dog" is a very serious insult. What's more, Do Khyentse gave Patrul the little finger—a sign of utter contempt—and began pelting him with stones. After hitting him square in the back, Do Khyentse stalked off and disappeared.

It took a moment for Patrul to understand what had just happened. Shaken, nearly in shock, he realized he'd completely missed the point!

It struck him that Do Khyentse had just given him a profound direct teaching on the true nature of mind. Filled with grateful devotion toward his teacher, Patrul sat down in a meditation posture and began to rest the mind in naked awareness—vast, spontaneously arising, clear as a cloudless sky, free of discursive thought.

Later in life, he would say that *Old Dog* was the secret initiation name kindly bestowed upon him by his master, Do Khyentse.

Indeed, Patrul later signed many of his texts "Old Dog."

» *A Piece of Advice* «

At all times and in all situations, examine your mindstream moment by moment: are thoughts positive or negative? When you recognize a thought to have negative content, be aware of its potential for harm and lay it aside. This is crucial.

Otherwise, when craving or other negative thoughts start to take shape, if you let them take hold, who knows where you'll wind up in the end?

You may not care about becoming a great scholar, but at least do your best to generate goodwill toward others and steadfast devotion to the Three Jewels.

Your future rebirths stretch out ahead much farther than this one life. The circumstances of those lifetimes will depend on your current aspirations, positive or negative. Don't jeopardize your future lives by seeking fame and status in this life.

The rest of this life will depend on how stable your virtuous aspirations are. See if you can transform your mindstream through the teachings.

You have come to a fork in the road: one path goes up, the other down. If you wait till you're on your deathbed to make your choice, you'll be out of luck.

Whether others have good or bad qualities is hard to know. Whether others applaud you or criticize you, you need to turn away from both craving praise and avoiding blame.

Though you may not accomplish great acts of merit, at least avoid evil actions, great or small.

Stop thinking badly of other beings. Don't speak ill of *anyone,* because you never know when the person you malign might be a sublime being.

In terms of food, clothes, and other material things, be content with what you've got and just stay put.

Otherwise, one day you'll end up a nuisance in everyone's eyes, a show-off in robes who just rambles on from one valley to the next, sniffing around like a stray dog.

Don't do that!

Written by Patrul.
May it bring virtue!

Patrul Tries to Offer Prostrations

While living in Rudam above Dzogchen Monastery, Patrul decided to come down to the monastery to make an offering of one hundred thousand prostrations to his teacher Mingyur Namkhai Dorje, the 4th Dzogchen Rinpoche. Mingyur Namkhai Dorje was a greatly realized being; his behavior was unconventional and unpredictable, not unlike that of the yogi Do Khyentse.

As soon as Patrul began to make his very first prostration, his teacher exclaimed, "*Ya!* Abu,[33] you're here!"

He got up from his throne and began prostrating to Patrul. Every time Patrul started trying to prostrate, his teacher sprang up in an instant and began prostrating to Patrul. A bit later, Patrul tried a few times to prostrate again, but the same thing happened over and over.

Finally, Patrul found a spot in back of Mingyur Namkhai Dorje's throne, well out of the way, and more important, out of his lama's line of sight. There, well hidden, Patrul at last was able to complete his offering of one hundred thousand prostrations.

Patrul's Teacher Demonstrates Clairvoyance

Thieves had broken into the main temple at Dzogchen Monastery and stolen some jewel ornaments from around the neck of a large statue. Everyone was extremely puzzled, since the temple had been locked and the ornaments were in a high, seemingly unreachable place.

When someone told the story to Mingyur Namkhai Dorje, he said, "Of course I know who the thief is, and I know how he did it. The thief sneaked in and somehow found a way up to that very narrow ledge that encircles the temple, the one high up, almost near the ceiling. He carefully walked along its edge till he came close to the great statue's head. Reaching over it with a long stick, he unhooked the jeweled ornaments from the statue, and lifted them up and away."

The monks checked the scene. They soon found footprints along the narrow ledge and they discovered the thief's long stick. Mingyur Namkhai Dorje refused to reveal the thief's identity, however, knowing that if the thief were to be caught, he would be badly beaten.

Later, some pilgrims came to meet Mingyur Namkhai Dorje and receive his blessing. They had only a brief audience, so they couldn't ask many questions. Instead, they requested Patrul to speak on their behalf.

Patrul agreed and later went to Mingyur Namkhai Dorje, obtained answers for all the pilgrims' questions, and presented their requests for prayers and protection. After doing so, Patrul got up to leave and began looking around as if he had lost something.

Mingyur Namkhai Dorje said to Patrul, "*Eh!* Looking for your bootstrap, are you? You'll find it at the end of that meadow over there near the small river flowing through Dzogchen Valley."

As Patrul made his way back from the monastery to the Shinje Cave, his trail led near the river. There, Patrul saw his bootstrap, which had fallen off his boot—just where his clairvoyant teacher had said it would be found.

Patrul Lectures Himself on His Practice

Patrul was living in a small black yak-hair tent in a meadow above Dzogchen Monastery. One day some people nearby heard him berating himself, saying, "Your practice today was *awful*! You don't deserve any food!"

After saying this, Patrul wouldn't let himself eat. Sometimes he'd even chastise himself by giving himself a good slap.

On other days, he was overheard remarking to himself, "*Hmm.* That was all right. Okay, not too bad today."

Patrul Receives a Special Transmission

At a time when Patrul was practicing meditation alone in a cave, he heard someone outside loudly calling his name:

"Patrul! Patrul!"

Wondering who it could possibly be, Patrul came out to see. There, standing by the opening of the cave was his extraordinary guru, the inimitable Do Khyentse Yeshe Dorje. He was stinking of *chang* and holding forth the severed leg of a deer that he had just hunted down and killed.

Patrul could not keep from staring at the deer leg and thinking to himself, "Do Khyentse really seems to have some sort of craving!"[34]

At this, the great yogi slapped him full across the face and screamed,

"*Pi-i-i!* You've been hanging out in this cave all this time, and *still* you're stuck in dualistic thinking?"

Do Khyentse spat in Patrul's direction and stalked off. Shocked, Patrul suddenly entered the naked state of immediate presence and experienced bare awareness free of concepts. Patrul said this was how he received direct transmission of the *Guhyagarbha Tantra* (Secret Essence Tantra).[35]

The Boulder Reminder

Above Dzogchen Monastery in the Glacier Wilderness (Kangtrö) there was a large boulder. When Patrul taught the dharma, he used to sit on top of the boulder so that everyone could see him. Once he started teaching, he was immovable, just like the large boulder. Rain or shine, Patrul would not get up from his seat until he had finished whatever teachings he was giving.

Patrul would point to the massive rock and tell his students, "When you see that immovable boulder, let the very sight of it bring into your minds an unshakable aspiration to benefit beings by attaining enlightenment."

Patrul and the Paramita of Patience

Patrul decided to go visit a hermit he'd heard about who had been living for a long time in total seclusion.

Patrul arrived at the hermit's retreat unannounced. With a smile and an air of eager inquiry, he sat down in a corner of the hermit's cave.

"Where have you come from?" asked the hermit politely, "and where are you going?"

"I came from behind," replied Patrul. "And I'll be going forward."

Puzzled, the hermit asked, "Where were you born?"

"On earth."

The renunciant hermit was not sure what to make of his unexpected and peculiar visitor.

A moment later, Patrul asked the hermit why he had been staying in such an isolated place, so far away from everything.

"I've been living here for twenty years," said the hermit, with some pride in his voice. "At the moment, I am meditating on the *paramita* of patience!"

At this, Patrul began laughing out loud and slapping his thigh in amusement.

"That's rich!" Patrul exclaimed, leaning over toward him like someone sharing a secret. In a confidential tone, he whispered in the hermit's ear, "For two old frauds, we're not doing so bad, are we?"

The hermit exploded in fury.

"Who do you think you are, coming here, shamelessly ruining my retreat? Who asked *you* to come? Why won't you let a poor practitioner meditate in peace?" screamed the hermit.

"*Hmm*," mused Patrul. "So much for your 'perfection of patience'!"

» *Drive Them Off with Stones* «

I bow down at the feet of my master.
When I, Old Dog, was off in retreat in the wilderness,
Some things said by my supreme refuge and protector
Came into my mind, and
I was moved to say what follows.

At first, when in the presence of my teacher,
Like an explorer who stumbles on an isle of gold,
I felt that all my wishes had come true.
That was *knowing the value of the teachings.*

Then, when in the presence of my teacher,
Like a thief dragged before a judge,
I felt keen remorse for all my shortcomings.
That was *getting a well-deserved scolding.*

Now, when in the presence of my teacher,
Like a pigeon nesting in a temple,
I feel too much at ease, like an equal.
That is *being better off keeping my distance.*

At first, when given instructions on meditation,
Like a famished man desperate for food,
I felt an urgent need to practice them at once.
That was *an outward show of meditation.*

Then, when given instructions on meditation,
Like someone trying to make out speech at a distance,
I felt confused about just what I'd heard.
That was *failing to clarify doubts.*

Now, when given instructions on meditation,
Like someone forced to swallow his own vomit,
I feel nothing but abhorrence.
That is *losing all taste for more.*

At first, on retreat in the wilderness,
Like a traveler who has just come back home,
I felt completely comfortable.
That was *joy in just being where I was.*

Then, on retreat in the wilderness,
Like a great beauty left all by herself,
I felt uneasy and on edge.
That was *much restless agitation.*

Now, on retreat in the wilderness,
Like an old dog who's just found the right ditch to die in,
I feel settled and content.
That is *playing the part of a corpse.*

At first, when I considered the view,
Like a vulture that seeks out the loftiest aerie,
The higher the view, the better I liked it.
That was *mouthing off about the view.*

Then, when I considered the view,
Like a man hesitating at a crossroads,
I feared I might take the wrong turn.
That was *remaining in doubt.*

Now, when I consider the view,
Like hearing a geezer babble to a baby,

I feel a bit bamboozled.
That is *losing all reference points.*

At first, when I considered meditation,
Like a couple newly in love
I felt nothing but desire.
That was *thirsting for practice.*

Then, when I considered meditation,
Like a weakling weighed down by a massive load,
I felt it was beyond me.
That was *not enough practice.*

Now, when I consider meditation,
Like a needle on a rock, balanced on its tip,
I can't settle even for an instant.
That is *being through with any more meditation.*

At first, when I thought about conduct,
Like a wild mustang hitched to a stake,
I felt tethered by my vows.
That was *the pretense of discipline.*

Then, when I thought about conduct,
Like an old guard dog broken free of its chain,
I felt free to do whatever I wanted.
That was *giving up vows.*

Now, when I think about conduct,
Like a great beauty who has let herself go,
I feel completely unconstrained.
That is *ceasing to care about conditions.*

At first, when I considered the goal,
Like hearing the silky sales pitch of a swindler,
It seemed like a fabulous deal.
That was *having great expectations.*

Then, when I considered the goal,[36]
Like the far shore of the ocean,
I felt it was way beyond me.
That was *having few hopes.*

Now, when I consider the goal,
Like a night burglar arriving at daybreak,
I feel that I've lost my chance.
That is *having no expectations.*

At first, when I gave explanations,
Like a great beauty sashaying through a market,
I felt entranced by my own eloquence.
That was *liking to hear myself talk.*

Then, when I gave explanations,
Like an old man retelling tales from his youth,
I felt I knew everything already.
That was *being a smooth talker.*

Now, when I give explanations,
Like an exorcist targeting a phantom,
I feel I'm just showing off my weak points.
That is *feeling humbled.*

At first, in my early debates,
Like someone who drags a weak case to court,
I'd have done anything to be the victor.
That was *giving in often to anger.*

Then, when I was debating,
Like a mediator trying to be impartial,
I was desperate to find out the truth.
That was *mobilizing all one's intelligence.*

Now, when I'm debating,
Like an outlaw running rampant in the badlands,

There's just no telling what I'll say or do next!
That is *losing all sense of restraint.*

At first, when writing a text,
Like the great masters' improvised songs of enlightenment,
Words came to my mind spontaneously.
That was *not modifying anything.*

Then, when writing a text,
Like a poet skillfully shaping his verses,
I worked on refining my craft.
That was *creating fine literature.*

Now, when writing a text,
Like reading a manual made by a moron,
I feel that the whole thing is pointless.
That is *not wasting paper and ink.*

At first, when in the presence of my colleagues,
Like young men gathered for an archery meet,
I felt keenly competitive with them.
That was *being the dupe of wanting this, not that.*

Then, when in the presence of my colleagues,
Like a prostitute at a party,
I felt I'd been intimate with each one already.
That was *having lots of friends.*

Now, when in the presence of my colleagues,
Like a leper who hangs out in public,
I feel I really shouldn't be there.
That is *living by oneself.*

At first, when I came upon riches,
Like a young child picking a flower,
I felt just an instant of delight.
That was *not being stingy with riches.*

Then, when I came upon riches,
Like water poured into a jug that leaks,
I felt there would never be enough.
That was *why I won't chase riches anymore.*

Now, when I come upon riches,
Like a pauper burdened by too many kids,
I see wealth as just a nuisance.
That is *being happy with nothing.*

At first, when I had a retinue,
Like creating an army of attendants,
I felt like a fine commander.
That was *helping others.*

Then, when I had a retinue,
Like a tutor herding a bunch of rookie monks,
I felt I'd completely lost my freedom.
That was *why I'm now severing those ties.*

Now, when I have a retinue,
Like bringing a thieving dog home,
I feel that everything will get ruined.
That is *why I'm better off alone.*

At first, when I taught students,
Like a slave who longs to be master,
I sought to become renowned.
That was *seeking adulation.*

Then, when I taught students,
Like pilgrims who depend on sacred sites,
I thought my students might depend upon me.
That was *seeking to benefit others.*

Now, when would-be students approach,
Like demons that pop up out of thin air,

I just scold them and chase them away—
That is *having to drive them off with stones.*

This is the end of the admonition known as "Drive them off with stones." May merit ensue!

Patrul and the Prescient Monk

Patrul was famous for his teachings on *The Way of the Bodhisattva.* He might take days, weeks, or months to comment on the entire text, teaching at whichever level of complexity was most suitable to the occasion, from brief and quintessential to extensive and complex. Often, he'd advise students to read the text before he gave his commentary. After he was done, he'd tell students to read it another hundred times.[37]

Patrul himself had received teachings on *The Way of the Bodhisattva* more than a hundred times. He taught the text more than a hundred times, yet even so, he used to say that he had not grasped its full meaning.

One night, a monk at Trago Monastery dreamed that he saw a lama who he felt was Shantideva in person, the author of *The Way of the Bodhisattva.* The next morning, when a wandering lama arrived at Trago Monastery, the monk recognized him: He looked just like the figure who had appeared in his dream the night before!

The monk approached the lama—who in fact was Patrul Rinpoche. Bowing respectfully, he requested that he teach *The Way of the Bodhisattva.* Bowing back, the lama agreed.

Patrul gave the teachings. When he left, the monk who had seen him in his dream went with him, accompanying him along the way for several days' walk.

Flowers Magically Appear

Patrul gave extensive teachings on four chapters[38] of *The Way of the Bodhisattva* to a crowd of several thousand people in Dzamthang. Instead of sitting on a throne, he sat on a grass-covered mound of earth called *porto,* a natural formation often found on the high plateaus.

After Patrul's teachings were over, local people noticed that flowers began to bloom on that grassy mound, wildflowers of many kinds and many colors.

There is a bright yellow flower that grows abundantly in high-altitude meadows in Kham in summertime. These lovely meadow flowers, called *serchen,* usually have five petals. But often, in places where Patrul had given teachings, people noticed that now each flower had not just five petals, but thirty petals or even fifty petals. People started to call these special blossoms "*Bodhicharyavatara* flowers."[39] They bloomed even in winter!

A Robber Sets His Sights on an Offering of Silver

Near the monastery of Dzamthang,[40] Patrul was sitting on a grassy mound, having just finished teaching *The Way of the Bodhisattva* to a large crowd of people. An old man who had attended the teachings came up to him and offered him a large piece of silver called "horse-hoof silver" because it is usually cast in the shape of a hoof.[41] Other than that silver ingot, the old man had few possessions, but he thought it would be a meritorious deed to offer his ingot to Patrul, toward whom he felt deep faith.

Patrul, as was his custom, refused to accept the offering, but the old man was persistent, laying the silver ingot at Patrul's feet and briskly walking away. Soon after, Patrul got up and left, leaving behind him all the offerings that people had made to him, including the silver ingot.

A thief learned that Patrul had been offered a silver ingot and followed him, intending to steal it. Patrul often traveled alone and spent his nights sleeping out under the stars. The robber approached the sleeping Patrul under cover of darkness and began going through his scanty belongings—a small cloth bag and a clay teapot. Not finding the riches he was looking for, the thief started feeling around in the clothing that Patrul was wearing.

Suddenly awakened by the thief's hand, Patrul cried out, "*Ka-ho!* What are you doing rummaging around in my clothes?"

Startled, the thief blurted: "Someone gave you a silver ingot! I must have it! *Give* it to me!"

"*Ka-ho!*" Patrul yelled again. "Look what a dismal life you lead, running here and there like a fool! Did you come all this way just for a piece of silver? How pathetic!"

"Now, listen up! Go, quickly, back the way you came. By dawn you'll reach the grassy mound where I was teaching. That's where you'll find the silver ingot."

The thief was skeptical, but he had searched the master's belongings thoroughly enough to know that Patrul was not in possession of a silver ingot. It seemed unlikely that the coveted offering would still be there, but nonetheless the thief retraced his steps all the way to the grassy mound. Searching around, he finally found the silver ingot that Patrul had simply abandoned there.

The robber, who was no longer young and was beginning to worry about his way of life, began a loud lament: "*A-dzi!* This Patrul is an authentic master, free from all attachment. By trying to steal things from him, I've created some very bad karma!"

Tormented by remorse, he retraced his steps again, looking for Patrul. When the thief found him again, Patrul cried, "*Ka-ho!* You're back! Still running around here and there like a fool? What do you want *this* time?"

Overcome, the thief broke into tears, "I'm not here to steal anything. I found the ingot, and I really regret having acted so badly toward you, a true spiritual master. To think that I was ready to rob you of the little you have! I beg you to forgive me! Please bless me and accept me as your disciple!"

Patrul said, "Don't bother confessing or begging my forgiveness. Just practice generosity from now on and invoke the Three Jewels. That will be enough."

Later, when some people heard about what the thief had done to Patrul, they tracked him down and beat him up.

When Patrul learned about this, he sharply rebuked the local people. "When you beat that man, you're beating me," he said. "So leave him alone!"

Patrul on Having Things

Patrul often pointed out the uselessness of worldly concerns and the inherently unsatisfactory nature of samsara. In particular, he emphasized the never-ending problems that came with owning possessions, saying, "Don't you get it? If you've got money, you've got *money* problems. If you have a house, you have *house* problems. If you have yaks, you have *yak* problems. If you have goats, you have *goat* problems!"

Patrul Practices in a Haunted Charnel Ground

Once, Patrul spent a day and a night in a charnel ground in Lauthang, in the Minyak area,[42] a dreaded place long known to be infested with vicious spirits. After he fell asleep, he began to experience terrifying apparitions. He supplicated his lama and all the teachers of the Dzogchen lineage. Suddenly, Patrul experienced a profound realization—he finally understood that all inner and outer phenomena are inherently empty of nature and that all are equally unreal from the point of view of ultimate reality.

Later, he reported his meditation experience to his teacher Do Khyentse Yeshe Dorje, who congratulated Patrul, saying, "*Yes!* You've cut down all four demons in a single blow!"[43]

Patrul said that after that night, his thoughts ceased to wander and his mindstream was no longer much disturbed by the negative emotions.

A Meeting of Two Minds

On a visit to Minyak, Patrul called on a great scholar, or Geshe, of the Geluk tradition, Drawa Geshe Tsultrim Namgyal. The two discussed many aspects of the *prajnaparamita,* the transcendent perfection of wisdom (one of the six *paramitas*).

Impressed by Patrul's erudition and profound understanding, the Geshe asked him his name.

"I'm Palge, a guy from Kham," Patrul replied casually. "Dzachukha."

After Patrul left, the Geshe said to his attendant, "In regard to the sutras, I'm a little bit learned, but in regard to both the sutras *and* the tantras, there's no one more learned than that Palge fellow! He's in a class by himself!"

"You've Ruined It!"

A shabbily dressed nomad lama had been wandering alone for some time when he arrived at the large encampment of a wealthy nomad family. He asked at the main tent if he might take shelter there for a couple of days. The family said he was welcome to do so, as long as he knew how to read. He said that, yes, he did know how to read. They gave him a place to stay in a little corner of the main tent near its opening, where he settled in and began reading and reciting some prayers.

Inside the main tent, everyone was busy preparing to receive a great scholar of the Geluk tradition, Minyak Kunzang Sönam, who was coming to preside over some very important ceremonies at the encampment. All the preparations continued for days.

Finally a day came when the nomad lama saw everyone suddenly rushing outside the tent. The great lama's party was just now approaching! It was time to welcome the great lama and receive his blessings.

People started to shout, ordering the shabby lama to come outside at once!

Minyak Kunzang Sönam arrived on horseback with a large and magnificent entourage. There were at least forty horsemen with him, each one carrying a long ceremonial banner. Everyone in the crowd had already begun prostrating to the lama.

Suddenly, Minyak Kunzang Sönam saw the shabby lama emerging from the tent. At once, the highly respected scholar dismounted from his rather tall horse and started doing prostrations to the shabby nomad lama.

The crowd was shocked to discover that the shabby nomad lama was in fact the great Patrul Rinpoche.

In front of the entire crowd, Patrul started scolding the great Minyak Kunzang Sönam: "Through the kindness of this family, I had a fine place to stay, but now *you've ruined it*!"

He threatened to leave at once, but eventually he yielded to the appeals of all present and did agree to stay on.

The great Minyak Kunzang Sönam made a promise that day never again to ride on horseback but to walk everywhere on foot and to lead the simple life of a hermit.

Patrul's Gift of Tea

Minyak Kunzang Sönam, the great Geluk scholar, was a close disciple of Patrul; he followed him for more than twenty years and was utterly devoted to him. Once, after they'd spent some time together, just as Kunzang Sönam was about to leave, Patrul presented him with a book[44] as a parting gift.

Patrul also presented him with a gift—a brick of tea—extending it with both hands, in the polite Tibetan gesture of offering. Patrul told him, "Make yourself some tea along the way."

Kunzang Sönam had so much devotion to Patrul that he wrapped the tea brick in a fine felt case and then wrapped the fine felt case in a colorful silk brocade pouch. Wherever he went, he took the silk brocade pouch with him; wherever he slept, he would hang the brocade pouch reverently above the head of his bed. From time to time, he would touch the pouch to the crown of his head and supplicate Patrul Rinpoche, while shedding tears of devotion.

Every first day of every new year, Minyak Kunzang Sönam would open up the colorful silk brocade pouch. He would then open up the fine felt case and take out the brick of tea.

"Today we shall make some of Patrul Rinpoche's tea!" he would say to those around him, breaking off a few leaves. He then would add, reverently, "Patrul himself gave this tea to me—with his own two hands!"

The Haunted Fortress

There was a terrible haunted fortress at Nyakrong, a district in Kham with deep rocky gorges and wild rivers. The sound of spirits wailing could be heard there even during the day. People never dared to go anywhere near it. Even the shadow of the fortress made them fall ill.

Once, after he had finished giving teachings on *The Way of the Bodhisattva,* Patrul predicted that if someone taught this sacred text a hundred times at the haunted fortress of Nyakrong, the evil spirits would fall silent and cause no further harm.

Tsanyak Sherab, a close disciple of Patrul Rinpoche, immediately volunteered to take on this challenge. Hearing this, the local villagers felt great pity and shook their heads, saddened at the thought that they would never ever see Tsanyak Sherab again, for he was certainly a doomed man.

When he arrived at the haunted fortress, Tsanyak Sherab chose a spacious room and laid his mat down on the floor. Then, after having generated compassion and bodhichitta, he began to teach all ten chapters of *The Way of the Bodhisattva,* speaking aloud to an audience that could not be seen.

That night, nothing happened. And so, day after day, Tsanyak Sherab kept on teaching. When the nearby villagers saw in the distance smoke arising from the fire Sherab had made to boil water for tea, they were shocked.

"It looks like he's not dead yet!" one surprised villager remarked.

A while later, one of the bravest men in the village decided to go to the haunted fortress and see for himself what was happening.

There he saw Tsanyak Sherab, still there and still happily teaching *The Way of the Bodhisattva.* He was still speaking aloud to an audience that could not be seen.

The brave villager returned to the village and told everyone what he had seen. People started to go to the fortress so that they, too, could listen to the teachings. Day after day, more and more people joined the audience at the fortress. By the time Tsanyak Sherab had finished teaching the entire text for the hundredth time, the whole village was sitting inside the fortress, listening with utmost devotion.

From then on, just as Patrul had predicted, there was no more trouble at the fortress of Nyakrong.

Jigme Gyalwai Nyugu and the Harmful Spirit

Patrul's root guru, Jigme Gyalwai Nyugu, was renowned for his compassion.

One time, an evil spirit decided it wanted to kill him. The spirit came to Gyalwai Nyugu's cave and peered inside. It saw an old man with white hair, eyes closed, sitting serenely in meditation, radiating loving-kindness and compassion.

The sight sent the spirit into such deep shock that its intent to harm vanished, and in its place was bodhichitta. It vowed never to kill again.

After that, whenever even the whisper of a thought of causing harm arose in the mindstream of the spirit, it was replaced in a flash by a vision of Jigme Gyalwai Nyugu, serenely radiating loving-kindness. Never again was it able to do harm.

Patrul and the Three Dargye Monks

Patrul was famously nonsectarian, never praising some schools and disparaging others. He refused to fuel the arrogant, vindictive sectarianism that had long been rampant in Tibet.[45]

Once, Patrul's wanderings took him on a road that passed by Dargye Monastery, a Geluk monastery in the Trehor region of Kham. Now, the monks of Dargye Monastery were notorious for their sectarianism. They used to harass all passing travelers, demanding to know which school they belonged to—Nyingma, Kagyu, Sakya, or Geluk. When they found out someone belonged to a school other than *their* school, they'd insult him rudely and sometimes beat him up.

When Patrul came walking near their monastery, three huge, fierce-looking monks approached him and demanded roughly, "Which school do you follow?"

Knowing they were out to pick a fight, Patrul replied tactfully and yet with perfect accuracy, "I follow the school of the Lord Buddha!"

Unsatisfied and still intent on determining his school, they went on, "How do you recite the refuge formula?"

Patrul recited: "I take refuge in the Buddha, the Dharma, and the Sangha!"

His answer gave the sectarian monks no satisfaction, as they were expecting refuge verses that would reveal Patrul's affiliation to a particular school and lineage.

"Name your tutelary deity!" they demanded, with increasing annoyance.

"The Three Jewels!" replied Patrul patiently.

Desperate for an answer, hoping to discover his school through his initiation name, the monks shouted, "Reveal to us your secret name!"

Now, it so happens that in Tibetan, the phrase "secret name" also refers to the male organ.

Lifting up his robes, Patrul amiably replied, in nomad dialect, "*Bulu-bulu!*" ("Dick!")

That finally shut them up.

Patrul at last was able to continue on his way, unmolested. He did so, loudly reciting, "*Om mani padme hung. Om mani padme hung.*"

Patrul Mentions His Past Lives

Patrul was once living and practicing in the lower part of the Yamantaka Cave near Dzogchen Monastery. Staying nearby in the nearby upper cave was a practitioner from Gyalmo Rong.

One day, as they got together, Patrul said to that fellow practitioner, "When a person practices in solitary places, far from all the hustle and bustle of the world, awareness may become naturally clear. It may even become easier to recall one's past lives. Has that ever happened to you?"

The Tro Sitrön mountain range, of which Dzogchen Glacier Wilderness (Kangtrö) is a part, seen from Yamantaka Cave. Dzogchen Monastery, Kham. (1985)

"Not so far," the practitioner said.

"I can remember more than a hundred of my past lives," Patrul confided. "Once, I was a prostitute in India, in the village where the *mahasiddha* Krishnacharya[46] lived. I offered Krishnacharya a bracelet of pure gold.

"After making that offering, I never again had a lesser rebirth."

Lungtok Meets His Root Master

When Nyoshul Lungtok first met Patrul, Patrul had been practicing the recitation of *Chanting the Names of Manjushri.* He was just reaching the verse with the words "Supreme teacher, worthy of homage!" when Lungtok came into his presence.

"This *is* an auspicious coincidence!" exclaimed Patrul with delight, and he repeated the verse: "'Supreme teacher, worthy of homage'!"

At once, like a father being reunited with his son, Patrul accepted Lungtok as his disciple and treated him with the deepest affection. For the next twenty-eight years, Lungtok remained at Patrul's side, serving as his attendant, hearing every word that Patrul taught, and receiving teachings on *The Way of the Bodhisattva* at least eighty times.[47]

An Insight into Patrul's Mind

Patrul asked his heart-disciple Nyoshul Lungtok, "Which lama do you supplicate?"

"I can't keep anyone in mind for long."

"Maybe not, but when you can concentrate, whom do you supplicate?"

"You."

"Me? Why me, of all people? Tibet has no dearth of lamas!"

"When I have positive thoughts, even for an instant, I know I owe them to you and your teachings. I keep in mind your inexhaustible kindness."

"That's okay, if that's how you see it. You can keep on doing that."

Patrul added, in his deep voice, "Within my mindstream, negative emotions hardly ever arise anymore!"

» *The Crucial Points of Practice* «

I take refuge in the guru.

I bow down before the Omniscient One,
Spiritual father, sons, lineage holders,
And my illustrious master,
Who taught me the meaning of Dzogchen,
The inconceivable naked essence,
Primordially free.
The total integration of view and meditation practice—
Beyond cultivating good qualities
And eliminating bad ones—
Is continuously to remain in wakefulness,
Naturally free, in this very immediate presence
Of awareness, just as it presents itself,
Unaltered, uncorrected.

To know a bit about meditation practice
Without knowing how to set thoughts free
Results in the meditative absorptions of the gods.[48]
Gaining certainty in one's realization
Comes with gaining skill in
How to set thoughts free just as they're arising.

Focusing wandering mind through calm-state meditation[49]
May muffle negative mental states for a while.
But as soon as circumstances change,
Ordinary discursive thoughts will just rear up again
Like poison that's lain dormant,
Until you've really understood the subtle crucial point—
How thoughts are set free just as they arise.

Like ripples on water,
Ordinary discursive thoughts
(Wanting this, not wanting that)
Pop up, all of a sudden.
But once you've learned how to liberate
Thoughts just as they arise,
They cannot take hold, and so they vanish.
This is a vital point that must be understood.

When "bad" thoughts arise, they will not accrue bad karma,
Since discursive thoughts
Set free just as they arise
Have not yet taken hold.
Who is helped or harmed by a mere flash of thought?

Until you master this crucial point—
How to set thoughts free just as they arise—
Your habitual mental chatter,
The constant undercurrent of thoughts,
Grows into a flood of negative emotions.

If you merely notice thoughts with mindfulness,
Positive thoughts keep creating hopes

Negative thoughts keep creating fears.
By doing this, you keep accruing and compounding karma;
This process is the true source of samsara.

This is why an instant of awareness
That sets thought free in its own condition
Is superior to a thousand calm-state meditation experiences.

Since primordial liberation, spontaneous liberation,
Liberation upon arising, direct liberation, and the rest,
Are each and all the crux of view, meditation, and action,
Develop meditation by practicing this crucial point:
Freeing thoughts into their own condition.

Apply this crucial point and there is no need
For any other view nor any other meditation.

As all beneficial thoughts arise,
You are free of attachment to them;
Though still striving for virtue, you are free of conceit.

As all negative thoughts arise,
They become unraveled naturally,
Like a tangled snake unwinding.

Should even the five poisons arise,
In an instant they are released into their own condition.

Neutral thoughts, too, self-settle naturally
Subsiding into the expanse of awareness.
Set free just as they arise, they leave no more imprint
Than the flight of a bird through the sky.

Deluded thinking is the very root of samsara.
Once you are certain how to bring discursive thought
Onto the path, through this self-liberation,
That is "freeing samsara and nirvana in the absolute expanse."
Until you master this vital point—

Becoming certain about this method of
Self-liberating discursive thoughts
And thus bringing all circumstances onto the path—
Though you may be able to blather on about emptiness,
Your "realization" is mere theory.
Your hidden negative qualities will be naturally exposed.
In the end, the five poisons will prevail
If you mistakenly regard their apparent solidity to be real.

Why? Only from the error of not knowing
How to liberate thoughts just as they arise.

Therefore, the most important point
About view, meditation, and action,
Which brings about the confidence of realization,
Boils down to mastery of this way
Of self-liberating [thoughts just as they arise].

Applying this in all circumstances of your life,
Keep bringing everything onto the path toward realization.

Even though I myself have not yet mastered this,
Inspired by the words of the omniscient master, the very
Buddha,
I have written down these words.

Take these words to heart, since
This is the most crucial, essential point of practice.
May all be auspicious!

Patrul's Offering to the Horseflies

Patrul emphasized meditation on the four immeasurables: loving-kindness, compassion, sympathetic joy, impartiality. He never failed to recognize the importance of regarding every being as having been, in some lifetime, our own kind mother who took loving care of us, and of developing a heartfelt benevolence, wishing that each and every being should find happiness and the causes of happiness.

While he was staying at the Changma hermitage (Willow Hermitage),[50] Patrul would go off into the forest on summer afternoons to a place where there were swarms of black horseflies. He would remove all his clothing and lie down on the ground. Soon his whole bare body would turn black because it was completely covered in black flies. Patrul would stay that way for many hours, not moving, just allowing swarms of ravenous horseflies to bite into his flesh and gorge on his blood.

Eventually he'd get up, get dressed, and say to his heart-disciple and attendant, "*Ya!* Lungtok! Time to go home!"

The next day, in the afternoon, Patrul would say, "*Ya!* Lungtok! Let's go back into the forest and make some more offerings!"

Patrul Finds His Limit

Patrul said to his student Nyoshul Lungtok, "My dear Lungtok, these days, when I practice contemplating the 'four thoughts that turn the mind to dharma,' and when I have to bring to mind the defects of samsara, I just can't make myself contemplate the sufferings of all six realms of existence. I am only able to contemplate the sufferings of beings in the three higher realms—the gods, demigods, and humans.

"But when I think about the sufferings of beings in the three lower realms—the animals, hungry ghosts, and hell-beings—I just can't stand the pain! I can't do it. It's just too *unbearable*!"

Developing Empathy, Understanding Emptiness

In the Yamantaka Cave in the forested wilderness above Dzogchen Monastery, Patrul gave teachings on the *Yeshe Lama*[51] to his long-time students Nyoshul Lungtok and Palchen Dorje, along with many other disciples.

At some point, everyone was outside doing the set of Dzogchen preliminary practices known as "distinguishing samsara from nirvana," when Nyoshul Lungtok was struck by seeing his fellow student Palchen Dorje,

Pilgrims gathered near the entrance to the Yamantaka cave. (1985)

who was moving around in an unusual way, reminding him of a pack animal such as a yak, holding its own tether in its mouth.

Seeing this, Lungtok was overcome with empathy, becoming keenly aware of how such beasts of burden must suffer. From this felt insight, he began to appreciate as never before how all sentient beings suffer so greatly in samsara. His feeling of compassion for their sufferings deepened.

Then, Lungtok did the practice known as "sounding the syllable *hung*." First, he sounded the seed syllable, then he visualized the syllables, multiplying and multiplying and expanding and expanding, until all of existence was pervaded by the seed syllable *hung*.

At that moment, the entire universe in all its vastness was revealed to Lungtok as immaterial and utterly transparent, truly empty in nature.

Lungtok's Dream

While he was receiving the *Yeshe Lama* teachings from Patrul, Nyoshul Lungtok kept having a recurring dream about a black ball of wool. In the dream he felt compelled to hold the ball very tight to keep it from unraveling.

One night, after the teachings, Lungtok had another dream in which Patrul appeared. The black ball of wool was there again. Patrul pulled on the end of the yarn, and the ball completely unraveled, revealing a golden statue of Vajrasattva. Patrul presented the statue to Lungtok.

In his dream, Lungtok thought to himself wryly, "If I'd known that statue was inside the ball of yarn, I wouldn't have tried so hard to prevent it from unraveling!"

Patrul Introduces Lungtok to the Nature of Mind

Often, Patrul and Lungtok used to climb up the slope toward Nakchung, a meadow high above Dzogchen Monastery, until they reached the base of a large fir tree. Each day, Patrul would go off to a new isolated spot and do solitary practice. Lungtok would stay at the foot of the pine tree and practice there. Eventually, he would make tea, and Patrul would return and sit down with him.

At dusk, Patrul used to go to an open space in a meadow at the edge of the cliff overlooking Dzogchen Valley. He would spread out his felt mat and stretch out on his back to do a session of threefold sky practice.[52]

One evening, after he'd finished practicing, Patrul said, "Say, dear Lungtok, didn't you tell me that you still haven't been able to recognize the nature of mind?"

"Yes, I did."

"There's nothing not to know. Come over here."

Lungtok did.

"Lie down like this and look up at the sky."

Patrul lay down on his back, and Lungtok did the same.

"Do you see the stars shining in the sky?" asked Patrul.

"Yes."

"Do you hear the dogs barking down at Dzogchen Monastery?"

"Yes."

"Do you hear the two of us talking?"

"Yes."

"Well, *that's it*!"

Lungtok would later tell his own students: "In that very moment, I was introduced directly to the wisdom of naked empty awareness! An unshakable certainty arose from the depths of my being, freeing me of any doubt." His master's presence and his own many years of meditation practice created an auspicious coincidence in that moment, producing a profound realization of primordial wisdom, awareness-emptiness inseparably united.

Lungtok Learns Backward

While in retreat at the Glacier Wilderness, high above Dzogchen Monastery, Patrul would spend the whole day practicing meditation. In the evenings, he would teach Lungtok from the *Seven Treasuries* by Kunkhyen Longchenpa.

When it got late, they both stood up. Patrul started walking forward as he continued to teach; he was walking in order to stay awake. Lungtok held the text out so that Patrul could see it; he walked backward as Patrul walked forward while reading from the book and then commenting on it.

The two kept on walking this way every night, one backward and the other forward, until eventually, Lungtok received from Patrul the entirety of teachings on the *Seven Treasuries.*

In later years, Lungtok remarked, "These days, even though people have the good fortune to hear teachings on the *Seven Treasuries* while they sit in

The Middle Lake of Dzogchen Glacier Wilderness, with a hermitage on the right side. (1985)

comfort, their bellies full, they don't bother to practice! Some don't even bother to ask for meditation instructions!"

To SUPPORT LUNGTOK'S STUDY AND PRACTICE, Patrul presented his student with his own set of Longchenpa's *Seven Treasuries,* the edition printed in Derge. He told Lungtok: "You have the good fortune and capacity to practice and fully realize the Great Perfection." In this way, he acknowledged Lungtok as his spiritual heir, with regard to inner realization.

After each session of teaching, Lungtok added notes based on Patrul's explanations, entering them carefully in red ink in between the lines of printed text.

These cherished texts with Nyoshul Lungtok's written notes were kept at Shugu Shar Monastery in his home place of Nyoshul in Palyul county of Kham. The largest volume of the collection, *The Supreme Treasury,*[53] has such handwritten annotations from beginning to end; the other volumes have a few notes here and there.

Lungtok Practices in the Glacier Wilderness

One day Patrul said to Lungtok, "Go to Dzogchen Kangtrö and meditate." Kangtrö, the "Glacier Wilderness," is an area of caves and places of retreat blessed by Padmasambhava. They are situated high up above Dzogchen Monastery at the snowline, near three lakes, one above the other, the highest lake being found at an altitude of around 5,000 meters above sea level.

According to Patrul's instruction, Lungtok went to the wilderness on the upper glacier above Dzogchen Monastery and stayed there in retreat for three years, dedicating his practice to the longevity of Mingyur Namkhai Dorje.

As his meditation cushion, Lungtok used a flat rock. For protection against the elements, he wore nothing more than e monk's robes made of cotton over an old, worn undershirt. He devoted himself to *chulen,*[54] a practice that entails taking in little solid food while receiving nourishment from extracting the essence of space through entering a deep, nonconceptual, meditative state.

Lungtok had visions of many deities; he attained realization of the *dharmakaya* within the Great Perfection and was able to perceive all phenomena, without bias or limitations, as manifestations of pure awareness. Here he practiced to completion the ultimate stages of Dzogchen, known as the four visions.

After three years, he returned to his teacher Patrul.

The Upper Lake of Dzogchen Glacier Wilderness. (1985)

Patrul asked, "Was it hard to survive?"

"I ate almost nothing," Lungtok told him. "I was happy to follow your instructions and to practice for the sake of Mingyur Namkhai Dorje's longevity."

"There is a saying: 'When a yogi keeps his *samayas* purely, gods and demons will provide sustenance!'" said Patrul, delighted. "You are the perfect example!"

The Great Master Patrul

Patrul Rinpoche was heading for Shri Singha[55] Philosophical College to teach Shantideva's *Way of the Bodhisattva*, and at the same time, a group of monks were on their way to Dzogchen Monastery to attend these teachings.

The party of monks came upon a lama in a meadow not far from the college.

Dressed in nomad style in an old sheepskin chuba, he was sitting on the ground by a little bonfire, making himself some tea.

The monks asked him, "Do you know if Patrul Rinpoche has arrived yet?"

"Yes, he's already here! He'll be teaching at Shri Singha!" the lama answered. "But, really, what's the point of going to hear *him*? That Patrul's nothing but a loudmouth! Honestly, he's a charlatan!"

Seemingly inspired, the shabby nomad lama continued bad-mouthing the great master Patrul Rinpoche at considerable length and with tremendous creativity and vigor.

Hearing these insults, the monks became furious.

"Shut your trap, *samaya*-breaker!" they screamed, "or we'll beat you to a pulp!"

The shabby nomad lama ceased his invective and resumed making tea.

The group of monks left and camped nearby for the night. In the morning, they headed for the college and came across the shabby lama once again.

He hailed them cordially, saying, "All right, let's all go together to Shri Singha! I hear that at least the *tea* they serve there is first class!"

The monks, still outraged, refused to talk to him. They went on to the college without him and found themselves seats in the assembly.

Soon there was an announcement that the great teacher Patrul Rinpoche was just about to enter. The whole audience rose to show respect, and in solemn, melodious voices, everyone sang verses in praise of Shantideva's *Way of the Bodhisattva.*

When the distinguished master took his seat on the teaching throne to begin the teachings, the monks realized with horror that the great master Patrul Rinpoche was none other than the shabby lama in sheepskin they had met earlier and threatened with bodily harm!

Patrul began his teachings by saying, "Last night, I met a bunch of furious monks. Where are they? I'd like them to come up here and sit in the very front row!"

Which, with chagrin, they did.

A Monk Makes a Full Confession

Once, at Shri Singha Philosophical College, it was the day for doing *sojong*, the confession ritual that monks are required to perform twice a month. The gong rang summoning people to the temple. Everyone began hurrying so as not to be late. Walking stick in hand, Patrul was heading toward the temple, too, dressed in a patched felt chuba, which he would wear in the summer.

A crowd was rushing in and climbing up the steps, shabby Patrul among them. Suddenly, one monk gave Patrul such a shove that he lost his balance and tumbled down the staircase. The monk who had rudely shoved aside Patrul had mistaken him for a thieving beggar trying to sneak into a ceremony meant for members of the sangha only.

Eventually, everyone entered the temple and found a seat. The monk, too, sat down. Then he looked up.

There was a throne on which was seated the person in charge of leading the *sojong* ceremony. Sitting upon the throne was Patrul, the shabby man the monk had very roughly shoved aside.

Trying to make the best of a bad situation, the horrified monk stood up at once, declaring, "Not only do I have an offense to confess, but I can confess it before the very person I offended!"

Patrul Waits in Line to Receive a Blessing

At a time when Patrul was traveling alone, on foot, he came upon the tent encampment of a group of lamas who were on their way to a large dharma assembly. He approached them to beg alms and asked if he might travel with their group. They agreed to let him join their party.

Looking like an ordinary wandering practitioner, he was treated as one. They gave the shabby nomad lama lots of menial chores to do: making tea, gathering firewood, serving tea to the other monks. With Patrul working hard as their humble servant, the group traveled through remote regions over several weeks until at last they reached their destination.

A prominent lama was to give an important Vajrayana transmission, and in keeping with the importance of the spiritual occasion, the gathering was very grand. In all aspects, it was a magnificent spectacle: a huge crowd made up of ordinary people dressed in their best clothes, high officials and their families, and handsome aristocrats in silken garments riding horses with polished silver-alloy bridles, elaborate saddles, ornate stirrups, and brightly colored saddle pads.

There were many high lamas and many very important monks, wearing tall ceremonial hats, brocades, and other monastic regalia.

The long ritual horns and conch-shell trumpets sounded like a celestial symphony. Each important lama was seated on a special throne whose exact height was precisely set according to rank and precedence.

The religious rituals began, and continued for several days. Once the assembly was over, all the monks, wealthy patrons, and laymen and laywomen got into line, waiting to make individual offerings to the presiding master and receive his blessings.

Patrul had been sitting at the back of the crowd the whole time, so he wound up at the end of the very long line, standing and waiting patiently for his turn to receive a personal blessing. (Patrul himself always declined to give such hand-blessings.) As the queue slowly advanced, people made prostrations, one by one, before the great master's throne. They each offered the lama a white silk scarf and then received his blessing.

At first, the great lama touched each person on the head, using his two hands to give his blessing. After some time, since there were so many people in line, the presiding lama stopped using his hands and began brushing each person's head with a long peacock feather.

Finally, it was Patrul's turn. He came forward to receive the great lama's blessing. Before touching the devotee's head with the peacock feather, the master peered down from his lofty throne at the bedraggled figure below him. His eyes widened with astonishment as he recognized the vagabond.

It was the great Patrul Rinpoche—who was, in fact, the great lama's own master.

The high lama somehow managed to clamber down from his extremely high throne. He stood before Patrul, raised his folded hands to his forehead, and began to prostrate to him.

As everyone present, including his former traveling companions, looked on and gasped in amazement, Patrul merely smiled.

Patrul Paints Some Tormas

When Patrul heard that Do Khyentse Yeshe Dorje had gone to Minyak, he decided to go there to meet him. After walking for a couple of weeks, he reached Do Khyentse's tent encampment.

Patrul found the kitchen tent, went in, and sat down.

A monk in the tent was making cone-shaped *tormas.* These cakes were used for offerings during Vajrayana rituals, some colored red and some white.

"Hey, you! Old lama!" the monk called out to Patrul. "I need to finish these tormas; give me a hand."

So, to help the monk, Patrul began to make tormas. He noticed that there was red dye for coloring the red tormas, but there was no butter, which was ordinarily used to give white tormas their color. Because there was no butter, Patrul decided to make all of the tormas red ones.

Eventually, the monk came over to Patrul and noticed Patrul's tormas. At once the monk began loudly scolding Patrul: "What have you done? You've made all of the tormas red!"

Patrul pointed out that he had only red dye and no butter.

"You've spoiled all my work!" the monk thundered. "You've made all of the tormas red! You even made the white tormas red! You're here to meet Do Khyentse, but if you can't even tell the difference between white tormas and red tormas, what kind of stupid questions will you be asking him?"

The torma-maker monk was so furious that he could hardly keep himself from beating Patrul to a pulp.

With an expression of pure innocence, Patrul asked, "Oh, by the way, do you happen to know what's the *point* of painting some tormas white and some tormas red?"[56]

At this, the monk, who had no idea what the meaning of the torma colors was, became even more enraged and started yelling, "Look at this old fellow! He can't even paint a torma correctly! On top of that, he's asking *questions*!"

Eventually, someone reported to Do Khyentse that a shabby nomad lama had come by to see him.

"What does he look like?" asked the great master.

"Well, he's dressed in a sheepskin coat with a red hem around the bottom."

Hearing this description, Do Khyentse exclaimed, "*A-dzi!* Could it be Patrul? Send him in!"

Patrul was ushered immediately into Do Khyentse's presence and began making prostrations.

Highly pleased, Do Khyentse greeted him with warmth and affection, saying, "*A-dzi!* You came!"

They spoke for a while. Then Do Khyentse asked, "Would you teach *The Way of the Bodhisattva* to benefit the local people?"

Patrul agreed.

He began the teachings on the next day to a large audience, even including the torma-making monk. He explained four important chapters: the benefits of bodhichitta, confessing one's faults, cultivating bodhichitta, and sharing the accumulated merits with all sentient beings.[57]

When he reached the section on loving-kindness and compassion, Patrul stopped to make a special comment.

"Of course, there are *some* people who want to beat the living daylights out of you just for asking a simple question," Patrul said, smiling cheerfully—"even though they themselves don't even know why some tormas are red and others are white!"

Patrul Passes Dargye Monastery Again

After Patrul had completed his visit to Minyak, his path took him in the vicinity of Dargye Monastery, which was well known for its sectarian sentiments.

A few monks standing outside the monastery saw a shabby nomad lama. Seeing his dress and demeanor, a few monks guessed that he likely belonged to the Nyingma school.

Thinking to taunt him, one monk stepped forward, demanding, "Where have you come from? Where are you going?"

This time, Patrul seized the initiative.

"Ah, you Gelukpas, you're just so *fantastic*!" Patrul replied. "All you Geluk tradition holders just keep going back and forth! You go all the way to the center of Tibet, to Ganden and to Sera, to study hard! Then, to teach, you come back again! Back and forth, over and over!"

He thought for a moment.

"Old Nyingma practitioners like me are such yokels," mused Patrul, shaking his head. "We just stay in one place all our lives, wrapped in a blanket, and in the end, we *never* come back!"

Pleased by what seemed to be flattering praise, the monks let Patrul go on his way, unmolested.

Not long afterward, the monks ran into their *geshe,* the monastery head. They told him that a wandering lama had just come by.

"He was a sweet Nyingma hermit," one monk said. "And he said very good things about us!"

Skeptical, the Geshe asked, "What exactly *did* he say?"

The monks told him.

The Geshe shook his head, saying, "No, those were *not* 'very good things.'"

The monks were mystified. The Geshe explained: "His allusion to our going back and forth meant we Gelukpas just keep cycling through samsara, over and over, as opposed to those Nyingmapas, who, through their so-called Dzogchen meditation practice, attain the level of 'no-return' [to samsara]!"

The Geshe told the monks to go after Patrul and bring him back, but wily Patrul was long gone.

Patrul and the Widow

While Patrul was traveling on foot across the vast plateaus of Golok, north of Dzachukha, he encountered a woman, mother of three, whose husband had just been killed by a *changthang dremong*, the huge bear of the Tibetan steppes, a beast much more dangerous than the *dremong* of the forests. Patrul asked the woman where she was going, and she told him she was headed to Dzachukha with her three children to beg for food, as the loss of her husband had left them destitute.

Then she began weeping.

"*Ka-ho!* Don't worry!" said Patrul. "I'll help you. I'm going to Dzachukha, too. Let's travel together."

She agreed, and so they walked together for many days. At night, they slept outside beneath the sky. Patrul would nestle one or two of the children into the folds of his sheepskin coat, and the woman would similarly hold the rest. During the day, Patrul would carry one child on his back, the woman would carry the second, and the third would walk along behind.

When the woman begged in villages and nomad camps they passed, Patrul would beg right alongside her, asking for tsampa, butter, and cheese. Travelers they met assumed they were a family of beggars. No one—least of all the newly widowed woman—guessed the identity of her shabby companion.

Eventually, they reached Dzachukha. That day the woman went off on her own to beg for food, and so did Patrul. In the evening, when they returned, the widow noticed that Patrul had a dark look on his face.

The woman asked, "What's wrong? You seem annoyed."

Patrul brushed it off, saying, "It's nothing. I had a task to accomplish, but the people here won't let me finish it. They're just making a big fuss about nothing."

Surprised, the woman asked, "What work could you have around here?"

Patrul replied, "Never mind, let's just go."

They came to a monastery on the side of a hill, where Patrul stopped.

He turned to the widow and said, "I have to go inside. You may come, too, but not right now. Come after a few days."

The woman said, "No, let's not separate; let's go in together. Until now, you have been so kind to me. We could get married. If not, let me at least stay at your side. I'd benefit from your kindness."

"No, that won't do," replied Patrul, adamant. "Up to now, I've done my best to help you, but the people here are troublemakers. We mustn't go in together. Come back in a few days; you'll find me inside."

So Patrul went up the hill to the monastery while the widow and her children stayed at the bottom of the hill, begging for their food.

As soon as he was inside the monastery, contrary to his usual habit of refusing offerings, Patrul ordered that any provisions offered to him should be kept and put aside for a very special guest he was expecting who would be needing provisions.

The next day, everyone in the valley had heard the news of the great lama's return.

"Patrul Rinpoche has come!" people said. "He'll be giving teachings on *The Way of the Bodhisattva*!"

Men and women, young and old, monks and nuns, male and female lay practitioners, everyone went hurrying to hear the great Patrul Rinpoche. People began to gather into a huge crowd, bringing along horses and yaks that carried their tents and provisions.

When the widow heard the news, she was thrilled, thinking, "A great lama has come! This will be my chance to make offerings and request prayers on behalf of my late husband!"

Along with everyone else, she climbed up to the monastery, bringing along her three fatherless children.

The poor widow and her family had to sit at the far edge of the large crowd to hear Patrul's teachings. She was so far away that she could not see his features clearly. At the end of the teachings, like everyone else, she stood on a long line, waiting to receive the great lama's blessing.

Eventually, she moved up in the long line till at last she came close enough to see that the great lama, Patrul Rinpoche, was none other than her shabby, kind, faithful traveling companion.

Moved by both devotion and amazement, she approached Patrul, saying, "Forgive me for not knowing who you were! You are like the Buddha in person! Forgive me for making you carry my children! Forgive me for asking you to marry me! Forgive me for everything!"

Patrul brushed off her apology lightly, saying, "Don't give it a second thought!"

Turning to the monastery attendants, he told them, "*This* is the very special guest I've been expecting! Please bring all the butter, cheese, and provisions that we have been setting aside especially for her!"

Patrul's Teachings Inspire All Beings

Wherever Patrul taught *The Way of the Bodhisattva,* harmful spirits were inspired to stop doing harm and to follow the bodhisattva path.

Once, in Dzakhok,[58] people noticed two lunatics possessed by evil spirits who, upon seeing one another, began to greet one another with warm affection.

Someone asked, "What are you two so happy about?"

The first lunatic replied, "Parma in Upper Dzachukha used to be completely infested with evil spirits. The whole place was just chock full of them, right down to the tiniest pebble! Patrul Rinpoche came there and taught *The Way of the Bodhisattva.*

"*Everyone* came to his teachings—gods, demons, spirits, lunatics, just *everyone*! That's where we two met! That's how we two got to be such good friends!"

Patrul Acts as a Servant

Once, Patrul was returning home to Dzachukha so that he could circumambulate the Palge Mani Wall. When he arrived, he came to a tent near the wall to ask for shelter. An old blind woman lived there, and she told Patrul he was welcome to stay. Patrul offered to serve as her servant, working for his keep. Every day he faithfully served her and made himself useful to her, making and pouring her tea, and emptying out her bedpan, doing whatever needed to be done.

Every day the old woman recited prayers aloud, supplicating the most famous lama of Dzachukha, Patrul Rinpoche, saying, "Oh, Patrul, with your compassion, please think of me!"

Palge Mani Wall, in Mamo Thang, Dzachukha province, Kham. The wall is around 1.8 km (1.1 mi.) long. Each stone is engraved with mantras, sacred texts, and images. (2005)

Every day, Patrul worked hard as the blind woman's servant; every day, after work, he went to the Palge Mani Wall to circumambulate and do his meditation practice.

A month went by this way.

One day, some of Patrul's disciples came by the mani wall, saw Patrul doing circumambulations, recognized him, and began to prostrate to him. The old woman was sitting nearby. Though she was unable to see what was happening, she was able to hear what was being said, and she heard them referring to her servant as "Patrul Rinpoche"!

Learning his true identity, she was embarrassed and of course would not allow Patrul to continue doing as he had done.

At this, Patrul scolded his students sharply, saying, "Your thoughtless prattle has done grievous harm to this poor old blind woman! She's lost a good servant, and all because of you!"

Patrul Takes Tea with a Little Girl

Patrul had been camping out in his little black yak-hair tent on the Plain of the Mamos near the site of the Palge Mani Wall. Early one morning, a small girl wearing only a miserable thin marmot-skin jacket stopped by Patrul's tent and wandered in. Patrul asked her why she was out so early in the morning. The poor little girl, chilled to the bone, said that she was trying to find a *dri* that had strayed away from the family's herd and was now lost.

"Come in here," said Patrul to the little girl. "Have some tea and tsampa."

When tea was about to be served, it suddenly occurred to Patrul that the small girl was not carrying a bowl with her. (Most Tibetans carry around their own wooden tea bowls in the folds of their clothes.)

Patrul picked up his own bowl from the table in front of him, filled it with tea and tsampa, and handed it to the little girl. Observers nearby were shocked to see Patrul hand the little nomad girl his tea bowl; on her part, the little girl was extremely reluctant to accept it. According to Tibetan custom, an ordinary person would never drink from a lama's bowl, as a teacher's personal items are treated with tremendous respect.

The poor little girl eventually took the bowl, not daring to transgress Patrul's command. Using it, she happily warmed herself with the tsampa and tea. After she finished, thinking that it would be polite to clean Patrul's bowl before giving it back, she very carefully wiped clean Patrul's bowl, doing so using the filthy fur of her wretched marmot-skin jacket.

Then, with reverence, the little girl handed Patrul's bowl back to Patrul.

"*Hmm!* My bowl was too dirty for you, was it?" teased Patrul. "Is that why you had to work so hard at cleaning it?"

Without even bothering to wash the bowl, Patrul poured himself more tea.[59]

Patrul and the Tossed Louse

Once, late in the afternoon, the vagabond Patrul arrived at a small nomad encampment. He saw a young nomad girl who was milking the *dzomos* and asked if he might take shelter there for the night. He was on his way to a local monastery to teach *The Way of the Bodhisattva.*

The girl told him she would ask her mother and went inside the tent to do so. Her mother peered out of the tent at Patrul and looked him over with suspicion.

She said to her daughter, in a warning tone, "You know, that sort of homeless beggar could very well be carrying some awful infectious disease! Or else he might be a thief!"

The mother hesitated, thinking it over, and then relented, saying, "Oh, all right, tell him he can stay in the tent—he can sleep way over there in the far corner."

They gave him some tsampa with hot tea, which he was very grateful to receive, as it was very cold. Patrul went to the far corner of the tent as instructed. He recited his prayers and then settled down to go to sleep.

The daughter noticed that for warmth Patrul had only his clothes and no blanket or bedding. She asked her mother if they had anything to give Patrul to keep him warm.

"Well, we have that old rolled-up sheepskin. It's full of lice, but it's better than nothing."

The nomad daughter unrolled the old sheepskin and gave it to Patrul, who gratefully took it and put it over himself.

Mother and daughter lay down to go to sleep on the opposite side of the tent some yards away. As the mother was settling down to sleep, she felt a little tickle on her waist. Tossing off her bedding, she discovered a little louse crawling around at her waistline.

Gently, she picked it up and gave it to her daughter, saying, "Take this louse and wrap it up in a bit of wool for the night. Tomorrow morning, take it outside and put it somewhere safe, out of the sun. Throw it someplace where it won't die!"

"'Throw it *someplace where it won't die*'?" interjected Patrul suddenly, raising his head from under the filthy sheepskin. "If there's a place like that, would you be kind enough to throw *me* there, too?"

Just Sitting on His Bed

Once, a learned Geshe came all the way from Central Tibet to Serchu Monastery in Dzachukha. He was going to give extensive teachings on *Three Principal Aspects of the Path*[60] by Je Tsongkhapa,[61] a seminal text on the graded path to enlightenment in fourteen lines of verse.

Patrul came to hear the Geshe's teachings. He sat unobtrusively at the back of the assembly, next to the door, on a little yak-fur mat.

When the teachings were finished, he stood up, rolled up his little mat, and went outside. Someone heard Patrul say, "I reached the same conclusion just sitting on my bed!"

In other words, what the Geshe had understood through years of scholarly study, Patrul had understood through doing meditation practice while seated on his bed.

A Tulku Has a Change of Name

While visiting Önpo in Lower Dzachukha one time, Patrul was staying in the tent of a nomad family. A Geluk lama named Tulku Lungtok came to see Patrul, requesting teachings on *The Way of the Bodhisattva.*

Patrul demurred, saying, "I'm not the type who can teach that—and you're not the type who'd get it!"

His request for teachings apparently denied, the lama got up at once and started to leave.

"*You* sure don't take long to make up your mind," Patrul observed.

Just then, a woman came in bearing an offering of two cups filled to the brim with sweet warm milk.

Thinking this an auspicious omen, Patrul relented and said, "All right, all right. I'll teach you." In the end, he bestowed upon this lama extensive teachings on *The Way of the Bodhisattva.*"

The Way of the Bodhisattva is known as the *Chöjuk* in Tibetan. This lama went on to teach the great text so often that he eventually became known as "Tulku Chöjuk Lungtok."

Patrul Tries to Meet Shabkar

The great Geluk scholar Japa Do-ngak Gyatso, commonly known as Alak Do-ngak, was a devoted student of Patrul. He was also a devoted student of Shabkar Tsogdruk Rangdröl, the great yogi from Amdo province in northeastern Tibet, whose writings were already widespread and widely revered. The life examples of both masters embodied the ideals of renunciation and compassion. Shabkar wrote:

When I stay, I have nothing to be attached to.
When I leave, I have nothing to leave behind.
Wherever I am, no one inquires, "Where have you been?
Where are you going?"
I, the renunciate yogi, am happy.

. . . .

Even more vast than the sky is the view, emptiness.
There, the sun of love and the moon of compassion arose,
And again and again I made boundless prayers
To benefit the teachings and beings.

Patrul finally decided to go to meet Shabkar at Yama Tashikhyil in the Rekong area of Amdo in Amdo. After walking for two weeks, he had reached halfway to his destination of Amdo, when he heard the news that Shabkar had just passed away.

Immediately, Patrul turned in the direction of Shabkar's place and made one hundred full prostrations. Spontaneously, he composed and sang a supplication for Shabkar's swift rebirth.[62]

He said to his traveling companions, "Compassion and love are the root of dharma. There was no one in this world more compassionate than Shabkar.

"I had nothing special to ask; I had no teachings to request from him, no teachings to offer him. I simply wished to see his face and acquire the merit of being in his presence."

The Land of the Insect-Eaters

When he heard of the death of Shabkar, Patrul had just arrived in Tsö in southeastern Amdo. He learned that this district was notorious as the "Land of the Insect-Eaters." Unlike the localities of Kham, it was traditional and customary in this locale for people to consume insects as part of their normal daily diet—all sorts of different kinds of insects, from worms and crawling bugs to flies.

When he learned of this, Patrul was shocked and dismayed, owing to his love for all sentient beings.

In somber tones, he was heard to make an aspiration prayer for a bodhisattva to be reborn in this insect-eating land, to guide the people in cultivating compassion.

(*Left*) Tsö Patrul (late 19th–early 20th c.), a lama from the Tsö region, was recognized as a tulku of Patrul Rinpoche. (*Right*) Patrul Namkha Jigme (d. 1961), the son of Tertön Dudjom Lingpa (1835–1903) and the brother of the 3rd Dodrupchen, Jigme Tenpai Nyima, has also been recognized as an incarnation of Patrul. Both these photographs have been published incorrectly in various places as being images of Patrul Rinpoche himself. (Source: Shechen Archives)

MANY YEARS LATER, a tulku was born in this region of Tsö. Recognized as one of Patrul's incarnations, he was called Tsö Patrul. Known for his altruism and compassion, he cared for the needy, inviting them to live near his residence. He fed hundreds of beggars, requesting that they first enter the gate of the dharma and begin doing the preliminary practices.[63]

Patrul Meets an Exemplary Monk

Having learned of Shabkar's death while on his way to visit him, Patrul turned and went southeast to Dzamthang, an important center of the Jonang tradition and the Kalachakra lineage.

In that place there lived a lama named Tsangpa Gelong Ngawang Chöjor, renowned as an exemplary monk who kept his 253 monastic vows very strictly and very purely. Patrul, who was circumambulating a temple near where this lama lived, saw the lama sitting by a window. Looking up, Patrul giggled. "*Tee-hee!* I bet that monk up there has broken more than a couple of vows!"

Hearing him, the lama immediately came downstairs. He began apologizing to Patrul.

"*A-dzi!* To the best of my knowledge, I haven't broken a single vow in my whole life, not in the slightest. But mind is always in motion, always changing with lightning speed. It's quite possible that things have happened in my mind without my awareness. It might well be that I've broken some vows without even knowing that I've done so! Would you be kind enough to teach me how to remain without distraction?"

Very pleased, Patrul said to him, "*Ha!* You have good ears! You actually *heard* what I said!"

PATRUL RECEIVED the transmission of the Kalachakra from Tsangpa Gelong Ngawang Chöjor of Dzamthang. Patrul gave instructions on Asanga's *Treatise on the Sublime Continuum*,[64] using Kunkhyen Dolpopa Sherab Gyaltsen's commentary, and also taught *The Way of the Bodhisattva* to more than a thousand people. Afterward, people said that all evil spirits that had afflicted this area were pacified and remained so for many years.

From Dzamthang, Patrul proceeded to nearby Yarlung Pemakö, the seat of the 1st Dodrupchen, Jigme Trinley Özer, in Golok. Dodrupchen had built a monastery there where he lived out the later part of his life and taught many of his famous students, including Do Khyentse.

At the time, Gyalse Shenphen Thaye, a main lineage holder of the Longchen Nyingthig, was living at Yarlung Pemakö, acting as Regent for Jigme Trinley Özer.

Patrul's Dedication to Practice

Patrul's heart-disciple Nyoshul Lungtok told his own disciples that Patrul practiced mind training (*lojong*) as a part of every session of meditation.

Nyoshul Lungtok said that Patrul practiced with such ferocity that he sometimes struck his chest with his fists, shouting, "I'll get this right, even if it kills me!"[65]

PATRUL PASSED many years in Golok, perhaps as many as ten. His spent his time in each of the four valleys: Markhok, Dokhok, Serta, and Dzika.

The 1st Dodrupchen had established a forty-five-day annual teaching and practice session on the *Guhyagarbha Tantra*. Patrul received the teachings and was also asked to be the teaching assistant, the tutor who helps the students review in the afternoon the teachings given in the morning. Following this, for the next two years, when Shenphen Thaye couldn't be at Yarlung, Patrul himself led the forty-five-day annual teaching and practice session.

The monks studied the commentary written by Minling Lochen[66] and chanted the root tantra by heart every day. The 3rd Dodrupchen later remarked, "Thanks to Shenphen Thaye and Patrul, those teachings on the *Guhyagarbha Tantra* brought the tradition of Vajrayana to this area, like the sunlight shining through cracks in the clouds."

At Yarlung Monastery,[67] Patrul Rinpoche established an annual tradition of month-long teaching on *The Way of the Bodhisattva* while practicing it at the same time.

Patrul Pacifies a Blood Feud

A violent blood feud had broken out between two fierce nomad tribes living in adjacent valleys of Markhok, in Golok. Upon hearing about it, Patrul climbed all the way up to the high pass up on the mountain ridge that separated the two valleys.

Patrul lay down on his back in the middle of the narrow path, right in the dirt, not speaking to anyone, pretending to be asleep, with his head resting on his small bag as a pillow. Anyone who wanted to cross over the pass from one valley to the next was forced to step over his body. According to Tibetan custom, it is extremely rude to step over anyone at any time, especially while wearing shoes. Patrul's physical position itself was forcing every traveler to carry out this insulting action, which made them all angry, in addition to their natural annoyance at having some stubborn, shabby nomad lying down smack in the middle of the path and blocking everyone's way.

For some days, Patrul lay out there in the dirt.

Patrul meditated on bodhichitta, compassion, and loving-kindness while the people passing back and forth showered continual abuse upon him, the unknown vagrant.

As they did so, Patrul prayed on behalf of each traveler that their disturbing negative emotions be pacified at once.

Eventually, every person involved in the blood feud had crossed over the pass at least once, by stepping over Patrul's body. And, as if by a miracle, the nomad tribes suddenly settled their feud and made a pact, avoiding further bloodshed.

At the request of the local leader Topgye from Washul, a nomadic area of Serta, Patrul went to Serta to teach *The Way of the Bodhisattva,* the *Mani Kahbum*[68] *by King Songtsen Gampo,* and other texts.

After hearing Patrul teach on compassion, the people of Serta were inspired to stop slaughtering animals for meat. Hunters stopped hunting, and bandits gave up robbing people. Since no one wanted to go against Patrul's advice, people's behaviors improved remarkably.

Patrul's teachings showered a rain of dharma throughout the provinces of Upper and Lower Markhok. He had the ability to sow the seed for liberation in even the simplest of people.

The irresistible power of his compassion transformed the minds of brutal warlords, bandit chiefs, and countless others who up until that point had had absolutely no faith in the dharma, people who had shunned virtuous deeds and indulged in reckless violence.

Patrul also taught in the dangerous ravines of Marong in Golok, where no one had ever seen or even heard of prayer beads *(malas)* and how to use them for mantra practice. Patrul taught everyone there how and why to recite the six-syllable mantra of Avalokiteshvara.

Patrul then went to Shukchen Tago,[69] a hillside with big juniper trees, and remained there for just over a year

Shukchen Tago, the ruins of the first small monastery built by Dodrup Trinley Özer, where Patrul Rinpoche spent a year reading the 103 volumes of the Buddha's words. (2016)

There was a small monastery, the first one built by Dodrup Jigme Trinley Özer,[70] with a library and a handful of monks. It was quiet enough to provide Patrul with near-solitude and an ideal place to stay, study, and meditate. It was also the seat of the 1st Dodrupchen, one of the most important teachers of Patrul's lineage.

In that library, Patrul read the entire Tripitaka three times, all 103 volumes of the Kangyur.[71] His method was to read one page, and then prostrate to it, three times. His memory was so exceptional that, having done this triple study, he remembered clearly most of the contents and could quote many passages by heart of the Tripitaka .

Patrul Practices in the Ari Forest Wilderness

Patrul and his heart-disciple Nyoshul Lungtok spent many years practicing meditation in the wilderness of Ari Forest, locally known as Ari Nak, in Dokhok (Inner Do Valley), a forested mountain slope on the bank of the Do River between Shukchen Tago and the present Dodrupchen Monastery.

They lived at the foot of a tree in an open field on a rise in the middle of the thick forest. No one ever went there, so they were able to practice undisturbed. They had nothing but the clothes they wore, a few texts, some butter, and a few bags of tsampa.

At noon, they'd have a simple meal of tea and tsampa. They'd tie up their bag of tsampa, hang it from the branch of a tree, and leave it there. Then Patrul would give a teaching on a few verses from *The Way of the Bodhisattva.*

When he came to the end of the verse, he'd stop. Then, Patrul would shout out, "AH!" twice, as a reminder to his disciple and to himself of the absolute nature, the emptiness of all phenomena, which this basic sound is said to indicate.

Then, Patrul would disappear into the forest alone.

Patrul would stay out in the forest through the whole night, with nothing to shield him from the elements except his thick white felt garment.

At noon on the next day, Patrul would suddenly reappear. He'd eat some tsampa, teach, and disappear again.

Patrul lived like that for months, practicing meditation in the wilderness.

In the mornings, Patrul sometimes sang along with the *jolmo,* the Tibetan thrush, whose poignant song sounds like a lament and is a natural reminder of impermanence.

"We must pay attention to that song," Patrul said to Lungtok. "*Alas, kye-ma, for me! Alas, kye-hu, for you!*"[72]

Ari Nak, the forest near which Patrul Rinpoche and Nyushul Lungtok spent several years in retreat. It has now been depleted by wood cutting. (2016)

Patrul praised Ari Forest as an ideal place to meditate, as it possessed the qualities described in the eighth chapter of *The Way of the Bodhisattva:*

In solitude, the mind and body
Are not troubled by distraction.
Therefore leave this worldly life
And totally abandon mental wandering.
. . . .
Penetrative insight joined with calm abiding[73]
Utterly eradicates afflicted states.
Knowing this, first search for calm abiding,
Found by people who are happy to be free from worldly ties.
. . . .
In woodlands, haunt of stag and bird,
Among the trees where no dissension jars,
It's there I would keep pleasant company!
When might I be off to make my dwelling there?
. . . .

When might I abide in such a place,
A place unclaimed and ownerless,
That's wide and unconfined, a place where I might stay
At liberty, without attachment?

When might I be free of fear,
Without the need to hide from anyone,
With just a begging bowl and few belongings,
Dressed in garments coveted by none?
. . . .[74]

Patrul and the Venue of Vultures

Once, when Patrul and Nyoshul Lungtok were living in a mountain wilderness, practicing meditation, they completely ran out of food. Patrul said to Lungtok, "Some nomads in the valley have thrown out a few sheep carcasses. Go down after dark and bring the carcasses back." Lungtok did as Patrul asked, and from these scrounged scraps they made a good meal to help them recover their strength.

The next day, Patrul saw a whole flock of vultures hovering over the spot where the sheep carcasses had been.

"Oh, Lungtok!" exclaimed Patrul. "You mustn't go down to get any more of those carcasses! We've been eating the vultures' food!"

Patrul Practices Tummo in a Blizzard

Once, in winter, Patrul and his heart-disciple Nyoshul Lungtok were crossing over a high mountain pass called Phagmo La. At the top of the pass, they were caught in a huge blizzard. Nyoshul Lungtok collapsed in the snow. Nearly frozen, he could hardly move at all.

Patrul sang a spontaneous song of realization.

"Hey, Lungtok!" said Patrul cheerily. "Now's your chance to practice *tummo*!"

Lungtok, however, was so overcome with cold he was unable to practice, so Patrul began the tummo practice by himself. After a short time, as a result of practice, Patrul's body began radiating heat.

Through this practice of developing inner heat, Patrul warmed Lungtok and brought him back from the brink of death. Then the two of them, master and student, began practicing tummo together. It wasn't long before the snowdrifts surrounding them melted away.[75]

PATRUL THUS STAYED for several years near the Ari Forest at Dhichung Cave in the back country of Do Valley.[76] At first, he and his student Lungtok were the only ones living and practicing in the forest. Over months and years, more practitioners came. They requested teachings and stayed to practice meditation.

Lungtok's Mother

Patrul spent many years practicing meditation in the remote forest wilderness of Ari Nak. His heart-disciple Nyoshul Lungtok was living in the area as well, assiduously practicing meditation.

About every seven days or so, Lungtok would leave his part of the forest and go to the place where his teacher Patrul was staying. Master and disciple would have tea together. Lungtok might offer Patrul his experiences in meditation, and Patrul would give Lungtok meditation instructions and teachings.

Once day, a merchant who came to the Ari Forest encountered Patrul. The merchant said to him, "I'm looking for Nyoshul Lungtok. I've been wandering around everywhere, trying to find him. I've brought him presents from his mother. Can you help me find him?"

"Good man!" answered Patrul. "You've come a long way, and you've gone to a lot of trouble to bring these gifts. However, Lungtok's gone off into the forest to do practice; he isn't due to come back here for a couple of days. You're welcome to wait here for him, if you wish. If you don't, you can leave his gifts with me."

"No, I promised his mother I'd give everything to him in person," said the merchant. "I promised to convey her messages to him as well. I can't go back until I've actually seen him. Isn't there any way you could help?"

Patrul thought for a moment. "Well, you *could* try going around the forest yelling, '*Eh,* Lungtok! Patrul wants you!'" suggested Patrul. "That's about the only way you'll get him to come out."

The merchant did as he was told. He went all around the forest, shouting at the top of his lungs, "*Ki-hi-hi* . . . ! Lungtok! Patrul wants you!"

Eventually, Lungtok heard him. As predicted, he emerged from the forest.

The merchant respectfully handed over the presents for Lungtok and delivered the message he'd brought.

Lungtok asked Patrul to give the merchant some spiritual advice, as well as protection cords[77] and blessed substances for both the merchant and Lungtok's mother. He gave the merchant a personal message for his mother as well.

Patrul asked Lungtok, "Do we have anything we might send your mother as a gift?"

Lungtok looked around but they had almost nothing, only a bag of tsampa and some tea.

Patrul thought for a bit. Then he said, "A while back, someone tried to give me some valuable things. I didn't take them; I just left them in a cave. Go there and see if anything is still there that we could give your mother."

Lungtok and the merchant went to the cave where the offerings had been made. There, on the damp moss, was a roll of fine Chinese silk brocade and a shiny ingot of silver. The silk brocade that had been left behind was spoiled by the damp and had already started to rot. Lungtok picked up the silver ingot and gave it to the merchant, telling him to bring it back to his mother as a gift.

Patrul Gives Teachings in the Forest

In the remote Ari Forest, Patrul gave extensive teachings, over more than three years, on Longchenpa's *Trilogy of Resting at Ease*[78] to Nyoshul Lungtok, Minyak Kunzang Sönam, and other fortunate students. He began with the first volume, *Resting at Ease in the Nature of Mind.*[79]

First, he gave the reading transmission and oral commentary. Next, he gave instructions on how to do the actual meditation. Then, he sent his disciples off by themselves to practice the meditations they had just learned. Patrul insisted that students become completely familiar with each practice.

After students had finished meditating, he met with each one individually. Having heard what personal experiences had occurred during meditation, he gave each student individual guidance.

Over three years, Patrul gave teachings. The first year, the teachings began in the summer, starting with the preliminary practices. The weather was warm, and there was plenty of food because the local nomads were able to make generous offerings of provisions for all the practitioners.

As time went on, the weather worsened. Supplies began to dwindle.

From white azalea roots, called *surkar,*[80] they began to brew a hot drink. Patrul called it "three-*kaya* tea." With one tea per *kaya* (*nirmanakaya, sambhogakaya, dharmakaya*), there was Manifested Tea, Tea of Divine Enjoyment, and Absolute Tea.

In the morning, nirmanakaya tea was a strong brew with strong color, smell, and taste. At lunch, sambhogakaya tea was made by adding water to the tea brew left over from breakfast. In the evening, tea was made from whatever little was left over from the weaker tea from lunch. In fact, it was not much more than boiled water—no color, no taste, no smell, nothing. This, Patrul said teasingly, was dharmakaya tea—the dharmakaya symbolizing the absolute nature, which is empty of intrinsic reality. There was, for sure, not much substance in the tea!

Master and disciples all lived on three-kaya tea for many weeks, not eating any solid food whatsoever. By the end of winter, food became very scarce. At one point, they all were living on nothing but a bit of roasted barley flour and tea for breakfast and at lunchtime a bit of roasted barley dough.

Eventually, that ran out, too.

Once or twice they came across the corpses of wild animals who had died of starvation during the winter. Sometimes they found cattle carcasses the nomads had discarded, from dead animals too skinny to be worth eating.[81] From these scraps, they made broth and shared it among themselves.

By the end of the teaching period, a plague of bloody dysentery broke out down in the valley. When this occurred, Patrul told his students to separate, go farther into the forest, and to stay there by themselves, doing individual retreat.

People fleeing the epidemic began to arrive. Patrul gave them teachings and encouraged them to remain and to practice the dharma. Eventually, Patrul had his disciple Palchen Dorje call everyone to come back from their respective places of retreat.

When they came back, they were very thin. Other than their dharma robes and the text, they had no possessions. Their demeanor was serene and composed. They wore long outer robes and carried monks' staffs and begging bowls. Patrul, pleased, came out to greet them, waving fragrant sticks of burning incense and saying, "My goodness! You look just like *bhikshus* from ancient India."

By the fifth lunar month, the high grassland meadows had turned green and lush. The local nomad families once again had an abundance of food and were again able to make their customarily generous offerings.

Someone had made and given as an offering to Patrul a large *tu,* a delicious sweet food made of dri butter, cheese, and molasses, formed into a solid cake shaped like a wheel.

Patrul gave instructions that the offering of *tu* be shared among the disciples. Each person was given a generous serving as a meal for the day, without even needing to have a fire.

Later on, Lungtok commented, "These days students lack diligence. Circumstances are good, but people fail to use that to their advantage—such a waste! In my time, we faced hardships all the time, but everyone worked hard at practicing nonetheless. So, especially when conditions for practice are good, practice as much as you can."

Far-Reaching Effects of Patrul's Teachings

When Patrul taught the second volume of Longchenpa's trilogy, *Resting at Ease in Meditation,*[82] all the students listening to him felt themselves being naturally drawn into profound contemplation, and they were able to rest easily in that state, without effort. His listeners first became aware that their own understanding was deepening, and then, as they noticed this effect among their fellow practitioners, their contemplation naturally became deeper still. Those present later revealed that they had witnessed even birds and wild animals responding to Patrul, sitting quite still yet alert, as if absorbed in natural awareness.

When Patrul taught the third volume, *Resting at Ease in Illusion,*[83] Lungtok said that he suddenly experienced the whole phenomenal world as being devoid of true existence—it was nothing but illusion, an all-pervading transparency, as fragile as a bubble on the point of bursting.

According to Lungtok, these teachings were unlike any other teachings. "We directly experienced his immense knowledge, the vivacity of his own meditation experiences, and the blessings of his realization, all together," he said.

Lungtok and the Bandit Chief

Patrul was living in the Ari Forest when he heard that Do Khyentse Yeshe Dorje had left his residence in Dartsedo, near the ancient Chinese border, and had gone to the Nyenpo Yutse mountain range in Golok.[84]

Patrul decided to go to meet his master. He said to his disciple Nyoshul Lungtok one evening, "Let's go for a walk!" Together, they set out for the Nyenpo Yutse mountain range and traveled for some days. One late afternoon, when it was time to stop and make camp for the night, Patrul sent Lungtok off to a nearby encampment, telling him to bring back some water so they could make tea.

Before he left, Patrul sternly warned Lungtok that he must be very careful. The whole area was known to be terribly dangerous. It harbored many bands of bloodthirsty bandits who preyed viciously on the local people.

Lungtok, concerned but courageous, went to fetch the water.

When he returned, poor Lungtok was shaking with fear. He told his master that the nearby camp belonged to a huge gang of robbers! They were rough and desperate nomad laymen led by a fierce bandit chief.

Just then, before Lungtok could even finish warning his teacher, the horrible bandit chief himself suddenly strode right into Patrul's camp! This tall, frightening figure was dressed in a long black chuba, and stuck into his belt like a sword was his long, razor-sharp nomad knife.

This ferocious bandit went straight over to Patrul, screamed at him, scolded him, and viciously kicked him several times.

Then, as suddenly as he had come, the bandit chief turned on his heel, stalked off, and disappeared into the night.

"We must get out of here at once!" cried Lungtok. "It's much too dangerous!"

Patrul smiled and said nothing.

Just then, a group of travelers passed by. They seemed to be heading directly for the nearby bandit camp. Before Lungtok could warn them about the gang, he overheard them chattering away. They were about to meet a great lama and were thoroughly excited at their good fortune!

With shock, Lungtok realized that the terrifying bandit chief with the razor-sharp nomad knife must be his master's master—the great Do Khyentse!

He was, of course, correct.

Do Khyentse's Hospitality

On a vast plateau in Amdo featuring one of the sacred lakes[85] near Nyenpo Yutse mountain range, there was a large nomad encampment of white tents surrounded by a flock of thousands of sheep grazing nearby.

This was the encampment of Do Khyentse Yeshe Dorje. He and the 2nd

Dodrupchen, Jigme Phuntsok Jungne, were herding their huge flock of sheep to faraway Dartsedo in Kham, something they did once a year.

Patrul and Lungtok presented themselves at the lamas' encampment.

They first went to the main tent, where some attendants brought them to meet Do Khyentse. Dressed in white lambskin, Do Khyentse was sitting with his gun by his side and a couple of small dogs sleeping on his couch. Next to him sat Dodrup Jigme Phuntsok Jungne, also dressed in white.

With his long, razor-sharp knife, Do Khyentse was slicing off pieces of meat from a roast lamb and devouring them.

Delighted to see Patrul, Do Khyentse had a carpet brought and put down for Patrul to sit on. He invited both Patrul and Lungtok to sit down and join him. Do Khyentse called his attendant and asked that a sheep be slaughtered. He gave orders that its finest meat be cooked especially for Patrul.

Now, Patrul never permitted animals to be slaughtered on his behalf. He was widely known for never doing harm to a single living creature, not even to the tiniest insect, and he disapproved of the custom of killing animals as feasts for Buddhist teachers. Patrul often urged people to give up this custom. He had once said that it was shocking to see ordained followers of our compassionate teacher, Lord Buddha, with their faces red with sweat, their cheeks greasy with drippings and juice from the dead flesh of helpless creatures.

Nonetheless, at Do Khyentse's order, an animal was chosen, it was slaughtered, and its flesh was cooked up as for a feast. The attendant returned with the meat, perfectly prepared, perfectly succulent. Do Khyentse offered the very choicest cuts to Patrul, who—again uncharacteristically—ate it all up without objection, doing so with apparent relish.

Patrul's disciple Nyoshul Lungtok, on the other hand, just looked appalled. Moved by compassion for the poor newly slain sheep, he could not bring himself to eat one single bite.

Do Khyentse looked at Nyoshul Lungtok and said, "Oh, I get it. You're probably not the kind of person who eats this. But anyway, here!"

Do Khyentse threw a big hunk of meat right at Nyoshul Lungtok's chest, saying, "*This* is for you!"

Slowly, painfully, with utter reluctance, Nyoshul Lungtok forced himself to eat the whole huge slab of meat Do Khyentse had tossed at him. For his part, Patrul, apparently in a festive mood, kept right on cheerily eating his very generous portion of freshly killed cooked mutton.

Having finished their meal, Do Khyentse and Patrul happily exchanged news and discussed various spiritual matters. Patrul made a request that Do Khyentse grant him a special initiation, the Queen of Great Bliss.[86]

"I've kept these teachings secret for years," said Do Khyentse. "I have not transmitted them to anyone for a long time. Today, I shall give you the transmission." He gave Patrul many outer, inner, and secret teachings, including an empowerment that introduced the disciple to the nature of pure awareness, called the *rigpai tsal wang*.[87]

Do Khyentse made a prediction that Patrul would live to be eighty years old and that he would bring benefit to every being who made a connection with him.

Patrul and Lungtok then took their leave.

After a few hours of walking, they reached a small hill, from which they could look back at where they'd come from and see the vast grassland plateau. Off in the distance, they could just barely make out a small patch of white, which was the big flock of sheep being herded to Dartsedo to be sold for slaughter.

Patrul said to Lungtok, "You know, those two, Do Khyentse and Dodrup Phuntsok Jungne, are, respectively, the true incarnations of Jigme Lingpa and Dodrup Trinley Özer. I've been teaching you for a long time and I've been teaching the dharma for a long time, but *I* can't guarantee that after you die, you'll be reborn in the pure land of Padmasambhava—Zangdokpalri, the Glorious Copper-Colored Mountain. But such is the power of Do Khyentse's blessings that at the instant of death, each and every last one of those sheep, without exception, will go directly to Zangdokpalri.

"Wouldn't you or I be extremely fortunate to be one of those sheep?"

The Gift from Lungtok's Mother

Patrul and Nyoshul Lungtok were staying in Karchung Khormo Olu, the secluded mountain retreat in Dzachukha where Patrul had been born.

Lungtok's mother sent him some butter as a gift, and as soon as Lungtok received it, he offered the lump of butter to Patrul. It was a very large lump indeed.

Patrul stared at the butter for a while. "Lungtok, why does your mother's butter look like the yellow hat of a dignitary?" he asked, adding, "Well, except it has furled rhubarb leaves around it, instead of being trimmed with fur."[88]

Lungtok explained to Patrul that the butter was made and shaped according to local tradition. Day after day, his mother had churned the rich summer milk into butter. After churning, each day's layer was set down. The next day's sweet milk would then be churned into butter, and when that day's layer was set down, leaves were carefully laid between the layers. Day after day, with loving intention to nourish her son, she would carefully slather on a new layer on top of the previous one, tenderly wrapping each in fresh leaves, as was the local nomad custom.

Impressed and moved by Lungtok's mother's painstaking work, Patrul returned the lump of butter to Lungtok.

"*A-dzi!*" exclaimed Patrul. "See how much love your mother put into making this? I wouldn't *dare* eat her butter![89]

Lungtok tried to give the butter back, saying, "*Please* accept this offering of butter."

"No, I mustn't," said Patrul. "Anyway, I'm sure it wouldn't agree with me."

Lungtok insisted. "Please take it. If you would be kind enough to accept this butter and eat it, it will create an auspicious connection. Take it and keep my mother in your prayers!"

Patrul relented and accepted the lump of handmade butter in order to create the connection with Lungtok's mother.

"That's It!"

It was some days after Patrul had accepted, at Lungtok's insistence, a special offering of butter sent by his mother. Suddenly Patrul asked Lungtok, "Do you miss your mother?"

"Not really," Lungtok replied.

"*A-dzi!*" said Patrul. "That's what happens when you fail to cultivate compassion!"

He continued, "Now go into that willow grove over there and train for seven days in accepting all beings as your mother, remembering their kindness. Then come back."

Lungtok then spent seven days contemplating the fact that every sentient being had, in some previous lifetime, been his mother, reflected on their selfless kindness to him, and developed the aspiration to bring them happiness and enlightenment. As a result, genuine loving-kindness, compassion, and bodhichitta arose in his mind for all beings.

He returned to his teacher and explained his experiences during meditation.

"That's it!" said Patrul, pleased. "That's what it takes! When mind training is done properly, particular signs arise in your mind! Shantideva said that with practice, everything becomes easy. People just don't do enough practice. If they did, they'd really make progress."

Not long afterward, Patrul told Lungtok, "Until now, I've told you not to accept any offerings. Now I want you to start accepting whatever you are given. Go home and see your mother for a while. Then come back."

Lungtok did as his master said. First he participated in the rites for Patrul's mother, who had just died, and was offered a stallion and ten silver coins. On his way home he requested alms, receiving several bricks of tea and even some cattle. All he had been given, he presented to his own mother when he arrived home.

Adzom Drukpa's Dilemma

By the time he was twenty, Adzom Drukpa was already renowned as a great lama.

Wanting to meet Patrul Rinpoche, he went to Mamo Thang Valley in Dzachukha. He arrived with a large retinue and set up his encampment not far from Drelkar Cave, where Patrul was staying.

The morning after he arrived, Adzom Drukpa and a monk walked up the hill toward Patrul's cave, which was halfway up the mountain on the slope of a cliff. On their way, the two happened to run into Patrul, who had left his cave to go down and fetch some water.

Without a word being spoken, Patrul recognized Adzom Drukpa instantly. However, he kept this to himself and greeted the visitors by saying, "I've heard that Adzom Drukpa has come here. Are you two part of that group?"

"Yes, we are," replied Adzom Drukpa.

"Well, then, come up, come in," said Patrul, and he led the visitors up a little path to his cave.

Inside the cave, the three were about to sit down when Patrul grabbed a furry little yak-skin rug and tossed it to Adzom Drukpa, saying, "Here! Use this!"

Adzom Drukpa accepted the yak-skin rug but hesitated. To seat himself on the rug—the personal possession of a great master—would be extremely disrespectful. But to decline to do what Patrul had told him to do would be even more disrespectful. It might even sever an auspicious karmic link between them.

Adzom Drukpa found a solution to this dilemma. He sat down on the floor of the tent, laid the yak-skin rug to his side, and leaned on it with his elbow, thus assuming a posture that was very acceptable among the people of Kham, conveying no discourtesy.

Just then a bird flew by the cave entrance and landed on some nearby nettles. As the bird began to sing sweetly, it came to Patrul's mind to ask Adzom Drukpa if he would perform phowa, the ritual transference of consciousness, on behalf of his late mother, Drolma.[90]

By Patrul's own account, his mother had been a good-natured, broad-minded, and truthful person. She was the first one to steer him toward the path of dharma. From the start, she made sure he was not spoiled by his position as a tulku and that he never misused the offerings given to him by the faithful.

Patrul made the request of Adzom Drukpa, and the young master gave his consent and performed the rituals on behalf of Patrul's mother.

Patrul Is Asked to Bestow Special Teachings

Adzom Drukpa made a formal request that Patrul bestow upon him the oral instructions on the *tsalung* and yogic exercises (*trulkhor*) according to the Longchen Nyingthig tradition.[91]

"Well, I don't know about that," responded Patrul noncommittally.

He looked thoughtful. "I've had these teachings. *Sort of*," said Patrul, vaguely. "But I think I've forgotten most of it!"

Then, in a gruff tone, he added, "*Hmf!* Well, we'll see."

That was the end of the conversation.

The next day, Patrul walked down toward Adzom Drukpa's encampment. Adzom Drukpa and retinue met him halfway. Everyone walked together down to the encampment, where Patrul was received with much pomp and ceremony.

Patrul was ushered into the main tent, which was luxurious and magnificent, covered in thick soft carpets, with piles of furs and lots of soft cushions covered in colorful Chinese silk brocades.

Patrul gave all this opulence a dubious look.

Adzom Drukpa, with a respectful gesture, directed Patrul toward the prominent cushion that was his personal seat.

"Let's go for it!" said Patrul, plonking himself down with one quick move. "This is all new to me! Until right this second, I'd never *been* to a celestial realm! This must be the 'Buddhafield of Utter Liberation'!"[92]

He paused, thought, then said, "Although few are fortunate enough to be suitable vessels, the teachings of the Mantrayana are widely available. Even so, from time to time, people come to me asking about the meaning of the *angra*. Even Geluk geshes have come to me, but there just hasn't been much that I wanted to say.

"Once, I came down with leprosy. I was very ill. I did some meditation practice and some yogic exercises, and I was cured. There's nothing to show that I was ever sick except for this little white scar," he said, pointing to a place between his eyebrows.

"Because of that experience, I feel confident that transmitting these teachings to you will be of benefit."

Patrul reached into the folds of his coat and pulled out a short skirtlike garment. It was an *angra,* a cloth costume made to be worn while doing yoga.

"This is my ninth *angra,*" he said, showing it to Adzom Drukpa. "I've worn out the other eight."

Then, over the next three weeks, Patrul taught Adzom Drukpa yoga.

He taught him all the details and specifics: positions, movements, breathing, and visualizations for practices involving *nadis*, *prana*, *bindu,* and *tummo.*[93] He gave guidance on why and precisely how to accomplish the various physical yoga exercises.

These two, master and student, performed all the yogic practices together until the transmission was complete. In this way, in what is known as the whispered lineage, one to one, this special knowledge belonging to the Longchen Nyingthig was passed on from master to student.

Visible Effects of Yoga

Patrul received direct instructions on the secret *tsalung* yogic teachings of the Longchen Nyingthig from Jigme Gyalwai Nyugu. He also trained extensively with the hidden yogi Drupwang Rogza Sönam Palge.[94] In this way, one on one, he had learned how to perform exercises involving channels and subtle energies.

Patrul used to train in these yogic exercises while seated in the center of his little black yak-hair tent. During one particular exercise, his head used to hit up against the tent's central pole.

Over time, the pole that his head repeatedly struck actually became noticeably dirty—a unique testament to Patrul's diligence and perseverance in practice.

Animate and Inanimate Dances

Nyoshul Lungtok went to a vase-accomplishment ceremony of the New Treasure tradition ceremony at Yel-le Gar.[95] During the ritual invocation, wisdom deities manifested through the monks, causing them to break into dance.[96]

When Lungtok returned, Patrul asked what had happened, and Lungtok told him what he'd seen. Patrul remarked, "Oh, today's was an animate dance! Sometimes inanimate dances happen as well!"

When Lungtok asked Patrul what he meant, he replied, "Once, at Shugu Shar Monastery, I performed the recitation practice for all thirteen mandalas of the Kahma. While I was doing the recitation of Vajrakilaya according to the Rog tradition,[97] a little copper *phurba* that was on the mandala as a support started dancing!"

"Why did that happen?"

"I don't know. I don't know if it was good or bad."

"Do you still have that *phurba*?" Lungtok asked.

Patrul replied, "I gave it to Tertön Sogyal Lerab Lingpa.[98] When he used that *phurba* to retrieve a concealed treasure from inside any kind of rock, he told me that it went right through solid rock easily, just like piercing mud."[99]

Patrul Laughs Over an Old Man's Corpse

Once, Patrul was giving teachings on the *Guhyagarbha Tantra* near Dhichung Cave. Among the assembly of disciples was an old man who was staying at a nearby nomad camp. He faithfully attended the teachings every day.

To get to the teachings from the nomad encampment, he had to cross the Do River. The water was too deep to ford on foot, so in the morning he crossed the river while riding on a yak, returning each evening after the teachings were done.

As often happens in Kham, one day a sudden downpour upstream created a flash flood—just as the old nomad was in the midst of crossing. It struck him with full force, and the strong current swept him away downstream.

The man's relatives found his corpse and carried it to Patrul, setting it before him, face up.

"Poor old man," said Patrul, shaking his head. "He died on his way to the teachings."

In Kham, nomads regard death by drowning as being especially inauspicious. They believe that those who die by drowning will surely be reborn in the lower realms.

The old man's widow and relatives were weeping uncontrollably.

"Please," the grieving widow begged Patrul, "embrace him with your compassion!"

"We must perform excellent prayers on his behalf!" said Patrul.

Patrul and his disciples began to recite the ritual for phowa, the transference of consciousness after death.

As they began their recitation, misty rainbow-colored clouds appeared and a gentle drizzle began to fall—what Tibetans call "a rain of flowers."

Patrul looked up into the sky.

Patrul looked down at the old man's corpse.

Patrul began to laugh.

He stopped reciting the ritual, though he was only halfway through. The other lamas and monks and students finished the ritual without him. No one dared ask Patrul the reason for his unusual behavior.

After a few days, one student got up the nerve and asked Patrul, "Abu, why did you laugh at that poor old man's corpse? Everyone knows that compassion is the main point of your teachings. Was that old man unworthy of your compassion?"

"Of course, he was!" Patrul said. "But I just couldn't help laughing!"

"At what?"

"Feeling great sadness, I had been making prayers that he be reborn in a celestial realm," Patrul replied. "Suddenly, I had a vision of him taking rebirth as a celestial being in the Paradise of the Thirty-three![100]

"I heard him ask the celestial beings why he was taking rebirth in their realm. They told him it was because he had been taking the Guhyagarbha teachings, doing so with one-pointed mind and pure faith.

"As gratitude for the teachings, he threw down this rain of flowers!"

Everyone there had experienced the gentle shower and had seen the sky filled with misty, rainbow-colored clouds.

"Knowing this, I looked down at his gray-haired corpse. I heard his widow wailing, saying, 'My husband has gone to hell.'

"The contradiction was so great that I just broke into laughter.

"Truly, the delusions of samsara are stupendous! They're like the apparitions of a conjurer! When people hear me laughing, they think I'm a little odd. But when I hear them wailing when their old man is already a celestial being, I think they're much stranger!"

AROUND THIS TIME, Patrul returned to the area around Dzogchen Monastery. He served as the 5th Abbot of Shri Singha College of Dzogchen Monastery. There and at Padme Thang, Nakchung hermitage, and elsewhere, for a number of years he taught *The Way of the Bodhisattva,* the *Mahayanasutralamkara* (Ornament of the Mahayana Sutras), the *Abhidharmakosha* (Treasury of the Abhidharma), the *Yönten Dzö* (Treasury of Precious Qualities), *the Domsum Namnge* (Ascertaining the Three Vows), and other texts.

Nine Brothers Delight Patrul

Once, Patrul came to the house of Lila Tulku of Dzogchen to meet his family. There were nine brothers in the family, and each had taken full monastic ordination, keeping the full set of 253 vows.[101] Each one of the nine *gelongs* ate from a traditional begging bowl, and all nine wore traditional yellow monastic dharma robes.

After visiting them, as he was going back to his retreat Patrul remarked, "From what I've seen today, I'm reassured that the Buddha dharma will last a little longer."[102]

Patrul Reads Tertön Sogyal's Mind

Once, Tertön Sogyal Lerab Lingpa was staying with Patrul Rinpoche, receiving teachings. Tertön Sogyal had begun his dharma studies at Dzogchen Monastery. Later in life, his many students would include Gyalwa Thubten Gyatso, the 13th Dalai Lama.

Sitting in the room along with Patrul and Tertön Sogyal was a young monk who had been studying a sutra and was now copying it down by hand, line by line. He was working on this verse:

By offering praise to the bodhisattvas,
Nonvirtue wanes and virtue waxes from within.

The young monk, however, had made a mistake in his copying. Puzzled on rereading what he had just written down, the young monk asked Patrul, "What can this line mean—'*By offering praise to the bodhisattvas, virtue wanes and nonvirtue waxes from within*'?"

Tertön Sogyal was barely able to stop himself from scoffing aloud at the boy's obvious error. He thought to himself, "Why does the great Patrul Rinpoche allow such a moron to bother him with stupid questions?"

"Yes, yes!" Patrul cried out to Tertön Sogyal. "It's so true, is it not? '*Nonvirtue waxes from within! Nonvirtue waxes from within!*'"

At once, Tertön Sogyal was ashamed to realize that his teacher Patrul had read his mind precisely and was fully aware of his unkind and arrogant thoughts.

Patrul's Miraculous Recovery

When Patrul was staying at the Shinje Cave above Dzogchen Monastery, someone saw him and said, "Your face is red. Your complexion is off—really, you look like you've had leprosy!"

"It's true," said Patrul. "I came down with a disease caused by *naga* spirits. So I practiced yogic exercises along with the meditation and recitation of Black Hayagriva according to the terma of Chögyal Ratna Lingpa.[103] Then I had a dream of a big snake coming out of my body. Visualizing myself as Hayagriva, I chopped the snake into pieces with my sword.[104] A week later, I was completely cured."

Patrul and Chokgyur Lingpa

On a steep cliffside in the Glacier Wilderness, the great tertön Chokgyur Lingpa was discovering terma teachings, which were part of the cycle of the Supreme Bliss, Union of All Buddhas.[105]

During this time, he was staying near Dzogchen Monastery. With him was the tulku of Yonge Mingyur Dorje,[106] who was serving as the tertön's attendant, receiving visitors, cooking his meals, making tea, and looking after him in general.

One day, at dawn, Chokgyur Lingpa said to his attendant, "Today, the great master Patrul Rinpoche will be coming. Please make special preparations."

A while later, after giving the tertön tea, Yonge came out of the master's room and noticed that a visitor had arrived, an old man with a large frame and prominent nose. He was dressed like a nomad from Golok, not in the robes of a lama. His simple coat was made of sheepskin, with the hairless pelt side turned out and covered in red felt cloth.

"I have to see Chokgyur Lingpa!" the old man said, and he proceeded to walk in.

As the tertön's visitors never entered his quarters unannounced, much less without permission, Yonge blocked the door, saying, "Wait! Wait! It doesn't work like that! I must first announce you to the lama!"

"Get out of my way!" said the old man, attempting to push Yonge aside.

Yonge grabbed the old man's sleeve and insisted, "You can't just barge in like this!"

The old man pulled back in the opposite direction, and the two began to tussle.

Suddenly, Yonge thought to himself, "Maybe this is not an ordinary old man from Golok. Perhaps I should go inside and ask."

What he had been told earlier about the day's visitor then dawned on him, but he had assumed that he'd be meeting someone who actually looked like a great master.

He turned around and saw that Chokgyur Lingpa had emerged from his quarters. The great tertön was flat out on the floor, doing full-length prostrations to the old nomad. The old man was bowing down, too.

"Then," Yonge later recounted, "after they both had bowed down to each other, they touched heads, just like two yaks."

Patrul Expresses Confidence in Chokgyur Lingpa

At Patrul's request, Chokgyur Lingpa gave the transmission for the Lama Gongdu (Union of the Wisdom-Minds of All Gurus) by Sangye Lingpa.[107]

When he finished, Patrul made a mandala offering to him in gratitude for the transmissions he had given. Patrul said to the assembly of disciples, "I'm convinced that Chokgyur Lingpa is an authentic tertön. His termas are immaculate. Today, we have been fortunate to receive this empowerment from Tertön Chokgyur Dechen Lingpa—it is the same as receiving it from Sangye Lingpa himself. He is the true representative of Padmasambhava in our time.

"In general, I put my confidence in the original teachings, as they are unequaled. I don't have much confidence in current termas, nor do I generally have visions or experiences as a result of meditation. However, after I practiced according to this terma,[108] there were definite signs of progress—dreams and pure visions with the signs mentioned in the sadhana. Therefore, although it is hard for ordinary people like me to judge others, I believe these terma teachings to be genuine."[109]

Since Patrul so rarely praised anyone, his lavish praise of Chokgyur Lingpa helped to establish his reputation as an authentic tertön.

The tertön named Patrul the spiritual heir of two cycles of termas: *The Perfectly Pure Union of all Buddhas* and *The Heart Essence of the Three Families*.[110]

Patrul's Pointing-Out Instruction for an Old Nomad

The tertön Chokgyur Lingpa, his consort Lady Dega, and all his children[111] received teachings on *The Way of the Bodhisattva* from Patrul, toward whom they all had much respect and devotion. Chokgyur Lingpa's children—his elder son, Wangchok Dorje, and his daughter, Könchog Paldrön (both children of Lady Dega), and his younger son, Tsewang Norbu (whose mother was a niece of Jamyang Khyentse Wangpo)—all considered Patrul to be their root teacher and studied at length with him.

Könchog Paldrön recalled an occasion when she and her family were in Patrul's presence[112] while he gave the pointing-out instruction to an old nomad from Golok.

Speaking in the old man's local dialect, Patrul gave this crucial teaching in brief, pointing to the true nature of mind:

Don't ruminate about the past!
Don't anticipate the future!

Don't cogitate about the present!
Not tampering with it
Leave mind just as is
This very instant
Aware
Relaxed
Beyond this, there's not a damn thing![113]

This essential advice became famed as Patrul's "Not-a-damn-thing instruction."

Yet, this quintessential teaching was not enough. The old man from Golok began pleading, "*Please* give me a blessing to ensure that I won't be reborn in hell!"

Patrul shook his head and told him that he could not do that.

"The only way to get to be reborn in a pure realm is through practice. It's not like flinging a stone!" said Patrul. "You can't just get there in a flash, like lightning!"

» *On the Nature of Mind* «

To an experienced practitioner, still mind is mind and moving mind is mind.
Once a practitioner has really recognized the empty nature of mind,
Moving mind and still mind are not two different things.
No matter what thought arises, no matter what appears,
it is empty of nature;
it is the play of primordial wisdom;
it is the profound understanding of the Victorious Ones

Just leave this as it is, without fabrication or modification.

Whenever thoughts arise, naturally, they will be set free spontaneously.

This itself is samadhi,
this is dharmakaya,
this is naturally arisen primordial wisdom,
this is Mahamudra, and
this is the transcendent perfection of wisdom.

Just as a rope already burnt by fire cannot tie anything up, discursive thoughts no longer bind.
Their nature is emptiness.
What appears as "thoughts" is the very radiance of emptiness.

Since there is no difference between thoughts and emptiness, the great Orgyen[114] said: "The nature of thoughts being emptiness, they should be understood as dharmakaya."

When one "meditates," *that's* the intellect. There's nothing to meditate *upon:* leave thoughts as they are, just as they present themselves.

When you start making all kinds of corrections, ordinary thoughts set in motion the chain reaction of delusion. So, don't correct or modify *anything*.

When you stray from leaving things just as they are, that itself is delusion.

So, all you need is to avoid wandering. The only point is never to wander, while maintaining no object of focus whatsoever.

If grasping thoughts are freed by themselves, outwardly, the objects of grasping (forms, sounds, etc.) will also be liberated of their own accord.

Sights, such as "beautiful" and "ugly" forms; sounds (pleasant or unpleasant to the ear); good or bad smells, tastes, or tactile sensations; joys and sorrows, desire and repulsion; friends and enemies; earth, water, fire, wind and all the rest, in short, whatever arises, whatever appears, *leave it all just as it is.*

Mindfulness should never be parted from compassion. At the beginning of the session, think that you are meditating for the benefit of all sentient beings. At the end of the session, dedicate the merit, wishing: "By this merit, may all sentient beings attain buddhahood."

The great Orgyen said: "Without compassion, the root of dharma is rotten."

This is extremely important.

An Offering of Silver

Once, an aristocrat from the Pulong family of Lhasa came to meet Patrul. Knowing how reluctant Patrul was to give formal audiences, much less to accept any offerings, he asked an old monk from Dzachukha for help.

The old monk knew that Patrul had been reciting the *Tantra of Immaculate Confession*[115] as part of his daily practice. Patrul had just come to the part where one does prostrations while reciting the liturgy when the old monk announced:

"A noble from the Pulong family of Lhasa wishes to meet you."

Patrul, in the process of doing prostrations, was fully stretched out on the ground. He stopped in that face-down position and told the monk, "Send him in!"

The aristocrat knew that he had to be quick. He came in and bowed down, touching his forehead to Patrul's feet, then planted a large piece of silver right behind Patrul's outstretched feet.

Having successfully made his offering, the nobleman ran off happily, before Patrul even had time to get up.

Patrul and Chokgyur Lingpa's Yellow Parchment

Once, the great tertön Chokgyur Lingpa gave one of his dakini scripts[116] to Patrul, as a blessing. Chokgyur Lingpa's document was written on a small piece of yellow parchment.

Normally, these scripts are supports that help a tertön to see clearly in his mind a whole cycle of teachings that he will later write down. Because all the necessary auspicious circumstances for this were not yet present, Chokgyur Lingpa had not deciphered this particular script.

An old monk, to whom Patrul had shown the parchment, tried to read it, but he could not understand the characters. Puzzled, he asked Patrul, "What does it say?"

Patrul answered, "The tertön himself can't make heads or tails out of it—how am *I* supposed to know?"

Another Offering of Silver

Every one of the three children of the famed tertön Chokgyur Lingpa became students of Patrul—his two sons, Wangchok Dorje and Tsewang Norbu, and his daughter, Könchog Paldrön. In particular, after receiving from Patrul the empowerment of the Longchen Nyingthig, they considered him as their root teacher.

Once, when Patrul was on retreat in a valley, Chokgyur Lingpa's son Tsewang Norbu came to a meadow, along with a few learned khenpos, to receive teachings. Patrul's listeners gathered around him. All of them had been spending time in retreat. Some stayed at the foot of a large tree, some stayed under a rocky overhang, some stayed in small caves, but none lived in a constructed habitation, as there were none there.

At some point, an old man arrived on horseback. He dismounted and prostrated three times before the lama.

Saying to Patrul, "Please save me from rebirth in the lower realms!" he placed an ingot of silver at Patrul's feet, even though he was well aware that Patrul did not accept offerings. He jumped back onto his horse and galloped off before Patrul had time to give the offering of silver back to him.

Seeing the bright ingot of silver on the ground, Tsewang Norbu thought to himself, "Well, no doubt Patrul will use this offering for some virtuous purpose or other."

Tsewang Norbu noticed that Patrul did not pick up the shiny chunk of silver; he ignored it completely. And when he finished teaching, he just stood up and went back to the place where he'd been staying, leaving the offering of silver behind.

One by one, his students got up and went off to the places where they did practice, not one of them even casting a glance back at the piece of precious metal.

The silver ingot was left behind, lying in the grass, round and bright like a full moon. Tsewang Norbu could not help thinking that it would be better to use it for some virtuous purpose than to just abandon it.

After having walked some distance away, he looked back again. The silver was still there, a sparkling dot in the green meadow. Walking down the hill, pondering, a tremendously powerful feeling of world-weariness, revulsion toward samsara, and true renunciation arose in his mind. Filled with faith and admiration, Tsewang Norbu thought to himself, "When I think of my guru and all these students who have renounced the attachments of this fleeting life, it reminds me of the behavior of Buddha and his disciples."

He thought of this story:

> Once, Lord Buddha and his disciples—including Ananda, Mahakashyapa, and many others arhats—were walking along, and came across a large piece of gold lying on the ground. As they passed it by, one after another would exclaim, "Poison!"
>
> A little girl who was collecting wood nearby heard them, and after they had gone, she looked and saw the nugget of gold, not knowing exactly what it was. She thought, "How strange! Here is a beautiful, bright yellow piece of stone. All the arhats stepped aside and avoided touching it, exclaiming, 'Poison!' That must be something I also should not touch."
>
> When she got home, the child told her mother, "Today I saw a curious kind of poison," and related all that had transpired. The mother wished to see for herself and went immediately. She immediately perceived that the so-called stone was a nugget of gold, which she brought home with her in order to use it to perform religious offerings. The news spread that the Buddha and his ordained followers had intentionally bypassed a piece of gold, leaving it behind and calling it "poison."

Remembering this, Tsewang Norbu felt inspired to have witnessed how naturally Patrul's behavior followed in the footsteps of the Victorious One and his disciples.

» *One Taste* «

Mistakenly taking apparent phenomena to be real
Means you'll be duped into clinging.
Once you know that outer phenomena and inner appearances
Are as real as the moon's reflection in water,
All phenomenal appearances have one taste.

When elderly eyes long for youthful strength
There's the toxic taste of attachment.
Once clinging to this physical body

Is freed in absolute space,
Youth and age have one taste.

When you take the three stages of life[117] to be real
And behave as if they are lasting,
The pain of death is bitter.
In the unique essence of awareness,
Death and birth have one taste.

When you are bound up by ties of affection
To your family members and friends,
Parting brings certain heartbreak.
Once you see samsara's nature as illusion,
Parting and meeting have one taste.

When you put your hope in gods,
Your fear of demons worsens.
Once you know the sacred nature of the world and beings,
Demons and gods have one taste.

When you keep following after discursive thoughts,
A thousand ideas will occur to you.
Once you notice mind without following thoughts,
You relax there, with no need to take action.

When you act just as everyone wants,
There's no end to your obligations.
When you act so as to go your own way,
You escape plans and projects for sure.

While others may speak well of you,
Though you're all too well aware of your flaws,
It's stupid to put on the airs of a saint;
It's time to get lost, you scoundrel!

The kingship falls into the hands of a fox;
King Fox eats royal fruit for a time.
Once King Fox is bitten by bitter-cold winds,
It's time to slink back to his den.[118]

If you stay on, as people from Marwa wish,
You'll never get to Do.[119]

Once you've made the choice to hit the road—
Do and Mar?—One pass, two valleys!

Ha! Sheer nonsense!
Hee! Pure babble!
Oh! Oh! Just blurted it out!

Karmai Khenpo Rinchen Dargye Requests Teachings

The great tertön Chokgyur Lingpa once told his student Karmai Khenpo Rinchen Dargye to go and receive teachings from Patrul Rinpoche. He told the Khenpo that Patrul was a master of inconceivable caliber and that to receive teachings from Patrul, particularly his teachings on Shantideva's *Way of the Bodhisattva,* would bring invaluable blessings.

Chokgyur Lingpa sent him to Patrul bearing a letter of introduction saying, "Please give my disciple clothing, food, and dharma."

Now, Rinchen Dargye was a great scholar, one of Chokgyur Lingpa's dharma heirs, and a fully ordained monk who was well known for keeping all his precepts purely, a fact of which he was quite proud. It was said that he had never allowed a lie to cross his lips and had never eaten meat nor touched alcohol. He rigorously upheld his vow not to ever touch a woman.[120]

The Khenpo came to Patrul carrying his monastic dharma robes on his shoulder, his begging bowl on his back, and his staff in his hand.

Just as the great Khenpo began doing prostrations, Patrul suddenly shouted, "Here's the King of Ghosts!"[121]

The Khenpo stopped and Patrul stood up.

The Khenpo tried again. Each time the Khenpo tried to prostrate to him, Patrul jumped off to the side, out of the way. He jumped left, then he moved right, making the whole thing impossible, completely evading the Khenpo's prostrations.

The Khenpo gave up.

The next day, mustering his courage, the Khenpo went again to Patrul and formally requested teachings.

Patrul shook his head.

"Oh, I can't give you any of those teachings!" said Patrul. "*I* can't teach you the dharma. *I'm* not a real teacher!"

The Khenpo left.

The next day, the Khenpo returned and renewed his supplication.

Patrul just stared at him. Then he shrugged and said, noncommittally, "Oh, well, stay, if you must, and we'll see what happens."

Dzachukha, one of the highest areas in Kham, was freezing cold at that time of year. For nearly a month, day after day, the great Khenpo stayed there, waiting, but Patrul did not give him one single word of teaching.

Eventually, Khenpo Rinchen Dargye came to Patrul and said, with some sadness, "Terchen[122] Chokgyur Lingpa sent me to receive teachings from you, but if you're really not going to give me any teachings, I'll leave. If you *are* willing to teach me, please know that I have strong faith in you. I haven't broken any *samayas,* and I don't harbor wrong views."

Patrul replied curtly, "Oh, well, then, all right, all right. Come back tomorrow!"

The next day, the Khenpo arrived, ready to receive his teachings at last.

With two hands and with extreme politeness, Patrul bestowed upon the Khenpo a complete set of monastic robes, saying, "*This*—is clothing!"

The Khenpo received the folded set of monastic robes and bowed.

Patrul said, "Come back tomorrow."

The next day, the Khenpo again arrived for his teachings.

With two hands and with extreme politeness, Patrul formally bestowed upon the Khenpo a huge leg of dried mutton, saying, "*This*—is food!"

Somewhat surprised, the Khenpo received the leg of mutton and bowed.

Patrul said, "Come back tomorrow."

The next day, the Khenpo again arrived for his teachings.

With two hands, and with extreme politeness, Patrul formally bestowed upon the Khenpo a text of *The Way of the Bodhisattva,* saying, "*This*—is dharma!"

The Khenpo received the text and bowed.

Patrul said, "Now, in accordance with the wishes of your teacher, I have just given you clothing, food, and dharma!"

There was silence.

"That's it!" said Patrul. "Tomorrow, you can go right back where you came from."

Aghast, the Khenpo began to prostrate before Patrul. He did so many times and then begged, "Please, please give me some instructions!"

Patrul adamantly refused. "Chokgyur Lingpa asked me very specifically to give you clothing, food, and dharma! Now you've got them! That's *it*!"

Khenpo Rinchen Dargye, however, did not go home. He remained and persevered in his daily requests for teachings.

At long last, Patrul relented. He began giving the Khenpo extensive teachings and continued to do so eagerly for several months, taking care of the Khenpo with loving affection.

Calling the great scholar insulting names like "King of Ghosts," avoiding his prostrations, and refusing to teach him—all this was Patrul's way of bringing to light the Khenpo's hidden vanity from having been so widely praised for the meticulous observance of his 253 *gelong* vows.

Patrul Receives Teachings from an Old Lama

An old lama was teaching Shantideva's *Way of the Bodhisattva.* Among his crowd of listeners was Patrul, who sat unrecognized, just another shabby nomad lama. After a few days, when the old lama had finished going through half the text, he stopped.

He told his disciples, "I've just learned that the great Patrul Rinpoche will be coming to Dzogchen Monastery to teach at the Shri Singha Philosophical College. He'll be teaching *The Way of the Bodhisattva,* his specialty. We should all go there to hear him."

The old lama knew that the shabby lama (Patrul) had been an especially attentive listener, and singled him out, saying, "You! You should go, too!"

They all went to Shri Singha for teachings. When they arrived, the old lama found himself a seat and sat down to listen.

Patrul came out and sat down on the teaching throne.

Seeing him, the old lama exclaimed, "Hey! There's my student!"

Acknowledging him in turn, Patrul replied, "Hey! There's my teacher!"

Then he added, teasingly, "There's my teacher! He's the one who taught me *The Way of the Bodhisattva*—but only halfway through!"

Patrul invited the old lama to come up near the teaching throne and sit down on the seat right beside him, which the old lama did, with a mixture of devotion and embarrassment.

Patrul Is Taught His Own Teachings

Patrul had decided to go to Kathok and gather merit by circumambulating the stupas at the Kathok Kumbum (the Hundred Thousand Images of Kathok).[123] The place was named in honor of master Kadampa Deshek's[124] vision of a hundred thousand Vajrasattvas dissolving into a huge boulder.

Among these many stupas, there is a trio known as the Three *Bums*.[125] These contain the relics of three patriarchs of Kathok: Yeshe Bum, Dorje Bum, and Changchup Bum. Appearing to be just another nomad lama, Patrul circumambulated these stupas all day, and no one gave him a second thought.

A few people noticed this shabby nomad lama stopping at each stupa, sticking his head inside, and saying a few words. Beyond that, there was nothing out of the ordinary about him.

When he first arrived, Patrul stayed with an old lama from Gyarong. The lama asked where he was from, and Patrul told him that he was from Dzachukha. He said that he was doing pilgrimage at the Kumbum to receive the blessings of this sacred place.

"Have you had any dharma teaching?" the old Gyarong lama asked Patrul.

Patrul replied, "Not much. I have received *The Way of the Bodhisattva* and a few other teachings, but that's about it."

His host said to him, "You seem intent upon virtue. Since you came here from so far away, you must be something of a diligent practitioner. If I were to teach you some dharma, would you be interested?"

"*A-ho!*" Patrul said, "Of course, I'd be interested! Who doesn't need the dharma?"

"There is a teaching called *Kunzang Lamai Shelung—The Words of My Perfect Teacher*—by the great Dza Patrul Rinpoche," said the old lama. "This wonderful text explains the preliminary practices and is very well known here; it will certainly help you a lot. Otherwise, if you make prayers and circumambulate the stupas, but do so without the correct attitude and understanding, all your effort won't result in much benefit."

"*A-dzi!*" exclaimed Patrul. "Truly, I need to know these teachings. Please be kind enough to grant them to me!"

So, day after day and chapter by chapter, the old Gyarong lama taught Patrul the *Kunzang Lamai Shelung*. From time to time, the apparently naive and illiterate Patrul would pose quite deep questions about the meaning of the text. The lama was puzzled to hear this simple person making such incisive comments.

After the old lama was halfway through teaching the text, Patrul moved from the home of the Gyarong lama and went to stay next door with an old woman. Every day, in the morning, Patrul would go out and circumambulate the stupas. Every day, after noon, he would go over to the Gyarong lama's place to receive teachings; every night, at dusk, he would return to the old woman's home.

While she was making tea in the evening, the old woman—who had heard about Patrul Rinpoche and was devoted to him—could be heard making fervent prayers of supplication, saying, "Think of me, Patrul Rinpoche! I am in your hands!"

One night, Patrul said to his hostess, "Old mother, there are many sublime beings throughout Tibet! Right here in Kathok, many realized lamas have appeared in the past; many high lamas are living here now. Why do you keep on supplicating this Patrul? Is he especially venerable or something?"

The old woman replied, "Oh, yes! There is no one more saintly than him these days. Many people in Kathok follow his teachings on the preliminary practices. Even I have heard those teachings."

Moved by faith, she folded her hands together in a gesture of respect.

But that didn't stop the mischievous Patrul.

"If you ask me," he went on, provocatively, "I think this Patrul of yours has an inflated reputation! He's probably just another one of those old nomad lamas, with nothing especially great or precious about him at all!"

"What an evil mind you have!" scolded the devout old lady. "How can you have such perverted thoughts about Patrul Rinpoche, calling him 'just another ordinary nomad lama'? You simply lack the good karma to see him as the Buddha in person!"

Patrul said nothing more.

Not long after that, some pilgrims from Dzachukha arrived at Kathok to circumambulate the stupas and saw a shabby nomad lama circumambulating the stupas as well. Being his fellow countrymen, the pilgrims immediately recognized Patrul. Exclaiming with delight, "Abu! Abu is here!" they all began bowing down to him in reverence.

Patrul was not happy about this at all.

He scolded the Dzachukha pilgrims, saying, "Until now, I was able to live here quietly, accumulating some merit. Now, with absolutely *no* need to have done so, you've gone and blabbed to everyone, saying, 'Patrul's here! Patrul's here!'"

"*That* will put an end to my tranquillity!"

Exactly as he had predicted, in no time at all the rumor spread over Kathok that the great Patrul Rinpoche had arrived, although no one could say for certain where he actually was to be found.

When Patrul came to the old lama's home to receive his afternoon teachings as usual, the lama said to him with excitement, "Hey! Everyone's saying that Patrul Rinpoche is here! Patrul Rinpoche has come, in person!"

Patrul showed no excitement at this news.

That day, at dusk, as usual, Patrul returned to the home of the old lady. She, too, said to him with excitement, "Patrul Rinpoche is here! Can you imagine?"

"You don't need to get all worked up!" scoffed Patrul. "What's so special about this Patrul Rinpoche? He's just an ordinary nomad lama. You'd be much better off supplicating the great lamas of Kathok!"

The old woman became very upset again, almost to the point of wanting to give Patrul a good beating. She scolded him sharply, saying, "You miserable creature, how dare you say such things. Even if Patrul Rinpoche, the Buddha in person, came right to your door, you wouldn't feel any devotion! You'd just dismiss him as an 'old nomad lama'! What a wretched fellow!"

Patrul said nothing.

Not long after this, Patrul was finally tracked down. The two high lamas of Kathok, Drime Shinkyong and Kathok Situ, formally invited him to teach *The Way of the Bodhisattva* at Kathok Monastery.

The devout old woman heard this news and was overjoyed that at last she would meet the saint to whom she had for so long addressed her supplication-prayers.

The next morning, the gong rang to summon everyone to the teachings.

Patrul left the old woman's house at the usual time in the morning, presumably going for his usual circumambulations.

The old woman hurried off to the monastery. There, sitting on the teaching throne, she saw the shabby nomad lama to whom she had been giving hospitality for some time.

Overwhelmed with shame, she began to prostrate at Patrul's feet, crying, "What bad karma I have accumulated! I've been scolding you, coming close to beating you up! I'll probably be reborn in hell! Please accept my confession! Whatever you tell me to do to purify my evil acts, I'll do!"

"There's nothing wrong," Patrul kindly assured her, "and there's no need for you to confess anything. Don't worry; you have a pure mind. A good heart is the root of all dharma. In fact, it is the very essence of *The Way of the Bodhisattva,* which I am teaching now. That's all that anyone needs."

Patrul began to teach, and as he did, the old Gyarong lama, too, realized that his very faithful student, the shabby nomad lama to whom he had been explaining *The Words of My Perfect Teacher,* day after day and chapter by chapter, was none other than its author, Patrul Rinpoche himself.

The poor lama felt so abashed that, without a word, he left overnight for his native Gyalmo Rong before Patrul or anyone else could stop him.

Patrul Asks the Great Kathok Situ for a Favor

The great Kathok Situ[126] invited Patrul to have tea and lunch at his residence. After he was seated in the master's grand apartment, Patrul looked all around and exclaimed, "*A-dzi!* How luxurious it is here! Everyone knows that Kathok Monastery and its lamas are prosperous, but you seem to be the richest of all!

"*Look* at these gorgeous inlaid boxes! These gold and silver ritual implements! These clothes made of beautiful silken brocades! These precious antique Chinese porcelain cups!

"*Look* at all these tiger-skin rugs and panther-skin carpets—what a terrifying display!

"Just look at all your vast estates! Your huge herds of livestock! There's nothing like this on earth; it's more like a celestial realm! How *dazzling*!"

Leaning over, Patrul whispered to Kathok Situ in a confidential tone, "By the way, I have not much on me besides a clay teapot. I've heard you are going away on a trip soon! Wouldn't you care to pack my little clay teapot up with all of your other stuff and take it along with you, just as a favor to me? Myself, I prefer to travel light!"

Aware of the reprimand implicit in Patrul's words, Kathok Situ replied, "Indeed, I shall take your clay pot."

Not long after Patrul left Kathok, Kathok Situ left Kathok as well, going off without a word to anyone. Renouncing all his possessions, his wealth, his retinue, and his comforts, he left his monastery behind and went to the White Glacier of Dokham,[127] a holy place where he spent the rest of his life in retreat. He lived in solitude and simplicity, wearing ragged clothes, keeping minimal provisions, giving up all worldly activities, and exchanging his porcelain teacups for a simple wooden bowl.

Later, Kathok Situ wrote to Patrul, saying, "Abu, following your advice, I have gone to a mountain solitude. By the way, I still have your teapot."

On reading his letter, Patrul said, with approval, "*He* has good ears! He actually heard what I said!"[128]

AFTER LEAVING KATHOK, Patrul Rinpoche gave extensive teachings on *The Way of the Bodhisattva* in many other monasteries in the nearby areas, including Getse Sershul Monastery, Lab Tridu Monastery, and Chuhor Monastery.

When teaching, he was always impartial, never praising some schools of Buddhism and disparaging others, not favoring one viewpoint over another. He refused to fuel the arrogant, vindictive sectarianism that had been so prevalent in his day.

He taught about each school according to its views, teaching either from his mind or from a commentary traditional to the school.[129]

Teaching in a very clear, complete way, neither too complex nor too concise, he would always discuss the essentials and link the teachings with actual practice.

The Key to Practice

Patrul told a group of his disciples, "You students are always asking me for teachings, but once you've received them, you don't bother to put them into practice. If you *did* practice, the best students would see results after a single day. Those of medium capacities would see results after a month. And even those of inferior capacities would see results within a year.

"You must understand the key points. If nothing happens when you practice, it means that you have not understood the key points. The bodhisattva Dromtönpa[130] said, 'To blend study, reflection, and meditation is the crucial, unmistaken key to dharma practice.'"

Patrul would give a session or two of teachings and then say, "Now you need to grow familiar with it," and he would send them to practice for a long time before teaching any more.

» Advice for Garwang from the Eastern Gorges of Gyalmo Rong «

Here are some key points written for those with minimal formal education who wish to practice the teachings.

First, if you want to practice the teachings, but have not done so, you have not yet made a deep enough commitment. With the recklessness of a lunatic, you must make a radical decision: to listen to the advice of a qualified spiritual master and to no one else.

Having made this deep commitment, begin the preliminary practices, using the "four thoughts that turn the mind to dharma" in order to tame your mind.

Next, no matter what happens to you, good or bad, recognize that ordinary worldly preoccupations do not have the slightest meaning whatsoever, not even so much as a tiny seed of sesame.

Until you are able to regard the ordinary affairs of samsara with a kind of natural revulsion—like someone sick with hepatitis served a pile of greasy food—you are likely to turn into a hyperactive renunciant, like an ox with its tail caught in a door.

If you're motivated to give up ordinary activities just from a fleeting impulse of renunciation, you'll wind up a failed "realized yogi," a jaded "great meditator," like someone who wastes his time soaking hard, ruined boots in water, hoping someday they'll soften again.

Until you have completely come to understand the "four thoughts that turn the mind to dharma" and have created a real capacity to renounce ordinary life, don't even bother mouthing mantras and giving up ordinary activities to do practice. This is important.

Conversely, once you begin to experience an unwavering weariness with samsara, an authentic sense of renunciation, immutable devotion and strong sense of self-confidence, you have taken the first step: adamantine freedom from the opinions of others.

This is the time to distance yourself from friends and from enemies, to give up plans, to ignore everything that you were supposed to get done, unswayed by the opinions of your friends or partners. *This* is the time to turn a deaf ear to both your superiors and your subordinates. *This* is the time to decide, on your own, to take up the reins of your destiny and make your escape, like a wild animal caught in a trap, working to set itself free.

As to the core of practice, the trainings involving body and speech (*like servants*) will not be most effective. It will be much more effective to work with mind (*master of all*).

Regarding the purpose of practice, know that without roots (*taking refuge and cultivating bodhichitta*), the trunk (*vows and precepts*) cannot flourish. Lacking these, the flowers (*view and conduct*) cannot blossom and the fruit (*the developing and completion stages*) cannot ripen.

The source of the whole path of dharma is taking refuge and generating bodhichitta (the wish to attain buddhahood, the enlightened state, for the sake of all sentient beings). These two are the root of the 84,000 sections of the dharma[131] and of the nine graded vehicles.[132] These two are the foundation, the essence, and the main trunk as well and the life force of the path. Without them, the dharma is nothing but a corpse (or even just a piece of a corpse), empty of any essence.

There is much to say about these two roots. Briefly, taking refuge means developing complete confidence and trust in the supreme Three Jewels. Developing bodhichitta means becoming aware that the infinity of sentient beings have, in some lifetime, been our parents, vowing to never forsake the aspiration to accomplish their happiness now, and determining ultimately to achieve buddhahood for their benefit.

Don't just grab at the fleece, the words; get a good grip on the legs, the practice. Having received the instructions from a spiritual master, practice Guru Yoga (merging with the guru's ultimate nature), transfer of consciousness (phowa), or any other practice of the direct and swift path for which you've received the empowerment.

If you can't manage that, having laid down the foundations (refuge and bodhichitta), recite the mani mantra with a good heart. That will suffice.

Also, unless you are propelled along the path by the life force of constant diligence and relentless perseverance, even though you are knowledgeable about the scriptures of the nine vehicles, this will not result in attaining buddhahood in a single lifetime.

However, take confidence in knowing that, one day, merely by having heard the words *the Three Jewels,* you will attain the enlightened state.

Written by Palge at Shri Singha.

Patrul Receives Teachings from the Mahasiddha of Trom

Accompanied by his disciple and spiritual friend Khenpo Pema Dorje, Patrul left Kathok and set out for East Tromgo in Tromtar in order to seek teachings from Chöying Rangdröl (Tsopu Drupchen Chöying Rangdröl), who lived in retreat on the steep rocky slopes of Trakchen Gyalmo Mountain. A highly realized practitioner, he was also known as the Mahasiddha of Trom.

Traveling in stages, Patrul and the Khenpo walked along the shore of the Black Lake (Tso Nagma) and reached the glaciers of the Rampart of Tromgo, in Washul Tromgo. Eventually, they arrived at the snow mountain range of Shar Shingo and a sacred mountain, one of whose sides is a sheer cliff known as Queen of the Fierce Rock (Traktsen Gyalmo).

Chöying Rangdröl did not have an extensive formal education. He had studied Kahma and Terma at Kathok Monastery according to the Kathok Nyingma tradition. When those studies were finished, he devoted his whole life to practicing meditation. He lived simply. For warmth, he wore an old sheepskin coat over a simple tunic. Day and night, he remained on his meditation mat, absorbed in doing practice.

He specialized in the Kathok-lineage treasure teachings of Longsal Nyingpo,[133] and it was these teachings that Patrul and the Khenpo had come to request.

As a result of his practice, Chöying Rangdröl had reached the highest stage of the Great Perfection teachings, the stage called "exhaustion of phenomena into the absolute nature."[134] Among his many students were the 3rd Drime Shinkyong (Jigme Yonten Gonpo, 'jigs med yon tan mgon po, 1837–1898), the 2nd Kathok Situ, and Nyakla Pema Dundul (who would later attain the rainbow body).

Patrul and the Khenpo came into the presence of Chöying Rangdröl.

After each making three prostrations, they formally requested the Longsal Nyingpo teachings and some other Dzogchen teachings according to the Kathok lineage.

Chöying Rangdröl agreed.

The first day, he began by giving teachings on the preliminary practices.

Chöying Rangdröl folded his hands at his heart and recited a few verses concerning the "four thoughts that turn the mind to dharma."

Then, he repeated the first verse slowly, three times:

Alas!
Within the six realms, having the freedoms and favorable conditions is rare;
Among humans, meeting the dharma is rare.
Finding the path is like finding a precious jewel.
Don't waste these precious opportunities!
Work hard at the essence of practice!

Tears rolled down the cheeks of this great master. Hearing these words and witnessing the master's tears, Patrul also began to weep. Chöying Rangdröl remained silent for some time. That was the first day's teaching.

The second day, Chöying Rangdröl taught in the same way, without recourse to texts, drawing directly on his personal experience. He said:

The life of sentient beings rushes past like a waterfall over a mountain cliff!

Folding his hands together, he paused and wept. Then, he went on:

Don't waste the favorable conditions and freedoms that you have been granted!
Don't let your life be spent in vain!

Seeing tears welling up in the eyes of both Chöying Rangdröl and Patrul, Khenpo Pema was dumbfounded.

"Here we have Patrul Rinpoche, a great scholar, someone who knows all these teachings like the back of his hand, but who, like this great yogi, is still moved to tears at the thought of the most basic of teachings! These teachings are completely rudimentary—no start, no finish, no structure—and no commentary whatsoever!

"Merely entertaining the thought of the preciousness of human birth, these two great practitioners are so deeply affected, they're *weeping*?" the Khenpo thought to himself, stunned and confounded. "It's incredible!"

Chöying Rangdröl Demonstrates Higher Perception

One day, after the teachings were done, Patrul, Chöying Rangdröl, and Pema Dorje were sitting together, conversing.

Chöying Rangdröl said to Patrul, "By the way, what is Dzogchen Mingyur Dorje up to these days?"

Patrul told him.

Chöying Rangdröl continued talking about Dzogchen Monastery, describing it, mentioning the names of the various temples, speaking of those people, good and bad, who lived there, finally saying, "Those people at Dzogchen are just not respecting Mingyur Namkhai Dorje the way they should."

At one point, Chöying Rangdröl casually mentioned that Mingyur Namkhai Dorje sat on a high throne, not far from the door, facing inward toward the shrine, during important ceremonies. This was an unusual arrangement and a singular characteristic of that particular monastery. (Usually, the throne faces the door with its back to the shrine or, more often, is on one side of the table, facing the assembly.)

Patrul nodded and said, "Yes, yes, that's right."

Pema Dorje thought to himself, "I wonder when Chöying Rangdröl visited Dzogchen Monastery, since he seems so familiar with it. Did he stay there in his youth, perhaps?"

So Pema Dorje asked Chöying Rangdröl, "Venerable lama, have you gone to Dzogchen Monastery?"

The great master hesitated a bit, then replied, "Well, I *suppose* you could say that I've gone there."

"How did you happen to go?"

"Well, every year at Dzogchen Monastery, you perform the elaborate ritual called the Tsokchen Dupa, the Great Gathering[135]—do you not? The one where Mingyur Namkhai Dorje sits on his throne, plays his small ivory hand drum, and sings, '*Vidyadharas, with your retinues, come!*'"

"Yes."

"Well, in response to such an auspicious invitation, all peaceful and wrathful deities of the hundred families, deities of the mandala, and us old forefathers *must* come! That's how and why I've been to Dzogchen Monastery.

"Other than that, I've never gone there."

At that moment, Pema Dorje realized that the great lama whom Patrul had come to meet was an actual *mahasiddha,* a *vidyadhara* ("awareness holder").[136]

Gyalwa Changchup's Prediction

Gyalwa Changchup, a clairvoyant realized being from Trom, once made this prediction:

"This year, a great spiritual being—Avalokiteshvara in human form—will come here from Washul Tromgo. Those who miss the chance to meet him are very unfortunate."

Despite this dramatic prophecy, no one gave it a thought when, later in the year, a lone person arrived, wearing the ordinary dress of a nomad, walking stick in hand. A few, assuming he must be some sort of lama, showed some devotion. Nobody ever guessed that the "great spiritual being" was Patrul Rinpoche himself!

Seeking an Audience with a Very Important Lama

Once, coming back from Kathok, Patrul came within sight of Dzongsar Monastery, where the great lama Jamyang Khyentse Wangpo had been in continuous retreat since the age of thirty-seven. He had taken a vow to remain in perpetual retreat, never again crossing beyond the threshold of his residence.

That day, Jamyang Khyentse Wangpo had told his attendants, "Today, whoever arrives, send them up to me."

Everyone assumed that some very important personage was expected to come that day to see Khyentse Wangpo Rinpoche.

Patrul arrived at the monastery. He was dressed, as usual, in his worn old sheepskin chuba, the dress of a nomad layman.

To Khyentse Rinpoche's attendants who opened the door, Patrul announced, "I want to see Dilgo Ngedön!"

Now, Patrul had not requested an audience with "Jamyang Khyentse Wangpo Rinpoche," but rather asked to see "Dilgo Ngedön," calling him by his family name from childhood.

Unfamiliar with that name, an attendant who was hanging around the doorway asked Patrul, "Who's Dilgo Ngedön?"

"Oh, he's an old dharma friend of mine. He's staying here at Dzongsar and I want to see him. I have a few things to tell him."

It took a while, but the attendant finally figured out that the person that Patrul was referring to must be Jamyang Khyentse Wangpo. He told Patrul, "Khyentse Rinpoche is in retreat. You can't just barge right in. Please wait here a bit. When he finishes his session of practice, I'll ask him if he will see you."

"So I can't get in to see him?"

"Well, you might be able to see him, but you'll have to wait, and I'll have to ask permission first. You can't just go straight in!"

"*Ya, ya!* Maybe he, little mouse-hare, may have lots of time to look around—but I, little grass-blade, have no time to laze around!"

With these words, Patrul got up and left.

The attendant thought, "What an odd fellow!"

At the session break, the attendant went to Rinpoche's quarters. Khyentse Wangpo asked him, "Hasn't *anyone* come by to see me today?"

His attendant shook his head and said, "No. No one special."

Khyentse Wangpo asked, "No one at *all*?"

"Well," the attendant conceded at last, "there *was* one gruff nomad who dropped by. He asked to see Dilgo Ngedön. He said couldn't wait; he hadn't a moment to spare."

"That must have been Patrul!" Khyentse Wangpo said, scolding the attendant. "Go and find him! Bring him back!"

Someone was sent after him. By then Patrul was well on his way to Palpung. He was about to cross the Horla Pass, a couple of hours' walk from Dzongsar, when the monastery's messenger finally caught up with him.

The messenger begged, "Please come back! Jamyang Khyentse Wangpo wants to see you!"

"Oh, he does, does he?" Patrul scoffed. "Jamyang Khyentse Wangpo, he's such a big shot now! Years ago, that Dilgo Ngedön and I both received teachings from Mahapandita Shechen Öntrul. Back then, he was just a young guy dressed in a yellow silk brocade coat. Now he's such a big deal that I can't even get in to *see* him?"

Without further ado, Patrul kept on walking toward Palpung, in the direction he was already headed.

Seeking an Audience with Another Very Important Lama

After leaving Dzongsar and forsaking his attempt to see Khyentse Wangpo, Patrul finally arrived in Palpung. He climbed up to the retreat center Tsadra Rinchen Drak, the "Jewel Rock Cliff Like Tsari" (a reference to the sacred place of Tsari), where he wanted to see the great Jamgön Kongtrul Rinpoche.

At the retreat center, Patrul found Jamgön Kongtrul's personal attendant and brusquely told him, "I have to see Kongtrul! *Now!*"

A bit shocked, Kongtrul's attendant responded almost exactly as Jamyang Khyentse Wangpo's attendant had done at Dzongsar.

"I'm sorry, but Kongtrul Rinpoche is in retreat. You can't just barge right in," explained the attendant. "Please wait here a bit. When he finishes his practice, I'll ask him if he will see you."

"So I *can't* get in to see him?"

"Well, you might be able to see him, but you'll have to wait, and I'll have to ask permission first. You can't just go straight in!"

"Wait?" said Patrul. "I don't have time to wait! Years ago, that Kongtrul and I received teachings from Mahapandita Shechen Öntrul. Back then, he was just some young guy wearing a goatskin coat. Now, he's such a big deal that I can't even get in to *see* him?"

With those words, Patrul got up and left.

Jamyang Khyentse Wangpo Countermands Patrul's Advice

Khenchen Tashi Özer was a highly learned scholar from Palpung Monastery. Studying with Jamgön Kongtrul and obeying his instructions, the Khenpo was a very strict monk who wore the yellow shawl, carried the begging bowl and staff, and kept monastic discipline very meticulously.

Later, he went to study with Patrul Rinpoche, who took one look at him and said, "What's with all these elaborations?"

The tradition was for a student to approach a master and say, "Please give me food, clothing, and teachings." This the Khenpo did, and Patrul told him to come back later. When the Khenpo returned, Patrul gave him some food, a book, and an article of clothing, saying, "Here you are. Goodbye."

Tashi Özer begged him for teachings for a long time and was finally allowed to stay. He spent quite some time with Patrul Rinpoche, studying and practicing meditation. Patrul suggested that he give up all possessions and comforts and dress in old robes of white felt.

Patrul said, "My son, become a renunciant. Be like the master Zurchungpa, 'a child of the mountains, wearing mist for clothing.' Wear only a plain white felt coat, give up riding on horseback, go everywhere on foot. Give up all elaborate involvements and live simply, like Milarepa."

Khenchen Tashi Özer took Patrul's advice, agreeing to live as a wandering mendicant. He gave his possessions away.

Patrul's lifestyle was so very unelaborate that his former fellow students Jamgön Kongtrul and Jamyang Khyentse, both now illustrious lamas, would say teasingly, "That Patrul's really much *too* simple. If only he'd do something *useful!*"

Not long afterward, dressed in the shabby white felt robes that Patrul had recommended, the Khenchen Tashi Özer traveled to Dzongsar to see the great Jamyang Khyentse Wangpo.

"Khenchen Tashi Özer has arrived," the attendant told Khyentse. "And it looks like he's become a disciple of Patrul!"

"Put him up in the monks' quarters," replied Khyentse Wangpo.

Unusually, he was not immediately ushered into Khyentse's presence, but was told by the lama's attendants that he'd just have to sit and wait for a while.

A few days went by and nothing happened, so Tashi Özer thought perhaps he should take the initiative and go see the master, but the attendant turned him away and told him just to stay in his room.

This "while" grew into a whole week, and then ten days.

Khenchen Tashi Özer grew increasingly worried. He knew that in the past Khyentse Wangpo had always been very kind to him and had allowed him into his presence at once. Being made to wait for such a long time surely meant that something had gone wrong. Tashi Özer searched his conscience for anything he might have done to offend Jamyang Khyentse, but could not find any obvious mistake with which to reproach himself.

"I wonder what has happened," he thought to himself. "He must be doing this to purify my bad karma and obscurations."

Although Khenchen Tashi Özer was a great lama in his own right, these doubts disturbed him deeply. Eventually, he felt so miserable that he wept.

Finally, Khyentse Wangpo sent for him.

When Tashi Özer came into the great master's presence, he saw that there was a high teaching throne set up right next to the throne of Khyentse Wangpo. On it was a full set of neatly folded monastic robes, all stacked up in a pile.

Jamyang Khyentse Wangpo glared fiercely at the white-robed Khenchen. Then he began to scold him angrily: "Aren't you the great Khenpo from Palpung Monastery? The rank of Khenchen, 'great scholar,' is a tremendous honor! What *are* those miserable rags you are wearing?" fumed Khyentse Wangpo. "This must be the work of that madman, Patrul!

"Take those rags *off*, put these robes *on*, and go take your seat on that throne!"

The Khenchen hesitated.

"What were you *thinking* when you threw away your monastic robes to put on that stinky felt?" demanded Khyentse Wangpo.

The Khenpo tried to resist, begging him, "Please don't compel me!"

Khyentse Wangpo threatened, "I'll beat you with my stick if you hesitate one second more! Now, promise me you'll never do such a mad thing again!"

Khenchen Tashi Özer gave in and did as Khyentse Wangpo wished.

After that, the great lama once again behaved with warmth and kindness to him, as he had always done before. Khyentse Wangpo foresaw that Khenchen Tashi Özer would benefit the teachings and beings more by remaining a scholar rather than becoming a wandering hermit.

Patrul and Jamyang Khyentse Wangpo

Despite their apparent differences, Patrul admired Jamyang Khyentse Wangpo very deeply. After reading the text of the Chetsun Nyingthig terma,[137] Patrul told a group of students that Khyentse Wangpo *was* Kunkhyen Longchenpa, and that if any of the students had a chance to see Khyentse Wangpo in person, there would be some sense of their having two eyes.

Every year for thirteen years, Patrul performed a ceremony for Khyentse Wangpo's longevity. Every year, Patrul composed a new long-life prayer on his behalf; every year, Patrul sent him a new statue of Amitayus, the Buddha of Boundless Life.[138]

Each year, when another new Amitayus statue from Patrul was presented to him, Jamyang Khyentse could be heard complaining, "Here's *another* command from that Patrul! Once again, he forbids me to die!"

Patrul Is Upset and Disappears

Jamyang Khyentse Wangpo had occasional differences of opinion with Patrul—even calling him "that lunatic" on some occasions. Nonetheless, he admired Patrul very deeply.

As an expression of his esteem, he composed a long devotional prayer in Patrul's praise, recounting his life story. This lengthy prayer served as basis for the later biography *Elixir of Faith,* written by Khenpo Kunpel.

Jamyang Khyentse Wangpo sent his composition in a letter to Patrul along with some *mendrup,*[139] a special edible substance made of medicinal plants mixed with many relics and consecrated during a week-long ritual.

Patrul was in the midst of giving teachings when he received Khyentse's letter. People in the audience witnessed him taking some of the *mendrup* and reading the letter.

Having read it, Patrul immediately became upset and shouted, "That Jamyang Khyentse Wangpo is such a horrible lama!"

Patrul suddenly stopped teaching, which was completely unlike him. He disappeared for several days.

When he at last returned and was about to continue teachings, people learned what in the letter had so upset Patrul—it was Khyentse's words of praise for Patrul.

As Khyentse's *mendrup* was distributed to all those present, Patrul praised Jamyang Khyentse Wangpo's boundless good qualities. Patrul then pointed out that praise and fame posed real obstacles to those who teach dharma. He explained that, after he'd read Jamyang Khyentse Wangpo's verses praising him, he needed time in order to reflect and make sure such lavish praise did not go to his head.

One of the verses from this long poem of praise is widely used to this day:

Outwardly, you are Shantideva, Bodhisattva;
Inwardly, you are Shavaripa, Lord of Siddhas;[140]

Secretly, you are Avalokiteshvara himself, supreme self-liberation of suffering;
Jigme Chökyi Wangpo,[141] I supplicate you.

Patrul and Lama Mipham

The great scholar Ju Mipham Gyatso, also known as Lama Mipham, was known to say that he had heard many learned and accomplished masters' teachings, but the only time he'd really had to study hard was when Patrul Rinpoche taught the ninth chapter of *The Way of the Bodhisattva* at Shri Singha Philosophical College. Mipham said Patrul's oral commentaries on this difficult and profound chapter on wisdom were the most important teachings he'd ever received.[142]

Subsequently, Mipham wrote *The Wish-Fulfilling Gem,*[143] a widely praised commentary on the famous ninth chapter of Shantideva's *Way of the Bodhisattva.*

A copy of this commentary found its way to Patrul. After he finished reading Mipham's commentary, Patrul said, "*O-ho*! This is what I taught at Shri Singha!"

Patrul in Awe

Once, Patrul was staying in Karchung Khormo Olu, living in a small yak-hair tent. His faithful attendant Sönam Tsering was living in a tent nearby.

At the time, Lama Mipham had just finished writing his now-famous "Prayer of Aspiration for the Flourishing of the Nyingma Teachings and to Please the Dharma Kings,"[144] which quickly became widespread. He wanted to show this new prayer to Patrul and ask for his opinion.

Lama Mipham had been staying at Juniong Monastery, his long-time residence, about a half-day's walk from Karchung Khormo Olu.

Arriving in the late afternoon, he went first to the tent of Sönam Tsering, Patrul's attendant. Sönam Tsering told Lama Mipham that Patrul had retired for the day and was no longer receiving visitors.

Handing the attendant his handwritten text, Lama Mipham told Sönam Tsering, "Take a look at this prayer tonight. Tomorrow, first thing, when you serve tea to Patrul Rinpoche, please read this prayer aloud to him."

That night, Sönam Tsering, fearing that he might not be able to read Lama Mipham's handwriting properly, rehearsed by reading the prayer aloud a number of times.

The next day, first thing in the morning, having tucked the text of the prayer into the folds of his upper robe, he went to serve tea to Patrul Rinpoche.

Patrul was in the middle of getting dressed. He had put on his white felt robe and was just about to tie up the very long woolen belt that he would wrap around his waist several times. He asked Sönam Tsering, "What was it that you were reciting last night for so long?"

"I was reading the prayer that Lama Mipham asked me to recite to you first thing this morning."

Halfway through tying up his belt, Patrul stopped what he was doing and said, "*Ya*, go on. Recite it!"

Sönam Tsering recited Lama Mipham's prayer while Patrul listened attentively, still standing, still holding either end of his long belt in his two hands.

In the middle of the recitation, while still holding the two ends of the belt, Patrul put both palms together at his heart.

"Oh . . . *oh!*" said Patrul with amazement. "How good this is! I had thought that in this Land of Snows, there was no one nearly as learned as Jamyang Khyentse Wangpo! However, here is someone very much like him! They are like a pair of purebred stallions galloping side by side!"

After having listened intently until the end of the recitation, at last Patrul finished tying his belt and sat down to drink his tea.

Estimations and Rankings

Someone once asked Patrul, "Who would you say is more learned, you or Mipham Rinpoche?"

Patrul paused and thought about it for a few moments.

Then he replied, "As to the sutras, we're even. As to the tantras, Mipham is a bit better."

Among You Three Great Masters

After the scholar Khenchen Tashi Özer studied with the renowned Patrul, he said, "How can there be another lama of this caliber anywhere on the face of the earth? He is tremendously learned and accomplished!"

Later, having studied with Jamyang Khyentse Wangpo, he said, "No one can possibly be more extraordinary!"

Lastly, when he had studied with Jamgön Kongtrul, he said, "Fantastic! This man is incomparable!"

One day, when the Khenchen was in the presence of Jamyang Khyentse Wangpo, he said, "Rinpoche, I'm a student of all three of you lamas, and I don't perceive anything other than great qualities in each of you. But tell me, among you three great masters—Jamgön Kongtrul Rinpoche, Patrul Rinpoche, and yourself—if you were to compete, who would be the most learned?"

"Patrul!" said Jamyang Khyentse Wangpo. "There is *no one* more learned than Patrul!"

"Among you three great masters, who benefits beings the most?" the Khenchen asked.

"Kongtrul!" said Jamyang Khyentse Wangpo. "He is the translator Vairotsana[145] in human form! He compiled the *Five Great Treasuries*! No one benefits beings like Kongtrul."

The scholar asked, "But among you three, who has the highest realization?"

Khyentse shrugged a bit and, without the least trace of arrogance or hypocrisy, said, "As for realization, that'd be me!"

Patrul Leaves Dzogchen Monastery

Having stayed in the area for some time, Patrul grew tired of the poor behavior of monks at Dzogchen Monastery. Many of the monks, although they were fully ordained, nonetheless drank alcohol and secretly kept wives.

Eventually, Patrul went to the 3rd Dzogchen Pönlop,[146] the abbot, to complain about this widespread failure of the monks to keep their monastic vows.

However, since one of the dissolute monks was the monastery's very powerful treasurer-administrator, Dzogchen Pönlop told Patrul there was nothing to be done and instead offered him some dried persimmons.

"Nope," replied Patrul. "I don't care for your dried persimmons!"

Patrul got up. "I'll be off," he said. "Stay well."

He packed up his few possessions and set out on the road.

Khenpo Pema Dorje soon heard that Patrul had left the monastery, and he was overwhelmed with sadness. Weeping, he wrote to Patrul saying, "You and I both are students of Gyalse Shenphen Thaye. If you go any farther than Dzachukha, you will break our *samaya*-bond!" And he sent the note off by messenger.

Dzogchen Valley seen from Patrul Rinpoche's Yamantaka Cave. (1985)

When the messenger finally caught up to Patrul, he was walking all alone, making his way slowly across the small pass at the edge of Dzogchen Valley. Patrul read the Khenpo's note.

"Oh, all right, all right," Patrul grumbled crossly. "I won't go any farther than Dzachukha."

It seemed from what he said that his intent had been to travel very far away, to Central Tibet or beyond—until he read Khenpo Pema Dorje's plea.

» *Advice to Myself* «

On the immaculate pollen bed of an open lotus
Seated on the disk of a full moon, the throne of white light,
The unshakable manifestation of bliss-emptiness in divine form:
Master Vajrasattva, sole deity, I trust in you!

Listen, Abu Shri, so distracted, with such bad karma!
Think how you've been fooled again and again by mistake after mistake.
Do you get it?
You're still making mistake after mistake, so watch out!

Stop living a false and empty life.
Drop those deceptions of your own mind
And endless projects that you don't need!

Don't make your head spin with the burden
Of strings of ideas that never come true
And endless distracting activities—
They're just waves on water.
Just keep quiet.

You listened to hundreds of teachings
Without understanding any.
What's the point?
You reflect upon them, then forget everything when you need it.
There's no use!
You meditate, but it doesn't cure your emotions.
Just drop it![147]

You've recited many mantras,
But you haven't mastered the creation phase.
You visualize deities as solid entities,
But haven't got rid of duality.

You seem to tame demons,
But you haven't tamed your mind.
So your nicely arranged four sessions of recitation.[148]
Just drop them!

Uplifted, mind seems so clear,
But it isn't at ease.
Underneath, mind seems so settled,
But it lacks clarity.

Your awareness seems to be unshakable,
But what's really stable? Your concepts!
So you can drop that point of concentration
And drop that steady gaze.

Your intense fervor looks like clear awareness
But just makes your preconceptions stronger.
Just dispense with your grasping mind
And give up your steady gaze
That's stuck like a stake in the ground.

Your words may seem sweet,
But they do not help your mind.
Your logic may seem sharp,
But it just foments delusion.

These instructions may seem profound,
But you don't put them into practice.
So drop reading books
That distract your mind and tire your eyes!

You sound your little drum: *tom! tom!*
It's just making a noise to show off.
You may intone: "Take my flesh! Take my blood!"[149]
But you haven't stopped cherishing them.

You may sound your cymbals: *ding! ding!*
But you have no concentration.
So drop that fancy kit
That just looks nice!

Today they want to learn,
But in the end they give up.
Today they seem to have understood,
But after a while there's nothing.

They may learn a hundred things,
But they don't apply them to their minds.

So drop those disciples
Who seem so important!

This year, they seem so considerate;
Next year, there's nothing.
They seem so humble but soon grow arrogant.
The more you treat them with tender affection,
The farther away they stray.
Stop being excited at new friends;
Drop those smiling chums.

. . . .

Endless chatter
Causes attachment and hatred.
You may express surprise or approval,
But it's really a way of speaking ill of others.

What you say may sound good,
But others get irritated.
So drop that gossip.
It only makes your mouth dry!

Teaching without personal experience
Is like having learned to dance from a book.
Even if they seem to listen to you with devotion,
From your side, it's pure deceit.

If you betray the teachings,
Sooner or later you'll be ashamed of yourself.
So drop those sermons
That have the appearance of fine rhetoric!

If you don't have them, you need them;
Once you have them, they're useless.
Not many pages to write, but once you start
There is no end.
If you wrote enough to cover the earth,

It's not enough.
Give up all this writing; it's useless.

Euphoric today,
Angry tomorrow,
People are prey to changes of mood.
They are never satisfied;
Even when they are, they are useless when you need them,
And bring you to despair.
So drop the politeness,
Flattery, and obsequiousness!

There are people who can handle
Religious and secular affairs;
Don't long for such companions, old Abu!
Don't you see that the old buffalo in his stable
Deep down just longs to sleep?
You can't do without eating, sleeping, and shitting;
Don't bother with the rest. It's not your business.
Do what's within your capabilities. Stay quiet in your corner!
Just drop everything! That is the essence!

Advice written by the yogi Trime Lodrö [Patrul Rinpoche][150] *for his close friend Abu Shri (who is none other than himself) to give him some suitable recommendations that he needs to put into practice. And even if there is nothing to put into practice, the essential point is to let go of everything. And not to be annoyed even if you don't attain the fruit of the teaching!*

Patrul's Pain

After leaving Dzogchen Monastery, Patrul went to Gemang Ritrö in Dzachukha and arrived at the home of Khenpo Yönten Gyatso, commonly known as Khenpo Yonga. After he'd been there for no more than a few moments, Patrul suddenly said, "Khenpo, would you mind if I stayed here for a year doing retreat?"

The Khenpo, surprised but overjoyed at the prospect, agreed at once, and for that year served as Patrul's retreat attendant.

After Patrul had been in retreat for some time, Khenpo Yonga was told that Dzogchen Pönlop, the abbot of Dzogchen Monastery, was coming to pay Patrul a visit.

The Khenpo warned Patrul about just who was about to arrive. Patrul, hearing this news, said nothing.

Dzogchen Pönlop arrived at Khenpo Yonga's place the next morning. Khenpo Yonga went outside to receive him formally, to help dismount his horse, and to politely escort him inside.

Pönlop found Patrul lying in on the floor, on bedding made of a hard mattress-cushion, his face covered with a thick nomad blanket made of long wool threads that look like fur. He was moaning loudly and piteously.

"*A-ho-ho! Ow!*"

Immediately, Dzogchen Pönlop asked, "What's the matter?"

From under the thick felt blanket, came Patrul's voice, wailing, "*Oww!* I'm in excruciating pain! *Ow! Ow!*"

Dzogchen Pönlop cried, "What's wrong?"

"I'm in pain!" screamed Patrul. "*Ow!* Help!"

"What's the matter?" cried Pönlop.

"I'm being torn apart—*by the five poisons*!"

Dzogchen Pönlop turned around and left.

Patrul emerged from under the covers, roaring with laughter.

Patrul Teaches Khenpo Yönten Gyatso

At Gemang, every day during Patrul's year of retreat, he practiced the sadhana called Dredging the Depths of Hell.[151] Patrul also taught Khenpo Yonga (Yönten Gyatso) a few pages from the two major commentaries on the *Guhyagarbha Tantra,* the commentary *Dispelling Darkness in the Ten Directions*[152] by Longchenpa and the *Ornament to the Thought of the Lord of Secrets* by Minling Lochen.[153]

When he was finished, he told the Khenpo, "You are heir to these teachings now and you must pass them on."

Khenpo Yonga followed this command, but whenever he would teach the *Guhyagarbha,* he and many disciples would get sick, and many other obstacles would arise.

At one point, Önpo Tendzin Norbu sent his three main disciples, Khenpo Yonga, Khenpo Kunpel, and Khenpo Shenga, to Mipham Rinpoche to clarify their questions about difficult points of the teachings. Khenpo Yonga told Mipham Rinpoche about the obstacles that had been arising whenever he taught this tantra.

Mipham suggested doing rituals to repair *samaya* each day prior to giving the teachings. He also said that they should memorize Longchenpa's 600-page commentary and recite it.

"In this way, you will be able to avert any obstacles," said Lama Mipham.

This approach to teaching the *Guhyagarbha Tantra* at Gemang Monastery became a tradition that has remained unbroken. Whoever presides over the teachings is a Khenpo who has memorized the long commentary. He recites it from memory and then comments on it.

During the Cultural Revolution, such religious activities were strictly forbidden under threat of severe punishment. Nonetheless, by gathering secretly in remote mountain retreats, the Khenpos of Gemang were able to maintain their tradition without a break.

Patrul Judges a Great Debate

Lama Mipham's *Wish-Fulfilling Gem,* his commentary on the ninth (wisdom) chapter of *The Way of the Bodhisattva,* sparked intense polemics from Geluk scholars of the time because it sharply criticized some important points regarding Je Tsongkhapa's explication of Madhyamaka.

The well-known Geluk scholar Alak Do-ngak was a student of Patrul's. The famed scholar Lama Mipham was also Patrul's student. Do-ngak challenged Mipham to a public debate on Madhyamika.

Patrul, famed for both his scholarship and his nonsectarian views, was asked to preside at the debate and judge the winner.

As he often did when teaching, writing, or debating, Mipham brought out his miniature statue of Manjushri, the Buddha of Wisdom, and placed it before him. Mipham carried the statue with him at all times.[154]

During the debate, people began to notice that there was something unusual happening—rays of light began streaming out from the heart of the little statue of Manjushri. The rays of light streamed into Lama Mipham's heart, connecting the two, heart to heart. This heart-to-heart light stream was very evident to all who were present. It continued to be seen for a long time.

When the debate ended, Patrul was asked to name the winner.

Patrul declined to choose a winner of the debate. He merely commented, "But I did see *some* things happening that spoke even louder than words."

Advice for Alak Do-ngak

After the debate between Lama Mipham and Alak Do-ngak was over, Patrul took Alak Do-ngak aside and took his student to task. "I said you should meditate on compassion and loving-kindness! Instead, you filled your head with scholarly nonsense!"

At this sharp rebuke, Alak Do-ngak wept openly.

Later, Patrul composed some words of advice for him:

First you met a supremely qualified guide,
Then you felt renunciation and joy for the dharma,
And now you're meditating in woodland solitude,
O my fortunate friend, you're fortunate indeed!

I met noble masters, but failed to follow them properly.
Whatever dharma I train in, I don't apply it to my mind.
I took to solitude, but couldn't be diligent or undistracted,
Turning into an old dog like me means remaining malign!

My friend, you've set out on the way to every happiness,
But as you tirelessly cultivate diligence and devotion,
Be ever watchful, alert for the demon of arrogant pride,
And your life will end happily too—do you understand?

....

These sincere words, which arose like a rainbow from the mouth,
Were offered from the mountain solitude of Dhichung by ragged Abu,
In order to dispel the sadness of a dear, like-minded friend.
May their meaning become apparent![155]

Two of a Kind

Patrul and Mipham had much in common in terms of lifestyle. Mipham used to wear the clothes of a lay practitioner and he also spent much time in solitary retreat in Dzachukha, Dzongsar, Denkhok, and remote places. He, too, could behave in unconventional ways.

Once, Mipham was traveling to Dzongsar Monastery to meet Jamyang Khyentse Wangpo. He was all alone, on foot, carrying a knapsack on his back. Suddenly, he was set upon by a gang of robbers who ordered him to take off his knapsack and hand it over to them.

Mipham said, "Please take it! You're welcome to what I have!"

He gave them his pack and then sat down quietly on a big rock and began saying prayers.

While he was sitting there, praying and relaxing, he felt in the folds of his robes for a little medicine bottle and took it out. The bottle, made of agate stone, contained a Chinese medicinal powder that Mipham used to sniff into his nose to relieve a sinus problem.

Seeing him do this, one of the bandits came over and said, "Hey, you! You look awfully happy for someone who's just been mugged! Why don't you hand over that nice little bottle, too?"

At this, Mipham rose to his feet and transformed completely.

"*I am the minister of great King Gesar!*" he roared. "How *dare* you miserable good-for-nothings try to plague me!"

Mipham picked up a big, fat rock, blew some mantras on it, put it in a slingshot, and hurled the huge missile at the bandits, as easily as if it were a pebble instead of a big, fat rock. Terrified, all the bandits ran away.

Lama Mipham picked up his knapsack (which the bandits had abandoned), put it on his back, and calmly continued his journey to Dzongsar.

Patrul Goes Begging for Food

Once, Patrul, dressed as usual like a nomad, went to the door of a wealthy nomad household to ask for some food. Seeing Patrul's shabbiness, the lady of the house covered her nose with her garment in a gesture of disgust. She summoned her daughter and told her to go outside and give Patrul some tsampa, warning her not to go too close to the beggar.

She said, "Just toss the tsampa to him and don't touch him—he might have something contagious!"

Hearing this, Patrul laughed out loud.

"What's flawless can't cause pestilence," he pointed out. "But don't worry—there's no one around here likely to catch what *I* have!"

After a moment, he mused, "Of course, when I was at Ngakchung, I suppose I *did* infect Lungtok. When I was at Dzogchen, you might say that I'd given it to Önpo Tenga."

Lungtok Leaves His Lama

When Lungtok was fifty years old, he and his master Patrul were living near the Plain of the Mamos. Patrul had a premonition that Lungtok's mother was going to die soon. He told his disciple to go see his mother before she died: "Go back to your homeland, stay there, and teach worthy disciples."

Lungtok was devastated at the thought of parting from his beloved master, having lived at his side for twenty-eight years, relying on him for light as the flame of an oil-lamp relies on its wick.

When the time came for Lungtok to go, Patrul took hold of his head in his two hands, caressing him, saying, "Dear Lungtok, there is no need for you to be sad. In my lifetime I will never meet the great Kunkhyen Longchenpa, but *you* will meet him—this is certain."[156]

Lungtok, who could not bear to leave, wept as he turned away.

After taking just a few steps, he turned and came back to his master. He leaned his head against Patrul's heart, weeping. Gently caressing his head with his hands, Patrul assured Lungtok that he was going meet the incarnation of Vimalamitra, and that this incarnation was to become Lungtok's student.

Lungtok, still distraught, got up and began to leave again. Then he stopped and turned back a third time.

Once again, Patrul tried to comfort him, touching the top of his head with gentle affection, saying, "There will be clear signs, so you will recognize him. You must transmit to him all the teachings you hold. If you do nothing else to benefit beings, this will more than suffice. If you can transmit the teachings to him alone, that will be your dharma achievement."

Having returned to Patrul three times, and having been comforted by him each time in the same way, Lungtok did finally leave his master's presence.

These two, master and student, would never meet again.

LUNGTOK DID AS PATRUL SAID. He was able to see his mother again before she died and was able give to her the offerings the faithful people of Dzachukha had given him.

From that time on, following Patrul's command, he remained in his native country, teaching countless disciples, including the young Khenpo Ngawang Palzang, the emanation of Vimalamitra and Longchenpa whose coming had been predicted by Patrul.

He also taught students of the great yogi Nyakla Pema Dundul[157] after their master attained the rainbow body.

Eventually, Nyoshul Lungtok had five great disciples: two Lingpas (tertöns) and three great Khenpos, among whom Ngawang Palzang was supreme.

Nyoshul Lungtok was the most realized disciple of Patrul. There is a saying in Dzachukha pertaining to Patrul's spiritual lineage: "If there is no Lungtok, Patrul is childless."[158]

How Patrul Taught at the Willow Hermitage

The Willow Hermitage (Changma Ritrö)[159] is on a sparsely forested mountain slope above the Dza River. It faces a vast expanse of treeless high-altitude plateau. In Patrul's day, there were no permanent shelters there, not one single solid house nor even a hut. Patrul and his students lived in tent encampments, exactly in the manner of the pastoral nomads of Kham. Master and students lived some in black yak-hair tents, some in white cotton tents just big enough for one or two people.

Before winter, everyone used to make small earthen walls around their tents as a barrier against fierce and icy winds. They'd dig up the earth below the tents, fill the hole up with sheep dung, small spherical pellets that provided very good insulation from the cold ground. On top of this layer of sheep dung, they spread rugs made from the furry skin of stillborn yaks. Master and disciples sat on these all day long, listening to the teachings and practicing.

» *Longing for Solitudes* «

In the settlements of the ordinary world
Samsara's fantasy phenomena
Continuously arise
As countless endless projects.
Undeceived by such illusions,
Seeing them as needless,
Abu's heart longs for mountain solitudes.

Practitioners, both lay and ordained,
In monasteries and villages alike
Are overtaxed by all the things they have to do.
Seeing their frenzy of work as pointless distraction,
Abu's heart longs for mountain solitudes.

As if they'll never die but live on forever,
People keep on making new plans,
Even when they're on the verge of death.
Seeing that their plans will come to nothing, one is saddened;
Abu's heart longs for mountain solitudes.

Acquaintances may provide fuel for one's passions and hatreds.
Colleagues may ensnare one into dishonesty and deceit.
Seeing so many "friends" who are not sources of virtue,
Abu's heart yearns for mountain solitudes.

Throughout the three realms of existence,[160]
Negative emotions are the deceiving enemies;
Throughout the six realms of samsara,
Distraction sends the wheel of cyclic existence spinning on.
Seeing that all these create only more suffering,
Abu's heart longs for mountain solitudes.

Unfailing protectors, Guru, and the Three Jewels,
Grant your blessings that, having gone into
The wilderness, I may survive there, and there steadfastly remain.

Supported by remaining in the wilderness,
May I achieve the blessings of mountain retreat:
Solitude of body
Solitude of speech
Solitude of mind.[161]

Patrul Receives an Extraordinary Guest

Once, Patrul told the people who were staying in his tent encampment that he was expecting a very important guest to arrive later in the day. He told everyone that, in preparation for this special visitor, they must make sure that everything was immaculate. Everyone worked hard to do so.

That afternoon, someone did arrive at Patrul's encampment. The new arrival was a crude beggar who was dressed entirely in rags. This tramp wore a very odd garland around his neck—it was a garland made out of the soles of dirty old boots, all strung together.[162]

At once, Patrul began doing prostrations to the odd beggar. Without hesitation, Patrul respectfully touched the top of his own head to his filthy guest's filthy feet.

No one said a word; everyone was dumbfounded. Not one person joined Patrul in paying respect to this derelict, much less joining him in doing prostrations.

With a polite gesture, Patrul showed the beggar into the main tent. Patrul told his students not to allow anyone else to come inside the tent and then he closed the tent flaps.

People listening could hear Patrul's voice from within as he began to perform the ritual called a *ganachakra,* a sacred feast offering.

They heard voices singing an invocation to Padmasambhava:

Hung! Rise up, Lotus-Born, with your host of dakinis!
Think about us, *sugatas* of all time and all directions.
Great and noble guide, Padma Tötreng Tsal,[163]
Come *now* from the realm of vidyadharas and dakinis!

Just then, an incredibly sweet incense-like fragrance began wafting outside the tent.

At this, some monks just couldn't contain their curiosity, so they opened a side flap on the tent and peered in.

What they saw was shocking. Inside the tent, they could see that Patrul was performing the *ganachakra* ritual, but there was not just one strange beggar—now there were eight of them!

After the *ganachakra*[164] ended, Patrul emerged from the tent. Emerging along with him was the tramp—just the one, still wearing his special leather garland made of boot soles.

Respectfully, Patrul escorted his unusual visitor up all the way to the next nearby mountain pass. From there, the beggar continued on his way.

When Patrul came back, his disciples questioned him about his unusual guest.

Patrul replied, "Since you were able to see him at all, you must have some good karma. Since you saw him, but only saw him as a beggar, you must have some bad karma.

"That was Dorje Drolö himself!"

Almost as an afterthought, Patrul added, "Padmasambhava's other emanations were invited. And all of them came!"[165]

Patrul Meets Two Murderers

Once, Patrul was staying in Drelkar Cave, the Cave of the White Mule, in Dzachukha. He was practicing meditation, wrapped in just a woolen cloak and wearing nothing else.

He heard someone screaming for help.

Patrul threw off his cloak and ran all the way down the hill.

At the bottom of the hill were two thieves, next to the body of a woman they had just stabbed to death. They were robbing the corpse of its jewelry.

Stark naked, Patrul rushed at the robbers, brandishing his wooden walking stick.

Terrified by this awful apparition, the thieves dropped the jewelry and ran for their lives.

The unfortunate woman had been seduced by one of the thieves a few days earlier and he convinced her to run away from home. She had been wearing many precious ornaments of coral, turquoise, agate, amber, and other valuable stones, as was the local custom in the prosperous area of Dzachukha.

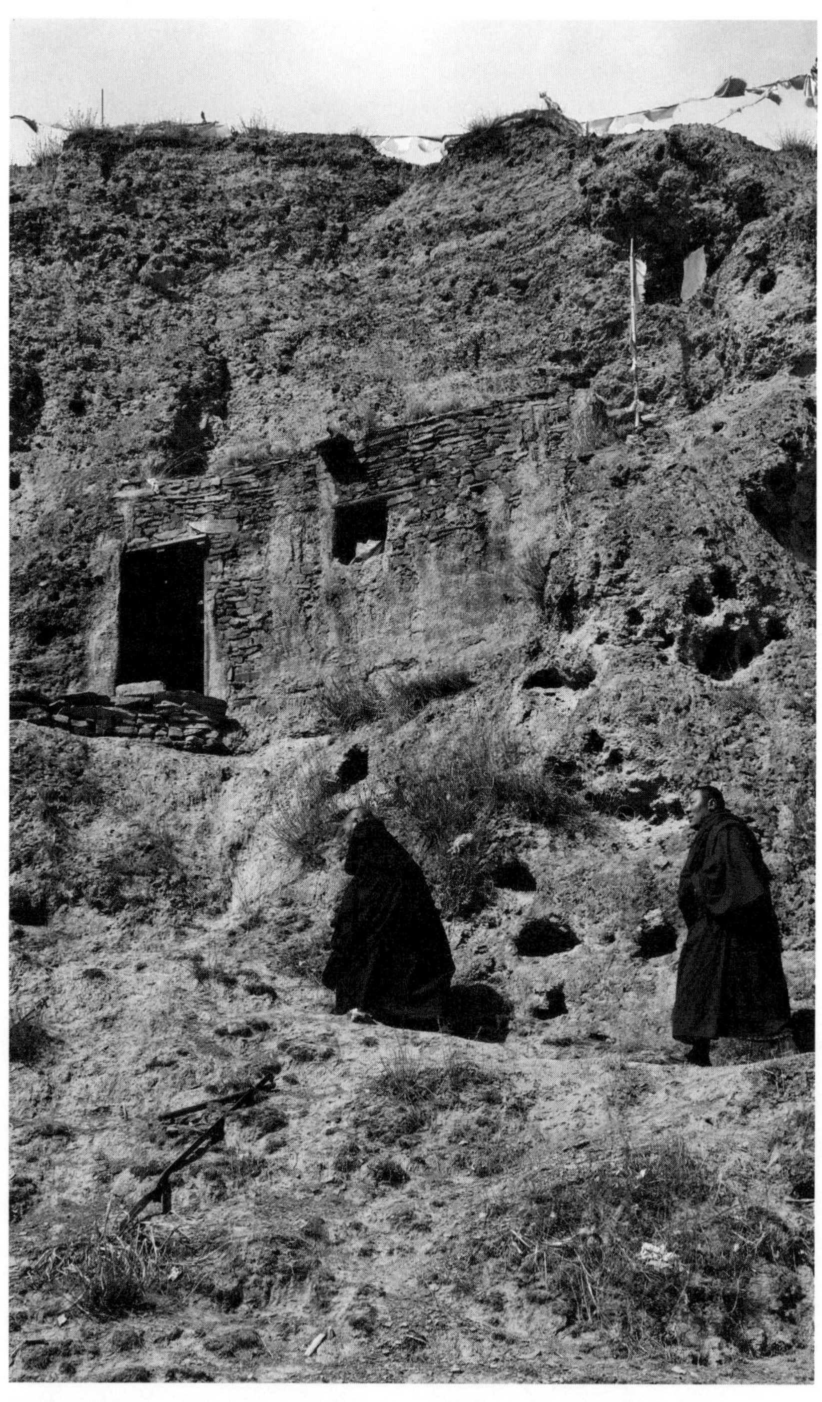

Drelkar Phuk, Patrul Rinpoche's meditation cave in Mamo Thang, Kham. (2016)

First, Patrul performed phowa to liberate the murdered woman's consciousness and recited prayers for her. Then, he collected all her jewelry and brought it to Dzagyal Monastery. On her behalf, Patrul offered the jewelry as adornments for the monastery's large statue of Maitreya Buddha.

Patrul Teaches the Great Perfection at Trama Lung

The power of the Dzogchen teachings lies in direct experience. Patrul often went out into the wilderness in order to practice some of these teachings.

At Trama Lung in the Upper Dzachukha Valley, where his master Jigme Gyalwai Nyugu spent years in retreat, Patrul gave detailed meditation instructions to Önpo Tenga (Orgyen Tendzin Norbu) and other fortunate students.

First, he taught the extraordinary Dzogchen preliminary practices called "distinguishing samsara from nirvana." Later, he taught the main practices, *trekchö* and *thögal*. After he had given a teaching and the instructions for how to do practice, everyone practiced, Patrul doing so along with his students.

Önpo Tenga later remarked: "Each one of us had been given these Dzogchen teachings before. Each one of us had already received these meditation instructions and practiced them. Some of us had even taught these teachings to others!

Dzagyal Trama Lung, Kham, the main retreat place of Jigme Gyalwai Nyugu. Here, on twenty-five occasions, Patrul Rinpoche received the Longchen Nyingthig teachings that led to his writing *The Words of My Perfect Teacher*. (2016)

"What we'd considered our 'understanding' turned out to be nothing but conjecture and fantasy. The detailed oral instructions Patrul gave us at Trama Lung were the result of his own meditation experiences. Following his instructions resulted in our having actual direct experience as a result of our practice. We were able to obtain results. They were direct and obvious, like seeing something that's right in the palm of your hand.

"You may be a practitioner of Dzogchen, someone able to recognize awareness as it arises,[166] but when you blend the deep devotion of Guru Yoga with practices such as 'distinguishing samsara from nirvana,' you make more progress.

"All this became clear at Trama Lung."

PATRUL STRESSED that without having fervent, devotion toward one's root teacher, there is no way to achieve the realization of Dzogchen.

As he got older, he practiced the Guru Yoga according to the Longchen Nyingthig all night long. People nearby could hear his deep voice singing "Precious One, Lotus-Born Guru, think of me!"

Food for a Day Is Plenty

While in Trama Lung, Patrul said to his disciple Mura Tulku Pema Dechen Zangpo,[167] "I was going to have a little cheese and tsampa to eat today. Either a dog took it or I gave it away to someone without realizing that it was all I had. Anyway, there's nothing left now. Would you mind sending me something to make a meal?"

Delighted to have the chance to serve Patrul, Mura Tulku went out to get some provisions. When he returned, he offered the food to Patrul.

However, instead of accepting it, Patrul gave it back to Mura Tulku, saying, "Oh, someone just gave me a little butter and a bit of cheese, so now I don't need any more!"

Patrul Is Distraught

After the death of Jigme Gyalwai Nyugu, many of his students continued to live at Dzagyal Trama Lung. They stayed in a cluster of little black yak-hair tents and devoted their lives to practicing meditation.

At some point, someone in charge decided that their location was not conducive to doing retreat: Dzagyal Trama Lung was just too cold, too windy, too wild, too high, too isolated, too uncomfortable!

They looked around and found another place, one that was more clement and much more comfortable: warmer, milder, lower, better!

Everyone moved down there, to a nice place in a nice valley behind Changma hill, the site of the present Dzagyal Monastery.[168]

When word of this relocation reached Patrul, he became distraught, saying, "That was an auspicious site, one prophesied by the dakinis and the great masters! If they had just stayed where they already were, the encampment would be overflowing with practitioners! The dharma of realization[169] would have flourished! The gathering of disciples would have grown so large that, in order to summon everyone for assembly and practice, gongs would have to be struck in all four directions! What a disaster!"

Patrul and the Learned Geshe

Once, a learned *geshe,* an erudite scholar from the Geluk tradition, decided to debate the renowned scholar Mipham Rinpoche. Mipham at that time was staying in Dzachukha at Juniong Monastery, so the Geshe headed off in that direction. Along the way, it occurred to him that he ought to test out his debate skills first by debating and defeating a few lesser Nyingmapa scholars.

One night, when he stopped, he asked the local people if they knew of any Nyingmapas around who knew enough philosophy to be able to debate. One man said, "Well, in a hut up in the forest there's Patrul. He knows a bit about books."

The Geshe was disappointed not to have found a well-known scholar to practice on. Nevertheless, he made his way through the forest and climbed up to Patrul's retreat hut. Patrul's retreat helper had warned Patrul of the Geshe's intention to visit and practice debating.

As soon as his helper told him the Geshe had arrived, Patrul picked up his worn-out sheepskin coat, turned it inside out, and put it on so that all the fur was on the outside. He lay down on his bed, putting his head at the foot of the bed and his feet at the head of the bed, on his pillow.

The Geshe knocked at the door, but Patrul did not answer. After knocking several times, the Geshe slowly opened the door. He saw Patrul lying in bed, with his feet on his pillow, and his head at the foot of the bed, wearing a sheepskin coat with its fur turned inside out.

The Geshe said, "Why are you lying that way? Can't you tell the head of a bed from the foot of a bed?"

"Dear lama, you're not very good at logic," Patrul replied brightly. "The head of my bed is where my head is. The foot of the bed is where I place my feet."

Rattled, the Geshe remarked, "Odd of you to wear your sheepskin coat inside out, with the fur on the outside and not on the inside."

Patrul shrugged and pointed out, "I'm wearing the fur on the outside and the skin on the inside—just the very same way the sheep do!"

After this spicy start, the Geshe questioned Patrul on the Nyingma views. Patrul responded with amazing ease and broad knowledge.

As he left and walked back down from Patrul's retreat hut, the Geshe thought to himself, "People told me this Patrul knew 'a little bit about books,' but if I couldn't debate and defeat *him*, how would I ever be able to debate and defeat the great Mipham? I'll just go down in disgrace!"

So the Geshe gave up and went home.

The Quick-Thinking Lama

Patrul was traveling through Kham, walking along a road that would take him back to his homeland, Dzachukha. He was not far from Gosa Monastery when he came upon a lama who was searching through the brush along the road, looking to the left and to the right, looking high and low, and doing so with a worried expression.

Seeing this, Patrul asked the lama, "What's wrong?"

The lama, whose name was Drochu Gome, told Patrul that one of his dzomos had run off and he was trying to find her.

The two traveled together, slowly going along the road in the direction of Gosa Monastery, the lama searching on this side and that, while Patrul walked along in his slow, stately way.

Eventually, they wound up at the place that was the lama's home.

When they arrived, Patrul politely inquired of the lama if he might stay the night. Drochu Gome, of course, was happy to offer hospitality to a wandering lama.

The next morning, it had snowed heavily. Drochu Gome noticed that his visitor's boots were sadly very worn. The leather was thin, and the soles were full of holes, making them quite unsuitable for such weather. The lama told Patrul he had an extra pair of boots, and he offered them to his guest. Patrul accepted and put the good boots on, giving the lama his old torn boots to throw away.

As he was taking leave, Patrul asked Gome whether they had met before. The lama replied, "No, we haven't, but I'm guessing you're the Venerable Patrul, aren't you? Would you be good enough to say some prayers for me?"

Patrul agreed, then went on his way, leaving Drochu Gome perfectly happy. He was happy because his wishes had come true—not because he'd finally found his lost dzomo, because in fact his dzomo hadn't gotten lost in the first place!

He'd heard that the great Patrul might be passing by Gosa. Knowing that formally offering hospitality to Patrul would most likely result in a refusal, he'd come up with a singular plan. He'd gone out to intercept Patrul on the road on purpose, completely fabricating a tale about having to look hither and yon for his poor lost dzomo—but it was all so he could bring Patrul closer and closer to his home, and then entice Patrul to accept his hospitality. And his plan had worked!

More than that, swapping his own new boots for Patrul's old ones, pretending to throw Patrul's old ones away, Drochu Gome managed to keep the boots, which he would treasure forever as authentic holy relics of a great saint, who otherwise would never, *ever* have allowed it!

The Lotus-Grove Play

In the beautiful Drichu Valley of Denkhok region in Kham lived a wealthy and influential family called Zimpön Tsang. Their handsome son, Tashi Gelek, fell deeply in love with the young daughter of Ju Tsang Gonpo Dargye.

Tashi sought the young lady's hand in marriage. The families agreed and the two were wed. They were an unusually happy couple, well disposed toward the dharma and they were devoted to one another. However, their happiness did not last long: a deadly epidemic swept through the entire Drichu Valley and many people fell ill suddenly. Of those stricken, many people died—including Tashi Gelek's young and beloved bride.

Tashi Gelek was completely heartbroken. The bereaved newlywed decided to go up the mountain to seek out the hermit Patrul and request his advice.

The Lotus Crystal Cave (Pema Shelphuk) on Pema Ri, above Denkhok and the Drichu (Yangse) River Valley. (1985)

Patrul at that time was living in retreat high up in the mountains, practicing meditation in the Lotus Crystal Cave,[170] a sacred site that overlooks the great river valley.

In response to Tashi's supplication, Patrul wrote *The Lotus-Grove Play,*[171] an allegory of two bees, a golden bee named Wide-Lotus-Wings and his true love, a turquoise bee named Sweet-Lotus-Melody, who live together in the lovely Lotus Grove.[172] Each is possessed of noble qualities: he is strong, young, intelligent, and generous. She is tender by nature, kind, calm, and full of virtues. As a couple, they are affectionate and harmonious. Their tenderness toward each other is continuous.

The male bee, aware of the transitory nature of the world, invites his partner to seek out dharma teachings. She, too, is aware of the unsatisfactoriness of conditioned existence, and eagerly agrees.

She says:

Exquisite, yet fleeting
—like samsara.
Magnificent, yet fleeting
—like the mirage of wealth.

Pleasurable, yet painful
—like the phantom pleasures of the senses.
Entirely lacking in essence
—that's samsara's realm!

The bees approach a great sage and formally request teachings, which the sage gives them, at great length, presenting the essential points of all the stages of the path from start to finish.

Emaho!
Wondrous!
The supreme light-guide on the path to liberation
Is the spiritual friend endowed with all good qualities.
In this degenerate age, his actions equal those of the buddhas
While his boundless compassion and kindness are even greater still.
Not to rely on an authentic spiritual friend along the path
Would be like a blind man gone onto a path without any guide.

[Human beings] aspire to happiness, yet they perpetuate the causes of suffering.
Filling your mind with love and compassion,
Vowing to dispel the suffering of all beings,
Don the armor of boundless courage!
Train in seeing others equal to oneself;
Train in exchanging oneself for others;
Then train in holding others dearer than oneself.

The two bees try to take these teachings to heart. They do so, for the most part, although they are rather careless about worldly enjoyments and desires.

One day, Wide-Lotus-Wings is flying through the sky while Sweet-Lotus-Melody sips delicious honey-nectar from a wildflower, when an unexpected thunderstorm rolls in. When the sky darkens, the petals of the wildflower suddenly close up, trapping Sweet-Lotus-Melody within them. Unable to free herself, she is terrified and helpless.

Her partner, Wide-Lotus-Wings, is terrified as well.

Sweet-Lotus-Melody cries out to Wide-Lotus-Wings and he hears her. She is already regretting her failure to practice the sage's teachings. As she slowly begins to suffocate, she begs Wide-Lotus-Wings to practice the dharma, so as not to have regrets at the time of his death, as she is having now. Wide-Lotus-Wings, unable to help in any way, suffers as he hears his beloved suffering.

Sweet-Lotus-Melody dies. Wide-Lotus-Wings' grief turns his mind toward dharma; a strong revulsion toward samsara arises in his mind.

The many verses that follow present the teachings, in what some view as a condensed version of *The Words of My Perfect Teacher.*

The bee learns how to become able to bring all circumstances onto the path:

When things are good, it's bad.
When things are bad, it's good.
When things are good, five poisonous emotions flare up.
When things are bad, past bad karma burns up.
Tribulations are the master's compassion.

When you're lauded, it's bad.
When you're belittled, it's good.
When you're admired, ego inflates even more.
When you're criticized, weak points become obvious.
Slanders are the deities' blessings.
. . . .
To practice dharma, these are essential.
To create certainty, these are essential.
To stay in solitude, these are essential.
To roam as a vagabond, these all are essential.

Hearing these extensive teachings and taking them to heart, the male bee vows to put them into practice.

Tashi Gelek, the young widower for whom Patrul wrote these words, did take them to heart, and devoted the rest of his life to practice.

Patrul Is Tricked by a Nomad Family

Once, back in Dzachukha, not far from the place where Patrul had pitched his own small yak-hair tent, the grandfather of a wealthy nomad family passed away. The family wished to ask Patrul Rinpoche to come to perform ceremonies on behalf of their grandfather, but they knew it was very unlikely that he would agree.

The eldest son, knowing something of Patrul's character, and in particular, the depth of his compassion, devised an interesting plan he hoped would succeed in bringing the family's wishes to fruition.

The son took his grandfather's dead body and wrapped it up in a huge grubby old piece of felt. Next, the son took his grandfather's collection of precious stones—corals, turquoises, and so on—and wrapped them up in a filthy worn-out leather pouch along with a precious black antique bowl. He tied the grimy pouch roughly onto the top of the shabbily wrapped corpse and tossed the whole thing out in the cold like garbage, not far from the main entrance to the family's tent.

The eldest son waited patiently until at last he saw Patrul walk past his family's tent. The son called out to him, "*Lama-la,*[173] please come in and have tea with us, if you wish."

Patrul agreed and entered the tent. He was offered a seat on a little yak-fur carpet, and then offered some tea.

While sipping his tea, Patrul asked the son, "What's that lump of stuff thrown outside your tent door?"

"That? Oh, that's nothing," replied the son breezily. "It's just the corpse of a servant who dropped dead just now. He was a poor old man without any family. There's no one here even to take it away to a charnel ground, so we just threw it out and left it right where it was. There's no need to send for a lama to do prayers and do phowa for him, because, really, who cares?"

At once, Patrul offered to do prayers and perform the ritual of phowa. He even offered to dispose of the dead body, by carrying it off to the nearest charnel ground himself.

As Patrul was hoisting the wrapped corpse onto his back, he noticed the grimy leather pouch and asked the son what was inside it.

"That? Oh, that's nothing," replied the son breezily, as before.

"The old servant had it with him when he first came. We have no clue as to what's in it—none of us even wanted to open up the filthy thing to look! Take it away and do with it whatever you want!"

Patrul took away the corpse and the pouch, too.

The sharp-witted son was very satisfied. Not only had he managed to take advantage of Patrul's notorious compassion to get him to perform phowa on his grandfather's behalf, but tricked him into taking an offering for having done so!

Patrul Is Tricked by Another Nomad Family

Once, after a young nomad girl died, her father wanted Patrul Rinpoche to say prayers on her behalf and perform the ritual of phowa. He was well aware that Patrul rarely performed such ceremonies, but he hoped he could find a way to get him to do it. Riding on one horse and taking another one with him, he left his own encampment and headed off to try to meet Patrul.

At that time, Patrul was staying in the Aja Valley of Dzachukha, a place so infamous for being rife with murderous bandits, no one dared ever to travel after dark.

The father had planned his trip very carefully. He wished to reach Patrul's encampment just as dusk was falling, and that is what he did. In this way, he succeeded in running into Patrul.

After they exchanged greetings, Patrul asked him where he was going.

The father replied, "I'm riding to Dzogchen Monastery to ask Dzogchen Rinpoche to do prayers on behalf of my daughter and to perform phowa. Time is short. I will get there even if I must ride through the night."

Patrul warned the father, "It's too dangerous! You mustn't ride *anywhere* in this area at night!. You'll be robbed for sure! Spend the night here and leave in the morning!"

The girl's father replied, "There's no time left. I must try my best to have these rituals done for her as soon as possible, even if robbers kill me in the process. I'm not likely to find a lama around *here* who'd do it, am I?"

At once, Patrul relented, saying, "Oh, all right, all right, then. You don't have to ride all night. I'll come and do it myself!"

Thus, the clever father managed to have the proper rituals for his deceased daughter performed by Patrul, just as he'd wished.

Patrul's Patrician Manners

Patrul was staying in the large encampment of a wealthy nomad when a few young nomad horsemen happened to ride past his tent. Looking toward Patrul's tent, one horseman remarked, "Nobody can talk to Patrul Rinpoche as if he were an ordinary, worldly person."

A second horseman said, cockily, "*I* can!"

The first horseman said, "If you can do it, I'll give you this horse!"

The second horseman accepted the bet.

The whole group rode over to Patrul's tent. The nomad who'd accepted the bet went right inside the lama's tent, while the other nomads stayed outside it, listening.

They all heard the cocky horseman breezily greet Patrul, saying, "Honored sir, how do you *do*?"

There was a long silence.

"And *you*, honored sir," they could hear Patrul replying politely in his very deep voice, "how do *you* do?"

There was an even longer silence.

Then the second horseman emerged from Patrul's tent, stepping out from the tent backward. His face was white as a ghost. Trembling, he looked absolutely shaken to his core.

He told his friends that the great Patrul Rinpoche had somehow known *exactly* why he was there and what he was up to.

"At first, after I said, 'Honored sir, how do you do?' I thought he hadn't heard me, there was such a long pause," said the horseman.

"Then, suddenly, formally, he doffed his hat and bowed down to me deeply, saying, in that low voice he has, 'And *you*, honored sir! How do *you* do?'

"I was so shocked by his impossibly courteous behavior, his sweeping his hat off his head with such a flourish, his bowing down before me, his terrifying shock of white hair, that I couldn't get a word to come out of my mouth! Not one!"

Patrul's Rude Manners

A very important, high-ranking aristocrat traveled all the way on foot from Golok to Dzachukha in order to have a chance to meet the great Patrul Rinpoche in person.

Not only did Patrul refuse to let him in, much less grant him an audience, but Patrul himself came to the entrance of his black yak-hair tent and began mercilessly scolding the very important personage, doing so loudly, fiercely, and at considerable length.

The notable from Golok responded, "Your fame is vast as the sky, and your name is known far and wide, sir—but you're just like fir bark thrown on a fire, the crackling kind that shoots off a shower of searing fiery sparks!"

At this, Patrul began to laugh. "You're right!" he said. "I had an uncle who was extremely rude. I must have inherited my bad manners from him!"

Some Love Him, Some Fear Him

Someone remarked to Patrul, "Some people love you and others fear you—they dare not say a word in your presence. Why might that be?"

Patrul thought for a while. Finally he replied:

"Maybe some people love me because I continuously cultivate compassion and loving-kindness. Maybe others fear me because I regard self and phenomena to be equally empty of intrinsic nature."

Explaining this story, a contemporary master[174] observed that people naturally feel attracted to someone whose heart is filled with compassion, while also feeling reverential awe ("fear") toward someone who truly understands the empty nature of all phenomena. Practitioners who have achieved such profound realization have a particular powerful yet quiet presence. They are like a mighty mountain that cannot be shaken by the winds of worldly hopes and fears.

Patrul's Respect for the Natural Course of the Elements

Patrul had harsh words for those tantric practitioners who performed magic rituals with the aim of changing the weather, either to bring rain or stop it, depending on the requests they receive from people.

"Wicked demons must have possessed the hearts of all these magic-makers," he once said. "They have delusions of grandeur, but their grandiose schemes accomplish nothing but the ruination of the land.

"Just look at what they do. Our three short months of summer are a pleasant season when we enjoy fine weather. The meadows are blanketed in multicolored flowers, the birds are singing, and animals frolic happily everywhere. That's also the time when these troublemakers come along and start cooking up all sorts of rituals for interfering with natural forces like the weather. They say they are summoning spirits, but all they summon is desolation.

"Their meddling harms both farmers and nomads alike. They bring about droughts and epidemics. And just think of all the animals they destroy with their magic—so many of them, right down to the smallest tadpoles, frogs, and fish. By harming all these beings, they bring nothing but bad karma on themselves."[175]

» *Words of Warning* «

You, Longchenpa, your spiritual son
And all those of your lineage,
Are supreme protectors,
Lords of bodhichitta.
Through your aspiration-prayers
Out of vast compassion
You gather in those wandering
Through samsara's realms,
Never letting them go.
To you, I pray.

Over aeons, these beings,
Each one once my mother,
Kept me kindly in their care;
Burdened by their heavy
Store of bad karma,
Suffering rains down.
To see this is unbearable;
My heart shatters!

Bad karma bad-deed "friends"
Are difficult to jettison;
Skilled at deception, beguiling
And causing confusion, they
Seduce my focus elsewhere.
Until my heart is set on practicing the holy dharma
I'll just keep on rotting in samsara's prison.

When I was young, unable to withstand
The influence of others,
I could not practice dharma.
When I was grown, caught up in sensual desires,
I did not practice dharma.
Now that I'm old, my faculties have failed,
I cannot practice dharma.

Now, what can I do?
Alas, alas!

In these degenerate times,
Thoughts and acts are crooked.
Hanging out with crooked folk
Goes against the teachings.
Even if I tried,
I'd never please them all.
Enough! I've had it!
I'm off to do mountain retreat, no matter what!

No matter how much I acquire, I never have enough.
No matter how much I accomplish, there is always more to do.
No matter how many I've flattered already, there are always more boots to lick.
Enough! I've had it!
I'll limit my dealings with others, no matter what!

However many pleasures I enjoy, my desire is never sated.
However much I learn, it's just words without meaning.
However much I fritter away my time, I never run out of distractions.
Enough! I've had it!
I'll cut out all this mental chatter, all these plans and hopes and fears!

What's the point of learning if it's not put into practice?
What's the point of reflecting if it just spawns fabrications?
What's the point of meditation that stirs up baseless hopes and fears?
Enough! I've had it!
I'll be laid back, naked, freed from concepts, no matter what!

If precepts are pretense and hypocrisy, what's the use of the Vinaya?
If practice is just hollow words, what's the use of Sutras?
If knowledge is just empty words, what's use of Abhidharma?
Enough! I've had it!
Like a lunatic, I'll just do whatever comes to mind, no matter what!

Hard to acquire, hard to protect—what's the big deal about riches?

Hard to govern, hard to please—what's the big deal about retinues?
Hard to acquire, hard to leave—what's the big deal about home?
Enough! I've had it!
I'll survive like a roadside beggar, living on handouts, no matter what!

What's the use of the *shravaka* who regards phenomena as the enemy?
What's the use of developing bodhichitta like a mawkish old lady?
What's the use of the tantrika warped by negative emotions?
Enough! I've had it!
I'll remain in the nature of mind, at ease, no matter what!

When I consider my own conduct,
I can do nothing but laugh.
When I consider the conduct of others,
I can do nothing but sigh.
Just now, whatever comes to mind is distressing.
Whomever I lay my eyes on, it's depressing.

When nature's elements rise up as enemies,
I feel completely fed up with the universe!
When hypocrisy, pretense and deceit rise up,
I feel completely fed up with those who inhabit the universe!
Regarding the endless river of bad karma,
Seeing how all of life is spent without meaning,
I feel completely fed up with people!
I just am completely fed up with it all!

You, my refuge and protector,
Are endowed with compassion
From the very beginning.
If you're unmoved by the tearful misery of beings
Wandering through samsara's realms for so very long,
Crushed beneath their burden of bad karma,
Who else will help them find relief?

"Yes, it is!"
"No, it's not!"
Nothing but useless babble!

"It's like this!"
"It's like that!"
Nothing but verbal deceit!
Duped by the theories of pig-headed academics,
I'd love to sweep their "view" out the door![176]

Seeing deities, seeing demons,
Genuine meditation experiences lessen.
All this visualizing of wrathful wild-eyed deities,
Their maws agape, turns you into a bedeviled spirit.
Duped into forcing myself to do stupid practices,
I'd love to throw "meditation" to the winds!

Aimed at achieving worldly goals, your Vinaya conduct
Just looks good from the outside.
Aimed at nothing but lust, your Mantrayana conduct
Only aims at private parts.
Duped into pursuing useless goals,[177]
I'd love to throw "conduct" down the drain!

When self-interest is entrenched,
How can you benefit others?
You give helpful advice to corpses
As to what to recognize in the bardo,
But you haven't yet recognized your own mind!
If you can't help yourself,
How can you hope to help others?
I'd love to throw "benefiting others" off a cliff!

Stuffed with preconceptions,
You hope to gaze into awareness,
But it's all completely concocted.
Your spaced-out *shamatha* practice
Just gets you tangled in the silkworm
Called "meditation experiences."
Making conceited assumptions
About having achieved those "high attainments"?
I'd love to throw "fruition" in the abyss!

Though you've neglected to practice,
You elucidate the teachings for others.
Your learning is your own worst enemy,
Ruining your mindstream with wrong views.
Endlessly arguing about terminology, you're misled by what
you've learned.
Seeing this, I'd love to toss "study and reflection" to the winds!

....

Having accomplished nothing
Within your own tradition,
You run off to seek another.
Then, not practicing that one,
You'll surely practice the next
Because that one's way more "profound"!
Your mind is all over the place,
Completely distracted,
Suckered in by a surfeit of scriptures!
Seeing this, I'd love to do nothing but practice!

You're a tight-fisted miser
Doing rites to bring riches, but
Only attracting the "demon of dearth."

Although you lack bodhichitta,
Having others in your charge,
You end up losing charge of yourself.
Slacking off on the supreme accomplishment,
You're so diligent about doing a bunch of rituals!
Seeing this, I'd love to tame my own mind!

Whatever plans I make, there's no time to achieve them.
Whatever I do, it turns out to be pointless.
I do this, I practice that: it's all self-deception.
Seeing this, I can bide my time till death without having a strategy!

....

Enough of discursive thoughts.
See how they've led me astray?
Enough of talking.
See how talk is a distraction?
Enough of doing things.
See how I get snared into activities?

I feel like roaming around like a stray mutt.
I feel like nestling in my den like an old fox.
I feel like doing whatever and making no plans.
I feel like rambling around like a tramp.

I don't need a lama, as I'm aware of my own mindstream.
I don't need a servant, as I can look after myself.
I don't need a mind buzzing with plans, since I know how
to take refuge.

Now, whatever happens, however it happens, let it be!

Like a corpse,
I am steadfast
And without ambition,
An "old dog" who looks like he's going downhill.

. . . .

In this way, may all be auspicious!

Patrul Gives Away a Fine Mandala

It was Patrul's general custom not to accept offerings. If he did accept an offering, he would soon give it away.

Sometimes people would make offerings to Patrul of religious objects, things practitioners needed for their meditation practice, such as vajra-and-bell sets, mandala sets, *damaru* drums, shrine offering-bowls, and so on. These he might accept and pass on to other practitioners, knowing they would be used for various virtuous deeds and for meditation practices.

There was a monk at Gegong Monastery named Kunpel who was a nephew of Patrul's sister's husband. He had no education when he arrived, as he came from an utterly destitute family. No one thought much of his prospects. Since he was unable to afford even candles or butter lamps, if he wanted to study at night he had only the light of the moon to read by.

Once, when this Kunpel happened to be present, someone offered Patrul a particularly fine mandala-offering set made of *lima* alloy (bell metal).[178] Others present were surprised when Kunpel had the nerve to ask Patrul if he would give *him* the fine mandala-offering set, and they were even more surprised when Patrul agreed.

"Of course!" said Patrul.

He handed Kunpel the mandala set, saying, "In the future, when you're giving dharma teachings to a great multitude, you'll be needing just such a fine mandala, won't you?"

Some listeners might have assumed Patrul was being a bit sarcastic. No one at that time (save Patrul, apparently) was able to foresee the future of this apparently ordinary monk from a decidedly destitute family. This monk was so poor that his feet were bleeding because he had no shoes, so poor that his clothing was dirty and patched—so poor that he really did have to study by moonlight. No one paid him much attention at all, never dreaming that through his devotion, diligence, courage, and the blessings of his teachers, such as Patrul, this poor monk would eventually transform into a renowned scholar-practitioner, the great Khenpo Kunpel, whom Patrul cared for like a son.

Beggars and Mani-Stone Carvers

Whenever Patrul saw beggars approaching, he'd become extremely happy, as if something absolutely wonderful was coming his way. He preferred the entreaties of beggars to ordinary normal conversation. When Patrul was able to give beggars everything they'd begged for, he became even happier than the recipients of his gifts were.

When poor mani-stone carvers, too, came and asked Patrul for help with food or clothing, tears would well up in his eyes; Patrul would actually become physically weak. If he happened to have something to give away, he would give it away in an instant, with great joy. When he had nothing to give, he'd say, sadly, "What's to be done?" and just stare off into space in anguish.

Once, a poor stone carver called Phurkyab came to Patrul and begged him for money. Sensing that the stone carver was a bit greedy, Patrul told him, "Just repeat the words 'I don't need this money,' and I will give money to you." Bewildered, the man did not dare to say anything at first. After Patrul repeated his instruction three times, the astounded man finally said, "I don't need this money."

Patrul then gave money to the beggar.

Later, someone asked Patrul to explain what he'd done.

Patrul replied, "Once, the lay devotee Anathapindada offered Buddha Shakyamuni a delicious, rich sweet called a *laddu*. A greedy brahman had been watching and begged the Buddha to give him the sweet. The Buddha replied, "Just say, 'Gautama, I don't need this *laddu*,' and I will give it to you."

The brahman did as he was asked, repeating the words that Buddha had told him to say, and then the Buddha gave him the *laddu*.

Later, the Buddha's personal attendant, Ananda, asked the Buddha to explain his actions.

Buddha replied, "For five hundred lifetimes, this brahman has never once uttered the words, 'I don't need . . . ' Since he has never said it, I requested him do so, repeating after me the words 'I don't need . . . ,' in order to create in his mind the habit of contentment."

Patrul Begs for More Beggars

Once, for a few days in a row, no poor people came to Patrul's tent door begging for help. Because of this dearth of beggars, offerings of food, money, and various other things started to accumulate in Patrul's quarters.

Unhappy at this increasing pile of religious offerings, Patrul told two of his students to leave at once, go find some beggars, round them up and bring them back.

Eventually, the disciples returned with a bunch of destitute mani-stone carvers.

"Isn't this *great*?" exclaimed Patrul, as he saw the stone carvers approach. He began gathering up all the offerings that had been piling up.

The instant the beggars came into Patrul's room, before they could even open their mouths to ask him for anything, Patrul started tossing money and other goods at them, shouting, "Here you go! Here you go!"

Soon, he'd given away every single offering that he'd had.

After the mani-stone carvers had taken all his offerings away, Patrul remarked, with great relief, "Isn't it *fantastic* finally to get rid of all that dreadful stuff that's just been lying around like an old corpse slowly going to rot?"

Patrul Accepts What He Is Given

For most of his life, when precious offerings were made to Patrul, he declined them. If not, he'd accept offerings politely and then abandon them on the spot, leaving them behind, on the ground, right where they were.

This was Patrul's general custom until the day he received this letter from Jamyang Khyentse Wangpo:

> Palge, you may not need wealth offered to you by the living on behalf of the dead, but don't just throw it away. Don't just let it go to rot in a wasteland.
>
> It is likely that these offerings were gained through the patrons' own blood, sweat, and tears. It won't do just to toss such offerings away. It's better to put them to use to achieve some virtuous purpose.[179]

Reading this, Patrul exclaimed, "Look what Dilgo Ngedön wrote to me! Sometimes he talks nonsense. Sometimes he talks sense. Today, I think he must be right!"

From then on, over four or five years, Patrul accepted all offerings of money, jewelry, and precious metals that were made to him from anyone and everyone, rich or poor. Patrul used these offerings to commission the careful carving onto stones of the mani mantra. So many stones were added that the new wall was much bigger than the original wall built by his predecessor Samten Phuntsok, in length, width, and height, thus fulfilling the prophecy that the next Palge incarnation would double its size. Patrul himself checked each stone after it was carved, supervising the work with such care that all the carved stones came out beautiful, impeccably clear, accurate, and well finished.

Patrul said, "Making any sacred object brings benefit to sentient beings. However, clay vases and statues are subject to ruin from rainwater; gold statues may be stolen unless well guarded; frescoes and thangkas are fragile; temples need caretakers; having caretakers means a need to support them and it is hard to find even one who does the job well. Sacred texts are easily damaged and easily mislaid. When someone gives offerings to support the carving of sacred texts on woodblocks, one still finds mistakes even after proofing them nine times. It is very hard to achieve a perfect set of woodblocks, without some words added or missing or mixed up.

"An offering of a wall of one hundred thousand mani stones is complete in and of itself. There is no need to worry about leaky roofs in summer or snow in winter. The wall does not need to be swept or cleaned. There is no need to protect it from pigeons or mice. There is no need to worry about how to support temple caretakers, and so on.

"Once the six syllables of the mantra have been properly carved, there is nothing more to check. There is no need to refer to models, since every single person knows the mantra by heart. The mani mantra has been blessed by the Buddha as being the condensation of 84,000 sections of his teachings into six syllables.

"In short, making other kinds of sacred objects is like trying to hold up the branches of a tree; to build a mani wall is like making the root of the tree. Even if this whole country were to be filled with invaders, there would be no need to worry about these stones being stolen or destroyed. The wall will last for many generations.[180]

"People used to say that if one lays a foundation for a mani stone, when the Lord of Death weighs our positive against our negative actions, the weight of this foundation will be added to our scale on the side of virtue.

"Truly, this mani wall is a finer offering than a foundation made of pure gold from the Jambu River. I don't have the means to make such precious offerings, but I can make prayers of dedication, with both my speech and my mind, thinking of the whole earth as being the foundation of these mani stones. If one were to weigh that merit, wouldn't it be substantial?"[181]

He blessed the mani wall stones to bring benefit to countless beings of countless generations who would eventually see these stones, hear of them, or even think of them. Patrul often said, too, that whoever made offerings, prostrations, or circumambulated these stones, and even those touched by the wind coming from their direction would never fall back into rebirth in samsara.

When he taught the *Guhyagarbha Tantra* to the 5th Dzogchen Rinpoche, Thubten Chökyi Dorje, Khenpo Shengpa (the reincarnation of Gyalse Shenphen Thaye), the great Khenpo Pema Dorje, Khenpo Könchog Özer, and about a thousand monks, Patrul asked that they all perform the consecration of the Palge Mani Wall during two full days.

Ahead of the ceremonies, Patrul sent a long silk ceremonial scarf and a silver ingot to the great omniscient vajradhara Jamyang Khyentse Wangpo at Dzongsar, asking him to perform a consecration of newly extended Palge Mani Wall.

Jamyang Khyentse Wangpo agreed, but said that he must do the consecration ceremony at a distance, since he was in permanent retreat and unable to travel.

He sent a small package of saffron-colored barley grains, which he said to toss on the tenth of the sixth month of the lunar calendar.

When the day came, everyone was ready for the consecration. Incense was lit.

Khyentse Rinpoche would be doing prayers from afar.

Patrul said, "He's not here in person, but old Khyentse does some unusual things once in a while, so, watch out!"

They performed the consecration ceremony, threw some of Khyentse Rinpoche's barley grains. When the ceremony was done a big cloud appeared overhead.

Just over the mani stones, suddenly, there came down a huge rain of grains of barley.

When compared to the handful of saffron-colored barley grains that Khyentse Rinpoche had sent before, they were exactly the same saffron-colored grains.[182]

After he saw this happen, Patrul said, "That tulku of the Dilgo family is just like an Indian *mahasiddha*!"

Then, lasting for three whole days, an amazing rain of flowers showered down on the Palge Mani Wall until it was covered in blossoms.

Patrul Practices Yoga

In remote places, Patrul practiced yoga according to the Longchen Nyingthig tradition. Before doing the twenty-one exercises, he would strip naked, assume a particular yogic posture, and hold his breath, as in the great vase exercise.[183] Holding his prana in the central channel, he eventually became able to recite the long *Chanting the Names of Manjushri* three times on a single held breath.

His student Khenpo Kunpel observed him do this.

Patrul sometimes snored while practicing or even nodded off. When, with a start, he woke up again, Patrul would say, "There's been a gap in my practice! I got distracted!"

Then, picking up the recitation *exactly where he'd left off,* Patrul would resume his practice.

Sometimes, when Khenpo Kunpel was doing this practice, Patrul happened to be sleeping nearby. If the Khenpo made even the slightest error, skipping a verse or even just misremembering a word, Patrul would snap out of sleep and correct him!

Apparently asleep, but actually resting in awareness, Patrul slept in the "clear light"[184] state—fully aware, vast, luminous, beyond thought.

Patrul Travels in an Unusual Way

Once, when there were a few other people nearby, Patrul was doing his daily recitation of *Chanting the Names of Manjushri.* As usual, he was reciting it in the Tibetan language.

Toward the end of the recitation, people listening were surprised to hear him switch suddenly from chanting in Tibetan to chanting in the Sanskrit language, doing so with apparent fluency, until the end.

Patrul gave a little start, and seemed to come back to himself. Then he said, as if in explanation, "All of a sudden, there I was! In Nalanda!"

Nalanda, of course, was the famed Buddhist university of India where Shantideva taught—a thousand years ago!

Patrul Receives Lo-nga Tulku

A lama named Lo-nga Tulku wanted to meet Patrul.[185]

He came to the place Patrul happened to be staying and started prostrating just outside Patrul's door.

Patrul saw him and grumbled, "Looks like someone's doing prostrations here. What's all that about?"

The lama got up and introduced himself, saying, "I'm Lo-nga Tulku."

Now, in Tibetan, *lo-nga* means not only a certain place, but also a reed that grows near water.

"*Lo-nga* Tulku?" said Patrul, feigning astonishment. "Hey! What degenerate times we live in! These days, even *reeds* reincarnate!"

Lo-nga Tulku was not put off. He knew that the reincarnation of Patrul's own teacher, Jigme Gyalwai Nyugu, was referred to as Trama Tulku.[186] Now, in Tibetan, *trama* means not only a certain place, but also "dry twig."

"Well, if there can be *twig* tulkus, why not *reed* tulkus?" his visitor quipped to Patrul.

"At least reeds are *flexible*!"

Although Patrul said nothing in reply, it was clear he was nonetheless pleased by the tulku's quick wit.

Lo-nga Tulku and Patrul's Carpet

Lo-nga Tulku sat down at Patrul's feet, and the two of them soon began talking. As they were speaking, Lo-nga Tulku surreptitiously began plucking some hairs from Patrul's felt carpet, hairs he wanted to keep as relics.

Noticing him, Patrul suddenly cried out, "What the hell are you doing *that* for?"

Guessing that Patrul might not approve what he was doing, Lo-nga Tulku spontaneously created a cover story, saying, "Oh! This? *Well*, there are epidemics plaguing our cattle these days *and* the cattle are also often attacked by wolves. I was thinking I might just tie some of these nice felt carpet-hairs onto their necks as a protection for them!"

Patrul was not at all fooled but rather was amused by the way Lo-nga Tulku had framed his request for relics. Not only did Patrul allow the tulku to collect the carpet hairs, but he tore off a piece of fabric from his own clothes and let him have that, too, as a relic.

Meeting the 3rd Dodrupchen

Once, while he was circumambulating stupas, Patrul was handed a letter from Do Khyentse Yeshe Dorje, asking him to oversee the education of the young Dodrupchen tulku.[187] Soon after that, when Patrul reached the east side of the circumambulation path, he encountered the newly recognized tulku in person.

Patrul had been reciting *Chanting the Names of Manjushri* as he made the circumambulation. At the moment the two came face to face, Patrul had just come to this verse:

Through great wisdom, in a single instant,
He realized and beheld all things.

"If this happened to anyone but me," Patrul later said, "it would be seen as an auspicious coincidence, a sign that this tulku will be a great scholar."

Meeting with a Yogi

A yogi named Ang Tendar—who was not just an ordinary practitioner but quite realized—went to visit Patrul.

"Where are you from?" Patrul asked him.

"I'm a disciple of Tsoknyi in Nangchen."[188]

"Well, well. I've heard of this Tsoknyi of Nangchen! He's supposed to have realized the view of the Great Perfection. Isn't he the one who is so fond of teaching in a way that, as Milarepa said, 'If you practice in the morning, you are a Buddha in the morning, and if you practice at night, you are a Buddha at night—and fortunate beings whose past actions have created suitable conditions do not even need to meditate—they will be liberated by merely hearing the teaching!'

"If this is your teacher, tell me this: how many of his disciples have attained the rainbow body?" Patrul teased.

"There was one student who *would* have attained the rainbow body," Tendar replied, "if he hadn't dropped dead from badly infected boils!"

Now, there is no way in the world *any* illness can prevent an advanced practitioner from attaining the rainbow body, so for a moment Patrul was left speechless.

Then they both burst out laughing.

First Teaching of the 3rd Dodrupchen

When the eight-year-old Jigme Tenpai Nyima came to Dzachukha to receive teachings from Patrul, Patrul was very kind to the little Dodrupchen. Every day, when he taught him, he had Dodrupchen seated on his own pillow (the one Patrul used to put under his head for sleeping), a gesture of extraordinary respect.

Dodrupchen stayed in the same house where Patrul was living, with only a wall between them. Every day, the little tulku could hear Patrul's deep voice chanting the prayer to Guru Rinpoche that is part of the Longchen Nyingthig, as part of his daily practice:

O Revered Lord, Precious Master!
You are the glorious embodiment
Of the compassion and blessings of all the buddhas.
You are the sole protector of all beings.
My whole body, heart, mind, and possessions
I offer to you without hesitation.
From this time until I attain enlightenment,
In all my happiness and suffering, good and bad, high and low,
O most revered Padmasambhava—please watch over me.

Early one morning, Patrul overheard young Dodrupchen crying.

Later Patrul discovered that Dodrupchen had fallen asleep during morning practice, so his tutor had spanked him. Patrul didn't like Dodrupchen's tutor, believing that his treatment was too rough for the amazing little Dodrupchen.

Patrul was so upset at what the tutor had done that he told Dodrupchen, "When you die, don't go to Zangdokpalri! If you do, Guru Rinpoche will send you back *here* again, as he is always worrying about the Tibetans. You must go to Sukhavati, Amitabha's blissful pure land, and not come back to these wicked people!"

When he had finished giving Dodrupchen teachings on *The Way of the Bodhisattva,* Patrul sent messengers all over Dzachukha Valley announcing that the eight-year-old would be giving public teachings on *The Way of the Bodhisattva.*

Before a big assembly of monks and laypeople at Dzagyal Monastery, Patrul himself offered the ceremonial mandala requesting the child to teach.

When Dodrupchen started his commentary, everyone was astonished by his knowledge and confidence. At first, Dodrupchen's soft voice didn't reach listeners who were sitting far away. Gradually, however, his voice grew stronger, and then everyone was able to hear him.

Patrul sent a message with happy news to Khyentse Wangpo:

> I had thought that the sun of dharma was about to set, but as far as the dharma of scriptural knowledge is concerned, the eight-year-old tulku

of Dodrupchen has given explanatory teachings on four chapters[189] of *The Way of the Bodhisattva*!

As for the dharma of realization, Nyakla Pema Dundul recently attained the rainbow body! Thus, the light of the doctrine of Buddha has not yet been extinguished!

Second Visit of the 3rd Dodrupchen

On Dodrupchen's next visit to Patrul for teachings, the young tulku was accompanied by a new tutor, Aku Lodrö, a gentle, respectful, gray-haired monk. Patrul was very pleased by this change and remarked to Dodrupchen, "Now, *he* seems like a proper tutor for an important lama!"

When the teachings were over, as an offering to Patrul Rinpoche, young Dodrupchen promised him that he would teach *The Way of the Bodhisattva* one hundred times in his life. Patrul was pleased by his offer, and it was a promise that Dodrupchen would indeed keep.

Patrul's Encampment

At first, there was just one tent, Patrul's little black yak-hair tent.

Over time, people came and set up tents of their own. Gradually, the tent encampment grew, from very few tents to very many. At its peak, there were hundreds of black yak-hair tents and white cotton tents gathered together in the style of nomads, sheltering thousands of devoted dharma practitioners who had come to hear Patrul teach. This encampment of practitioners was known as Patrul Gar.

Patrul taught everyone staying there what he called the Three Opportunities, a practice to refine one's intentions.

The first opportunity occurs upon waking: don't get up in a rush, the way a cow or a sheep in a pen does, but take a moment while still in bed to relax your mind. Look within, and check your intention.

The second opportunity at Patrul Gar occurs on the way to the teachings. People must squeeze through a narrow passage to get past a stupa on the way to the teaching tent. The moment of squeezing past should be used as a reminder to cultivate bodhichitta and a wish to benefit others, by avoiding evil actions and performing beneficial actions.

The third opportunity occurs during the teachings, another chance to know one's goal and set one's intention:

Each instant, put your heart into it again.
Each moment, remind yourself again.
Each second, check yourself again.
Night and day, make your resolve again.
In the morning, commit yourself again.
Each meditation session, examine mind minutely.
Never be apart from dharma, not even accidentally.
Continually, do not forget.[190]

When people staying at Patrul Gar just weren't getting the point, Patrul would actually send them away.

"You are fooling me and I am fooling you; it's pointless!" Patrul would say. "Get out, go away do something useful with your life! Go away, get married, do business, have children! What's the point of not being a practitioner *and* not being a worldly person? Go be a worldly person, just remember to have a good heart!"

WHEN HE WAS SEVENTY-ONE, Patrul began keeping enough food to last for a week, rather than only keeping enough for a single day, as had previously been his custom.[191]

Other than that, he'd send offerings to the stone wall fund. Sometimes, when extra food was offered to him, he would decline to take it, and leave it right at the spot where it had been offered.

Because of these abandoned offerings, Patrul attracted groups of beggars who would follow in his wake and pick up the food or other offerings that Patrul had left behind.

Wangchok Dorje's Renunciation

Wangchok Dorje, also known as Tsewang Trakpa, was the elder son of the great tertön Chokgyur Lingpa. He met Patrul when he was a child. Like his sister Könchog Paldrön and his half-brother Tsewang Norbu, he quickly became a devoted student of Patrul.

Wangchok Dorje spontaneously recognized the nature of mind at an early age, entirely on his own. His intelligence was strikingly brilliant, and his insight left people speechless. From the age of sixteen, he had been composing amazing songs of realization and profound dharma commentaries. He was even able to read the script of the dakinis.

He was tall and strong, with a noble bearing. His hair was very unusual. He wore long braids wrapped around his head. It was described as a "magnetizing tiara," meaning that his hair had never been cut and that a dakini dwelled in every strand. His hair shone with a dark blue luster, and when he washed it, it never tangled.

When Wangchok Dorje was twenty, in 1880, he traveled to Patrul's encampment. Since so many of Patrul's students were great masters in their own right, Patrul's camp was said to be like a den of snow lions who later spread the lion's roar of dharma in all directions.

Wangchok Dorje arrived at Patrul's encampment with great pomp and circumstance, in the style of his tertön-father. He came on horseback, accompanied by a retinue of forty horsemen, bringing with them an entire herd of yaks.

It was quite a contrast to the simplicity of Patrul, who had few personal possessions and still lived in the black yak-hair tent of a nomad. Patrul was dedicated to his monastic vows and thus also had no consort.

Patrul often spoke glowingly about the life example of the master Zurchungpa,[192] who was like "a child of the mountains, wearing mist for clothing."

Wangchok Dorje heard Patrul praise the virtue of adopting the simple way of life of early practitioners of the Kagyu lineage, abandoning elaborations and worldly preoccupations.

Patrul said, "If you wish to be a good dharma practitioner, just sit on a low seat and wear ordinary old clothes. No one ever said there's any point to sitting up high looking down on others, dressed up in fancy brocade."

Inspired, Wangchok Dorje said, "That's fine by me!"

Without missing a beat, he divested himself of all his possessions.

He dismissed his entourage and sent all his horses back to Chokgyur Lingpa's monastery. He gave up women. He gave away his ornaments. He gave away his fine silk brocade garments and put on an old chuba of cheap felt and sheepskin.

He cut off his gorgeous long hair and shaved his head. He took the *getsul* vows of a novice monk. Eventually, word of Wangchok Dorje's transformation reached Jamyang Khyentse Wangpo.

Distraught, he said, "This must be the work of that madman, Patrul!" Khyentse Wangpo is said to have wept like a little child.[193]

IN 1881, WHEN HE WAS SEVENTY-FOUR, Patrul began performing a purification ritual called Dredging the Depths of Hell.[194] For a year and a half, he practiced before the reliquary stupa holding remains of his teacher Jigme Gyalwai Nyugu. Patrul then made one hundred thousand fire offerings. During this time, he gave many advanced teachings and instructions to his closest disciples.[195]

The Return of Wangchok Dorje

Wangchok Dorje stayed at Patrul's encampment for three years, studying and practicing the teachings. When three years were over, Wangchok Dorje went back to Dzongsar.

He made the return journey on foot, not on horseback. He was accompanied by two helpers, not a grand retinue of forty horsemen. Carrying a wooden staff, looking like a beggar, he arrived at Dzongsar with a single hornless yak as a pack animal laden with a few books and some tea.

When Wangchok Dorje, head shaven, wearing a shabby sheepskin chuba, came into the presence of Jamyang Khyentse Wangpo, the great lama took one look at him and said, "You *have* cut your hair!"

Wangchok Dorje said, "I wish to live as a renunciant practitioner, wandering everywhere, with no fixed abode."

Khyentse Wangpo, displeased, snapped, "Don't *say* that!"

He told Wangchok Dorje, "Don't go off wandering; just settle down somewhere in retreat. Go back to Neten Monastery and stay there doing practice. But first, give me that hair!"

Someone must have saved the long hair that had been cut off at his ordination, for Wangchok Dorje did present a lock from his shorn topknot to Khyentse Wangpo, who kept it very carefully ever after in a reliquary at Dzongsar Monastery. Later, Khyentse Wangpo referred to this relic in writing, saying that each one of these hairs was the abode of one hundred thousand dakinis.

Wangchok Dorje settled down in a small house in the middle of a meadow. He continued to live in retreat as a celibate monk, saying he preferred to be "a good practitioner."

After some time—some say days, some say years—Wangchok Dorje suddenly came down with a bad fever and quickly expired.[196]

Pema Trinley, who had been Chokgyur Lingpa's cook and by that time was Jamyang Khyentse Wangpo's bursar, had the unenviable task of breaking the bad news to Khyentse Wangpo.

On hearing of Wangchok Dorje's death, Khyentse Wangpo was deeply upset. Feeling that there had been no need for the son of a realized yogi to cut off his hair, Khyentse Wangpo cried out, "Crazy Patrul made Wangchok Dorje cut his hair and turned him into a renunciant!

"Now *look* what has happened! How tragic! This proves how little merit there is in the present age of decline.[197]

"Padmasambhava himself predicted that this son of the tertön would spread his termas from the Chinese border in the east all the way to Mount Kailash in the west, benefiting beings like an immense sheet of white silk cloth unfurling. Now Patrul has messed up everything!"

Khyentse then struck his fists against his chest, expressing despair in typical Khampa fashion.

"The auspicious coincidences didn't hold up," he moaned with a very morose expression. "*He* was supposed to be the one to reveal and propagate the remaining termas!"

Khenchen Tashi Özer Tries to See Patrul

Khenchen Tashi Özer came back to Kham from Central Tibet accompanied by a group of pilgrims, including a young nun who was the tulku of Dorje Phagmo of Yamdrok.[198] The group traveled to Upper Getse, a place in a valley above Dzagyal Monastery, where Patrul, now nearing the end of his life, had just spent six months alone practicing in a small nomad tent made of black yak-hair, just as he had done for many years.

Everyone told them it would be impossible for them to actually meet Patrul, since he was no longer seeing anyone at all.

But Khenchen Tashi Özer reassured his group, saying, "Don't worry, we will get to see him."

When this group drew near, they heard Patrul's voice yelling at them from inside his tent, saying, "*O-ho!* Here's the great Khenpo Tashi Özer! Now he's showing off by bringing along some high-born young nun from Central

Tibet! *A-yi!* You're all going to be the death of me, all you people who just won't leave me in peace!"

They pleaded with him to be admitted to his presence.

From inside the tent came the reply, "See what I mean? You don't listen to a word I say!"

"We *will* listen to what you say!" they insisted.

Patrul shouted back, "Oh, all right, then! Go down to Dzagyal Monastery to the *kudung,* the body relic[199] of Jigme Gyalwai Nyugu. He was Avalokiteshvara in person. To be in the presence of his *kudung* is like being in the presence of the Jowo of Lhasa.[200] If you make offerings there, you will encounter no obstacles in this life and will progress toward liberation throughout all of your future lives. All prayers made in the presence of his relic will be granted!"[201]

So the group of pilgrims did just as Patrul had advised. They went to Dzagyal Monastery and offered prayers, lamps, prostrations, circumambulations, and *ganachakra* feasts, and did so for three whole days.

They then came back to Patrul Rinpoche's tent, still worried that they would not be permitted to see him in person.

"Don't worry," said the Khenpo, trying to reassure the others. "This time we will surely be allowed to meet him."

As soon as the group came near the tent, trying to enter, Patrul scolded them just as harshly as he had done before, yelling, "All you people will be the death of me!"

The Khenpo answered, "We listened to you and we did everything you asked. We went to Dzagyal Monastery and made prayers and offerings before the relic of Jigme Gyalwai Nyugu, just as you said we should.

"But you were wrong about something! You said that any prayer made before the relic would be granted—but *our* prayers were *not* granted!"

"*What?*" cried Patrul. "*Which* prayer of yours didn't come true?"

"We prayed that we should be able meet Patrul Rinpoche—*in person*!"

There was a long moment of silence.

Bound by his own words, Patrul was forced to relent, saying gruffly, "Oh, all right, all right. Come on in!"

He opened the curtain of his tent, let them enter, and gave them teachings, just as requested.

Khenpo Könchog Drönme Tries to See Patrul

Khenpo Könchog Drönme[202] knew that Patrul was no longer receiving visitors, and that when people insisted on seeing him, he'd give them a magnificent scolding. Yet, no matter how much Patrul scolded, it just made everyone's faith and respect increase. The Khenpo very much wanted to ask for teachings despite the inevitable—at least, he wanted to give it a try.

Patrul happened to be staying at the time in a small tent that was set up at one end of a larger nomad encampment. The Khenpo was well aware that this camp, like most nomad camps, was protected by Tibetan mastiffs, ferocious dogs that would be unchained at night to roam freely and guard the encampments from marauders.

The thought of being mauled by mastiffs did not dissuade the Khenpo. He was determined to try his very best.

One night, quiet as a mouse, the dauntless Khenpo managed to climb up and along a long, narrow crater. It was set at such an angle that no one—neither dog nor man—was able to see him. This long crater came to an end very near to Patrul's little black yak-hair tent.

When the Khenpo was just above Patrul's tent, he emerged, ran down a little slope, and slipped into the tent.

As he came in, Patrul heard the noise and yelled, "Hey! Are you a thief?"

"Yes! I'm a thief!" said the Khenpo. "I'm a thief and I've come to steal your wisdom!"

Forthright and brave himself, Patrul appreciated these qualities in others.

Thus, the intrepid Khenpo was able to receive from Patrul the very meditation instructions he had wished for, instead of receiving a blistering scolding.

In 1884, the mother of the King of Derge came to Mamo Thang to meet Patrul Rinpoche. Patrul gave to her and her retinue, along with a gathering of thousands, the teachings on Accomplishing the Pure Land (the prayer for rebirth in Sukhavati, Amitabha's Western Buddhafield of Great Bliss)[203] and on the *Mani Kahbum*. Afterward, people made offerings of gold, silver, and other valuables, but Patrul refused to accept them and gave them back.

Trama Tulku Receives Instructions

Kunzang Dechen Dorje—the reincarnation of Jigme Gyalwai Nyugu known as Trama Tulku—came and spent the whole day with Patrul. He wanted to know how much longer Patrul would live. Patrul told him, "I'll live for three more years. When I die, wherever you are, near or far, you must come. Please don't touch my corpse. Please don't have a stupa made for it."

AFTER HE FINISHED TEACHING Accomplishing the Pure Land in Gegong, Patrul said, "You are confused about 'faith' and 'wrong view.' As to 'faith,' place your faith in the dharma. As to 'wrong view,' for example, that would be when you place your faith in a particular individual rather than having faith in the dharma itself."

For six months, he gave extensive teachings on *The Way of the Bodhisattva* to Khenpo Kunpel and a small group of disciples.

After this, he rarely taught. When people asked him for teachings, he would send them to Önpo Tenga or another of his close disciples. If people insisted, he'd scold them, but all his scolding just made people more devoted than ever.

Patrul's Last Great Public Ganachakra

At Dzagyal Monastery, Patrul arranged a lavish feast offering for the people of Dzachukha. He invited the 5th Dzogchen Rinpoche, Thubden Chökyi Dorje, to come. Everyone was invited, lay and ordained, tulkus and khenpos with their retinues, monks, nuns, and local people.

Lamas, monks, and nuns performed the ritual known as the Gathering of the Vidyadharas.[204] Laypeople circumambulated the temple and made prostrations.

Tea and curd and small sweet potatoes called *troma* were offered to everyone.

Elaborate religious offerings were made, and blessed substances were distributed to a crowd of thousands.

An auspicious gentle rain fell, rainbow arcs appeared in the sky, thunder rumbled.

Some people saw the form of Guru Padmasambhava appear in a mass of rainbow light as the last rays of the sun set over the mountain ridge.

IN 1886, PATRUL returned to Karchung Khormo Olu, the very place where he was born and where he stayed many times throughout his life—a sacred place that the faithful considered the equal of Samye Monastery and Khangri Thökar.[205]

About this time, Patrul's behavior started to shift. When he was asked for advice, he no longer made any suggestions, but again and again, just said, "It's up to you. Do whatever you think is best."

Last Days and Hours

Patrul began experiencing problems with his health.

From the thirteenth day of the fourth lunar month of the Male Fire Pig Year (1887), he reported feeling a bit unwell.

To whatever people would ask him, he would reply, in a rather unusual fashion: "Do what you like. You know better."

His physician, Jampel, who was also the chieftain of Ling La (a nomadic community), was summoned. Long-life ceremonies were performed on Patrul's behalf.

While treating Patrul, Jampel asked him, "Abu, I gather from what you've said on various occasions[206] that we should pray to be reborn in Amitabha's Western Buddhafield of Great Bliss. Is this so?"

Patrul paused a bit, then replied, "Well, for you, West. For me, East"—perhaps referring to Vajrasattva's Eastern Buddhafield of Manifest Joy.

Later, Patrul asked his attendant Sönam Tsering, "Who asked that the Offering to the Arhats be recited last night?"

Sönam Tsering replied that the disciples had decided among themselves to do so. Patrul said, "When you performed that ceremony, I fell asleep for a bit. When they got to the verse of the arhat Yanlagjung,[207] I woke up and heard a voice say, 'You will benefit beings in the East!' Could someone like me be of real benefit to beings?"[208]

Sönam Tsering did not ask what he meant.

According to his attendant, on the 17th of the fourth lunar month of the Male Fire Pig Year (1887), Patrul took a little food, recited the *Tantra of Immaculate Confession,* and did a few prostrations. He performed the five-fold yogic exercises.[209] He also did an exercise to increase the free flow of wisdom prana through the channels at the heart chakra.

On the 18th, in early morning he ate some curd and drank a little tea. At sunrise, he took off his clothes, sat upright in a meditative pose, crossed his legs in the vajra posture, and rested his two hands upon his knees.

When Khenpo Kunpel dressed him again, Patrul said nothing.

In addition to his attendant Sönam Tsering, three people stayed by Patrul's side that night: Khenpo Kunpel, a person named Kungyam, and Patrul's doctor, Jampel.

At one point, Sönam Tsering recounted, Patrul gazed straight into space and snapped the fingers of both hands.[210] He rested his hands under his robe in the *mudra* of equanimity. Then Patrul entered in the infinite, luminous space beyond birth and death, pure from the very beginning.

As is said:

> A fully-realized yogi may look like an ordinary person, but his mind remains in pure awareness without effort . . . when he leaves his physical body, his consciousness becomes one with the dharmakaya, just as the air in a vase merges with the surrounding space when the vase is broken.[211]

After Patrul's Death

After Patrul passed away, in accordance with his expressed wish, a delegation was sent to invite Trama Tulku, the incarnation of Patrul's teacher Jigme Gyalwai Nyugu, to come. Another person was sent to fetch Patrul's student Önpo Tenga from Gemang Monastery. When Önpo Tenga arrived, he said

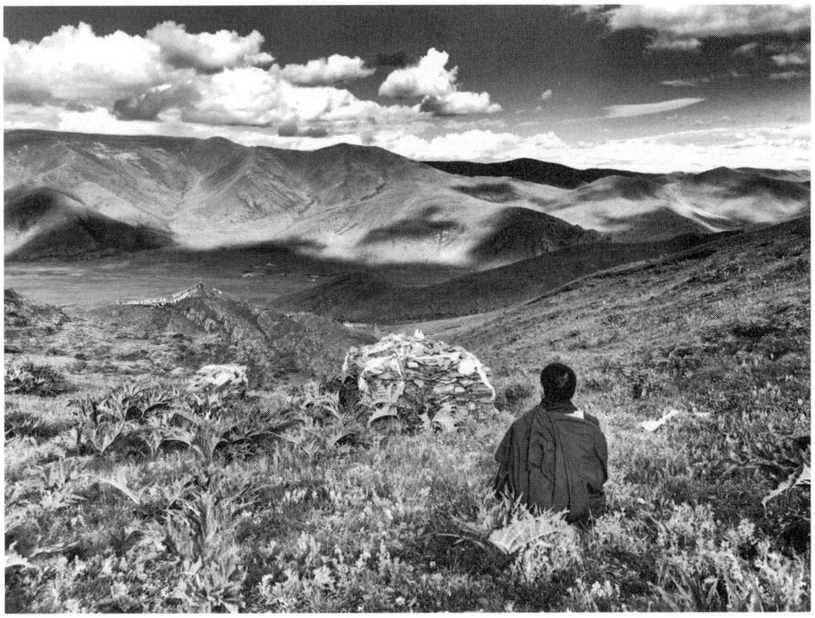

The ruins of the small stupa where Patrul Rinpoche's cremation took place at Karchung Khormo Olu. (2016)

that no one else should be sent for until Patrul's post mortem meditation, or *thukdam*,[212] was completed.

As soon as Trama Tulku arrived, on the 20th day of the lunar calendar, Patrul Rinpoche's *thukdam* meditation came to an end.

Önpo Tenga, Sönam Tsering, and the others took care of all that needed to be done. Khenpo Kunpel and Palshu Lama Tseli[213] were sent to gather Patrul's personal effects.

Khenpo Yönten Gyatso of Gemang arrived. Mura Tulku, who had been staying in Lower Dzachu, also arrived. When he entered Patrul Rinpoche's room, he was completely overwhelmed by grief and fainted. As he regained consciousness, he was heard to say, as if speaking directly to Patrul, "I thought that you were gone!" From that moment, Mura Tulku entirely stopped grieving. Önpo Tenga commented that Mura Tulku must have had a vision of Patrul Rinpoche, graced by the direct transmission of the master's realization.

The ritual Dredging the Depths of Hell was performed by Patrul Rinpoche's closest disciples.

After that, many lamas of all schools began arriving. They performed various offering ceremonies. About two thousand students assembled. Each was given a small piece of Patrul Rinpoche's clothing as a relic.

Many people vowed on the spot to give up unvirtuous actions and to accomplish virtuous deeds. With neither attachment nor animosity, filled with sadness, disillusioned with samsaric existence, everyone devoted themselves to practice, night and day.

The cremation was performed on the 25th day of the same month, the day of the month that is dedicated to the dakinis.[214] Rainbows appeared in an otherwise perfectly clear blue sky. Everyone there witnessed this and saw many other wonderful signs as well.

Over the next few days, rain fell in abundance, just as in summer. Lush grass grew and flowers bloomed. The Dza River was suddenly in spate. Although many of all ages had to ford the swollen river, there was not a single mishap, and people felt that this was due to Patrul Rinpoche's prayers and protection. Later, even during times of drought, rain would always fall on the anniversary of Patrul Rinpoche's *parinirvana*.

On the 28th, the relics were collected from the cremation pyre. Later, these remains were deposited in square stupas built on each corner of the Palge Mani Wall, the Hundred Thousand Mani Stones, and consecrated according to tradition.

Patrul Rinpoche's relics: monastic upper shawl, prayer wheel, tea kettle, bellows, and Buddha statue, kept at Khormo Olu by some descendants of Patrul Rinpoche's sister. (2016)

Patrul once wrote:

One: Praise is nonsense—empty and unfounded.
Two: Fame just results in a swollen head.
Three: Creating a cache of riches out of offerings
creates a rich cache of bad karma.

Having given up all these three,
May I, Old Dog, die like a dog.

Patrul's Unique Qualities

Outwardly, there was little to distinguish Patrul from an ordinary person. Even after he had become quite famous, Patrul was able to travel incognito. Because of his unremarkable appearance and humble demeanor, he was rarely recognized.

When Patrul stayed somewhere, he did so with no particular agenda in mind. When he decided to leave, he just took off, without specific destination. He would stop and stay anywhere he felt like stopping—in forests, in caves, in valleys, in the snow mountains, out in the middle of nowhere, or in a nomad's black yak-hair tent—staying as long as he wished and no longer.

He once described himself like this:

Mad yogi of the wilderness,
Darling child of the world,
Protector of beings,
Nurturing loving-kindness and bodhichitta.

He was completely meticulous in terms of preserving the authenticity of transmissions of the teachings.

In regard to the teachings based on the sutras, he would not teach a text unless he had had reading transmission. Once, people asked him to teach Nagarjuna's famous *Letter to a Friend*;[215] he refused, saying, "I can't teach it. I don't have the transmission—I can't teach it."

As for the Mantrayana, the teachings and practices based on the tantra texts, he would not teach a word unless he had the proper transmission, having received the initiation and completed the meditation practice.

When it came to the Dzogchen teachings, he was particularly strict. He told his heart-disciple Nyoshul Lungtok not to teach Dzogchen until he was fifty years old.

When Patrul taught the dharma, people's minds were completely transformed. An entire assembly of students would become tranquil, everyone naturally resting in contemplation. A seemingly simple point, when taught by Patrul, became a door opening up a hundred profound spiritual understandings. His language was direct and immediately applicable to one's inner experiences. Because of his immense knowledge, the warmth of his blessings, and the depth of his realization, receiving teachings from Patrul was unlike receiving teachings from anyone else.

He knew *The Seven Treasuries* of Longchenpa almost by heart. After his forties, he mostly stopped teaching from written texts and just taught straight from his memory During the thirteen years he taught at Shri Singha Philosophical College in Dzogchen, he never had to make use of a single page of a text, even when presenting the most complex Buddhist philosophy.

Nevertheless, his teachings were crystal clear and delivered without the slightest hesitation.

It is said: "The waning of the words of the Tathagata, the sutras of the Victorious One, comes about from neglecting to read the scriptures." Patrul always kept this in mind and showed great eagerness for all activities related to hearing and teaching the dharma. He was pleased, too, when others listened to or taught the dharma. He encouraged renunciation and weariness with the world; he skillfully led people toward virtue. Not wanting people to waste their lives, he would ripen those who had not yet taken the path of dharma.

When Patrul came to a monastery, he would arrive unexpectedly, so as to avoid any fuss or formal reception. He would stay in an ordinary cell, like all the other monks.

Before Patrul, outside monastic libraries, only a very few owned texts such as *The Way of the Bodhisattva.* His teachings were cherished by many people, lay and ordained. He most often taught *The Way of the Bodhisattva,* the *Five Treatises of Maitreya,*[216] *The Three Vows,* and the *Treasury of Precious Qualities.*

Patrul taught each school according to its own views, teaching either from his mind[217] or from a commentary traditional to the school, without ever displaying even a hint of sectarian views. In his characteristically clear and complete way, neither too complex nor too simplistic, he presented the essentials and then linked the view with actual meditation practice.

Many people, even monks as young as ten, became able to recite and even teach the whole *Way of the Bodhisattva.* Countless people, both monastic and lay, came to understand that to have a good heart and to develop bodhichitta was the very root of the Buddha dharma. No matter if a person's station in life was high or low, Patrul gave them all the same advice: "Have a good heart and act with kindness. There is no higher teaching." When people asked Patrul to give them a name, he usually gave one that began with "Nyingje" (Compassion).[218]

Whoever showed a sincere interest in learning and practicing the dharma, Patrul never spared any effort to teach. Whenever a student gained some understanding, Patrul was even more delighted than was his student. Whoever had made some progress on the path he advised to cultivate bodhichitta and the three wisdoms (listening, reflecting, and practicing the teachings) to protect them from falling into wrong views.

To students of the highest capacity he gave the most profound teachings, such as the *Guhyagarbha Tantra,* Longchenpa's *Resting at Ease in the Nature of Mind,* Jigme Lingpa's *Treasury of Precious Qualities,* commentaries on these profound treatises, and the Great Perfection (Dzogchen).

Through Patrul's tireless efforts, the teachings of the Mahayana, long neglected, once again became widespread. Teachings on the *Guhyagarbha Tantra,* long in decline, were again restored to new brilliance. The Dzogchen teachings, long sullied by concepts, shone again like gold. As a result, many of his students became accomplished practitioners.

Patrul said that four of his disciples had qualities that surpassed his own: Minyak Kunzang Sönam, superior in conduct; Tendzin Trakpa of Gyarong, superior in logic; Önpo Tendzin Norbu, superior in his way of explaining the teachings; Nyoshul Lungtok, superior in his understanding of the view.

Mantrayana practitioners he warned: "Some practitioners, though they have studied and understood a bit about emptiness, and they have visualized a deity and recited its mantras for many months and years, may take rebirth as harmful spirits because they deviate from the teachings and fall under the spell of malicious intent. However, practitioners whose main practice is compassion will never run those risks."

Like shoots of new grass springing up, he inspired people to purify themselves through spiritual practice, using the four powers of confession.[219] In this age of degeneration upon degeneration, the appearance of a teacher like Patrul Rinpoche was like a bright moon appearing in the darkest night, radiating compassion, showing that the good karma of sentient beings had not been completely exhausted.

Patrul's personal conduct was perfect and complete. He walked in a simple, dignified way, neither too fast nor too slow. If he had to look back, he would not just twist his head, but slowly turn his whole body from the right side and look. Outwardly, he was the very embodiment of the sutra teachings; inwardly, he had the unwavering compassionate mind of a bodhisattva; secretly, he immaculately kept the commitments of the Vajrayana.

Patrul was so scrupulous about his own behavior that he could honestly say, as Jigme Lingpa wrote "From offerings of gold and silver right down to offerings of needles and thread, I have never misused material wealth offered, but have always and only used it to achieve virtuous goals."

Unlike most lamas, Patrul refused to give hand-blessings, saying, "What's the point of my touching your head with my hands as a blessing? What you really need is to become a good practitioner of meditation and to change your mind, from within."

He declined to give elaborate rituals of empowerment. If students needed specific empowerments, he would send them to other masters.

Having shattered pride and arrogance, Patrul completely abandoned the luster of greatness, just as one might fling away snot into the dust. He acted in a simple, direct, carefree way, like a young boy running down a road.

Yet his mind was so profound and steady and his spiritual resplendence so unique that the most powerful and wealthy rulers and high lamas were all humbled and overwhelmed in his presence.

Patrul spent his life as a hidden yogi, preferring solitude and anonymity to fame. Genuinely humble, he developed through his practice an unshakable confidence and inner freedom that left him serene under all circumstances. Patrul lived relaxed in total presence, equally content upon a high brocade-wrapped throne addressing thousands or emptying a frail old lady's bedpan.

As Önpo Tenga said, "We don't really take cause and effect seriously, so our practice bears little fruit. Otherwise, we would all become like Patrul Rinpoche."

The whole of Patrul's life was pure and stainless, appropriate and splendid. However one looks at it, his life example enhances one's confidence in the teachings.

He did not indulge in useless ordinary talk, so he spoke seldom, but when he did speak, he spoke in a deep voice in a direct, even blunt manner. Those who had the good fortune to spend time close to him said that he never said a word unconnected to the dharma. His entire existence was devoted to practicing and transmitting the teachings.

His attentive, awakened presence inspired awe and respect; only those who really wished for uncompromising spiritual guidance would even dare to try to meet him.

When he scolded people, or when, more rarely, he teased them and made fun of them, it was always spiritual instruction in disguise.

He never boasted about his own inner realization, but sometimes in his songs one finds indications of his profound meditative experiences, realization, and inner qualities.

One of his spiritual songs ends like this:

Having entered—the path of liberation,
Exhausted—all deluded thoughts,
Progressed—in inner experiences and realization,
Purified—delusion,

Received—the blessings of the deities of the Three Roots,[220]
Destroyed—primitive belief in solid reality,
These words of whimsy were set down by a shabby fellow,
Who now may rest content in the continuum of dharmakaya.

He felt a deep tenderness toward all sentient beings as a mother feels limitless tenderness toward her own child.

Patrul's words were as authentic as gold, free of hypocrisy and free of pretense. He lived a life free of contradiction; his values and goals and conduct were always consistent in following the path.

He was never obsequious in the presence of the noble and powerful, nor was he ever contemptuous of the simple, the humble, and the poor.

He was always eager to praise the good qualities of those who behaved in harmony with the teachings. He was fearless in pointing out the defects of anyone behaving in ways that were in contradiction to the dharma, with the exception of those persons he saw as irredeemable. Even when he was at his most severe, scolding someone in a formidable and overwhelming way, his words were totally free of animosity and attachment. If one made the effort to understand what he sought to convey, the meaning of his advice was always profound.

He had no time for devious people who put on an outer display of politeness to mask their deceitful true intentions. He had nothing to lose and nothing to gain from worldly affairs. Patrul never strayed away from the most upright speech and conduct. His mind was as vast and unfathomable as the ocean.

Patrul was knowledgeable about almost everything—he possessed all kinds of manual skills, such as building and crafting, while also able to deal skillfully with very complex worldly situations and customs. At the same time, he remained free of attachment and kept himself above mundane concerns and expectations.

He was the master of renunciates and, as such, was completely free from worries.

At first, Patrul could seem brusque or intimidating, but the more one spent time with him, the more one could truly witness his utter lack of partiality—his total absence of hope and total absence of fear. Always open and relaxed, Patrul was, in fact, very easy to be with, able to regard all circumstances, good or bad, as one taste.

Eventually, one could not bear to be apart from him.

» *Calling the Lama from Afar: A Song of Devotion and Yearning* «

A supplication to summon the blessings of the three lineages

To my master, I respectfully bow down.

The expanse of primordial ground is immutable.
In the pure realm of samsara and nirvana being inseparable,
Amid the vast expanse of unmodified empty awareness
All phenomena are fully exhausted in *dharmata,* the absolute nature.
Dharmakaya guru, Drime Özer,[221] primordial buddha,
All-pervading lord of the sugatas' mandalas, think of me!

In the pure realm of appearances and emptiness being inseparable,
The development and completion stages are united.
Amid the vast expanse of Mahamudra, all the paths and levels
Are perfect and complete in the basic ground.
Sambhogakaya guru, Khyentse Özer,[222] radiant, mirage-like natural presence,
Lord of primordial wisdom, think of me!

The myriad manifestation who transform beings
Have all one taste in primordial wisdom,
Great bliss, unconditional compassion endowed with skillful means.
Nirmanakaya guru, root master, embodiment of compassion,
Lord of bodhisattvas, think of me!

The Trikaya lineage is embodied as one
In the mind-to-mind transmission of the Victorious Ones.
You are the manifestation of ever-present primordial wisdom,
The essence of awareness-emptiness, the ground of emanations
For the ocean of mandalas that are the nondual phenomenal world.
Union of all refuges, master, buddha, think of me!

The ultimate reach of the wisdom of the buddha, the enlightened
state,
Is the primordial expanse, inseparable from awareness.
This perfectly pure expanse is shown by the ocean-like supreme
dharma.
Those who have realized this wisdom constitute the supreme sangha.
Root master, Three Jewels gathered as one, think of me!

The nature of the dharmakaya buddha
Is the wisdom-mind into which all phenomena become exhausted.
The arising mandala of the sambhogakaya
Is the radiance of awareness reaching its ultimate point.
The display of nirmanakaya
Is awareness itself as it arises and expands.
Root master, Trikaya gathered as one, think of me!

You are the union of all masters, skillfully manifesting in various
forms;
You are the Lord of the ocean of mandalas of the indivisible expanse.
You have soared through sky of the true nature, through the power of
your realization.
Root master, Three Roots gathered as one, think of me!

Undaunted by samsara,
Your heart is endowed with unstoppable compassion.
Free from clinging to nirvana,
The expanse of your wisdom-mind is one with that of the Victorious
Ones.
You have ripened the seed of the view into the fruit of Realization.
Root master, all buddhas in person, think of me!

You skillfully appear to beings to be taught in whichever form is
helpful.
Your compassionate wisdom and great purity are the hallmarks of a
bodhisattva.
Your meditation and postmeditation are perfected in primordial
wisdom.

Accomplishing the excellent deeds of the Victorious Ones,
Fearless bodhisattva, scion of the Victorious Ones,[223] think of me!

Toward sentient beings who, bereft of happiness, endure the stark reality of suffering
Your heart swells with the four immeasurables,[224]
Permeated by unconditional compassion that is of one taste with supreme joy,
Intrepid scion of the bodhisattvas, think of me!

....

With a hand that sets aside delusion,
Having pointed out the excellent path,
You guide us on the path,
You exemplify the path through your practice,
And you practice generosity, thus engaging in the six paramitas.
Endowed with knowledge of the four skillful ways of attracting
Beings needing to be transformed,[225]
Fearless scion who accomplishes benefit for others, think of me!

....

The perfectly pure expanse—the essence of the enlightened state—is the ground dharmakaya.
The purifying path's realization is the dharmakaya of equipoise.
The fruit of purification—twofold purity[226]—is the ultimate dharmakaya.
Guru who displays the three lineages gathered as one, think of me!

Through the view, you remain in the true nature, unimpeded awareness-emptiness.
You enjoy the fruit, primordial liberation, free from rejecting and wanting.
Master who demonstrates the excellent unmistaken path of unfabricated primordial wisdom
In which are united view, meditation, action, and fruition—think of me!

To sentient beings who, misled by misbelief and
Beset by the proliferation of delusion triggered by ignorance,
Have strayed onto the wrong path
You point out the sound and unmistaken way, free from confusion.
Guru who guides us on the path of liberation, think of me!

....

Once freed into their true nature,
Negative discursive thoughts do not
Proliferate as they ordinarily do.
Once introduced to the nature of mind,
Realization arises of its own accord.
Without wanting, without rejecting,
One engages in supreme action.
Guru who grants the primordial wisdom of the dharmakaya,
think of me!

....

In the effortless [natural] state,
One's intention is achieved
Without any need for striving.
The practice of primordial wisdom, free from concepts,
Is pristine simplicity that crushes delusion into dust.[227]
The very state of one's own awareness
Is the meditation equipoise that requires no meditation.
Guru who introduces us directly to our innate wisdom-mind,
think of me!

....

Seeing the wisdom in which [all obscurations] come to an end
Is the ultimate fruition.
The resulting insight embraces all that is to be known,
Thus making one a guide to all beings.
Having reached the level that transcends samsara and nirvana,
Lord of compassion, whose kindness I can never repay, think of me!

Think of me, master!
Keep me in your mind!

This plaintive song in verse, calling the lama from afar,
Arose through the strength of deep devotion.
Most kind one, may my verses of entreaty
Imploring your compassion and your care
Reach your wisdom-hearing.

The path of devotion results in instant liberation for those with faith.
Within the continuum of dharmakaya, daily activities,
 postmeditation
And realization are inseparably united,
Setting free all sentient beings—each one once our past mother
Through ever-increasing buddha-activity.[228]
May effortless accomplishment occur!
Guru, think of me!

At the request of Lhundrup Dorje, Abu Shri set down whatever came to mind.
Since this advice concerns the excellent qualities of the master, there may be some benefit in it. If there is benefit, let it be dedicated to the infinity of beings.

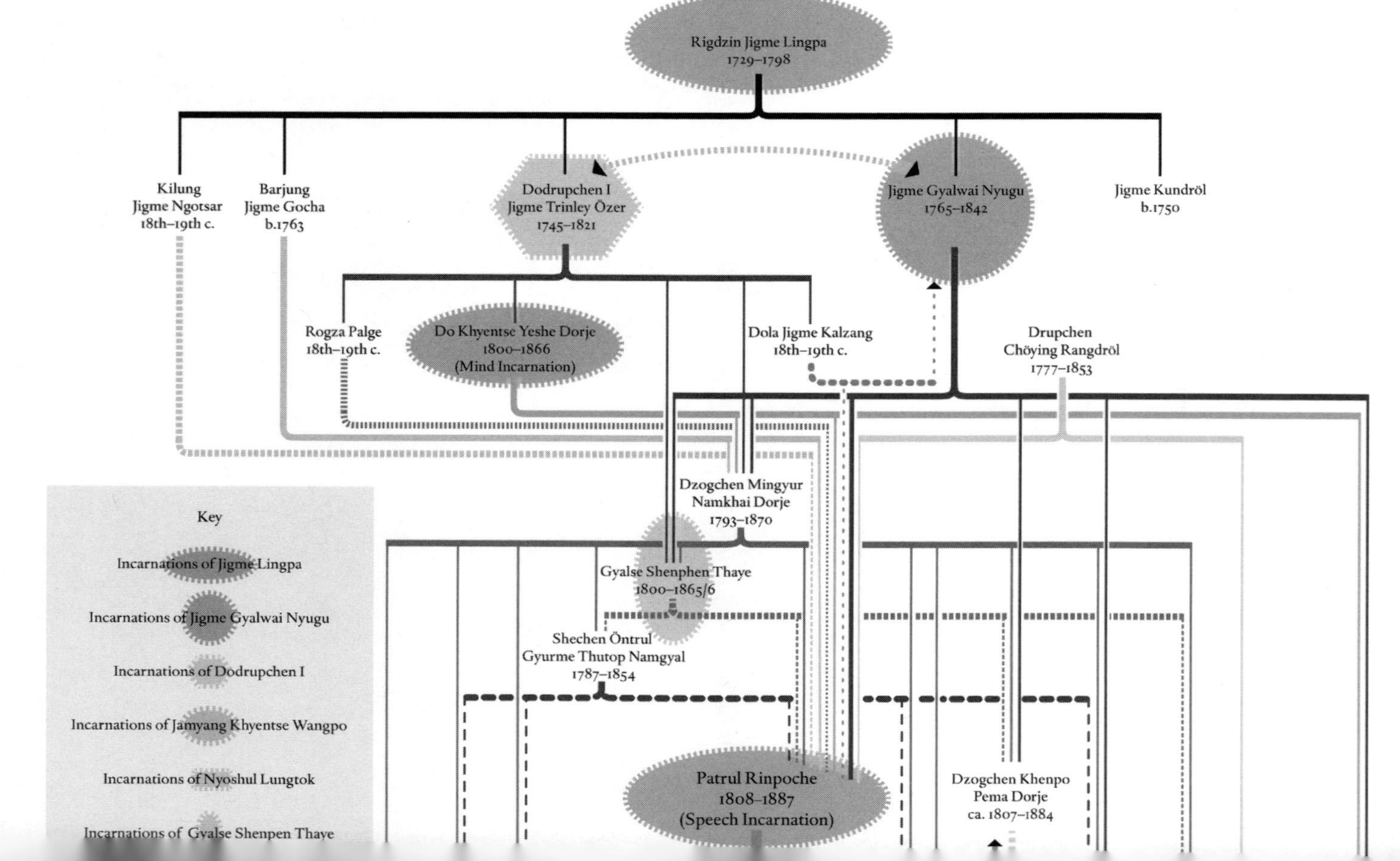

Rigdzin Jigme Lingpa
1729–1798
Kilung
Jigme Ngotsar
18th–19th c.
Barjung
Jigme Gocha
b.1763
Dodrupchen I
Jigme Trinley Özer
1745–1821
Jigme Gyalwai Nyugu
1765–1842
Jigme Kundröl
b.1750
Rogza Palge
18th–19th c.
Do Khyentse Yeshe Dorje
1800–1866
(Mind Incarnation)
Dola Jigme Kalzang
18th–19th c.
Drupchen
Chöying Rangdröl
1777–1853
Dzogchen Mingyur
Namkhai Dorje
1793–1870
Gyalse Shenphen Thaye
1800–1865/6
Shechen Öntrul
Gyurme Thutop Namgyal
1787–1854
Patrul Rinpoche
1808–1887
(Speech Incarnation)
Dzogchen Khenpo
Pema Dorje
ca. 1807–1884
Key
Incarnations of Jigme Lingpa
Incarnations of Jigme Gyalwai Nyugu
Incarnations of Dodrupchen I
Incarnations of Jamyang Khyentse Wangpo
Incarnations of Nyoshul Lungtok
Incarnations of Gyalse Shenpen Thaye

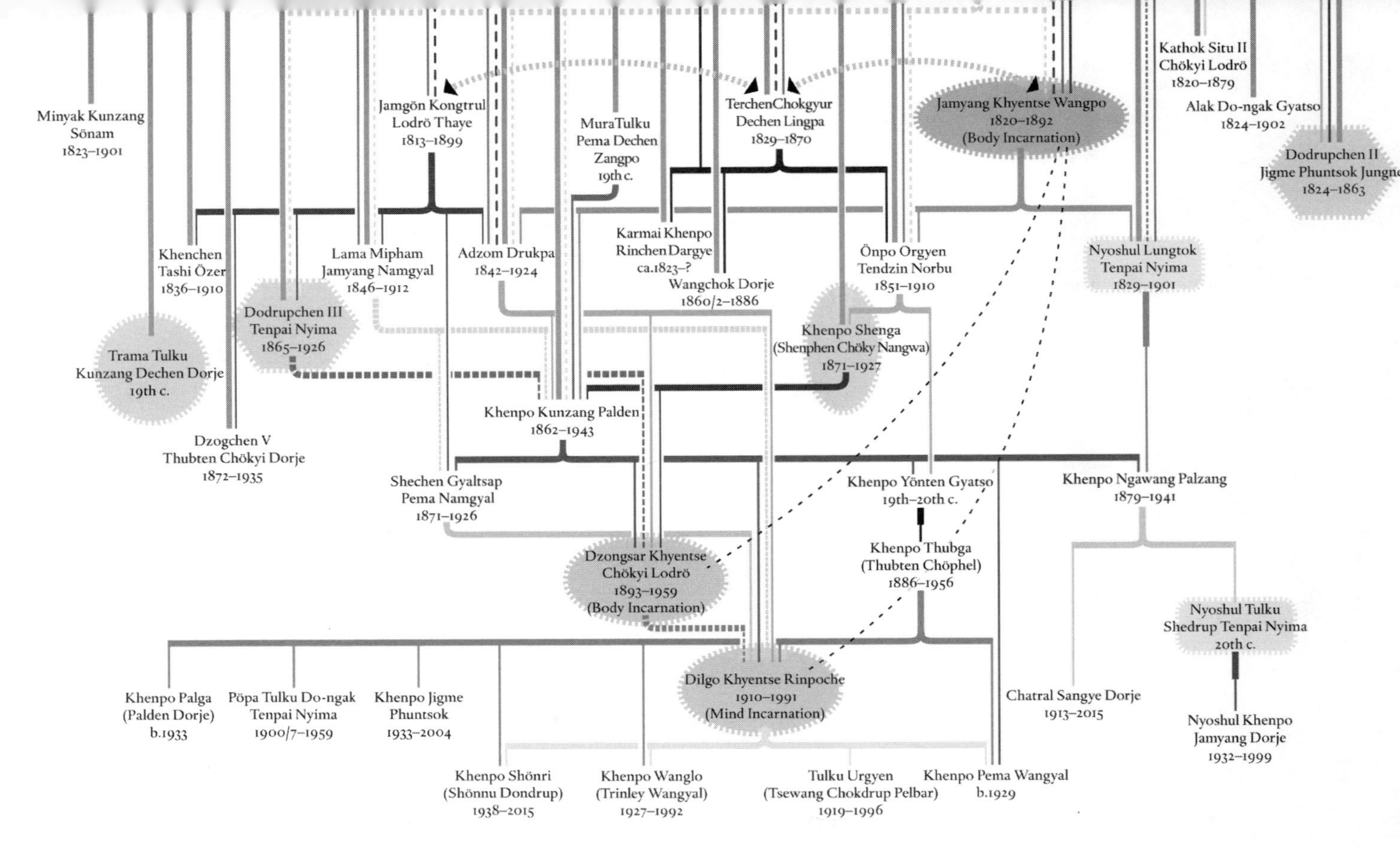
Kathok Situ II
Chökyi Lodrö
1820–1879
Alak Do-ngak Gyatso
1824–1902
Dodrupchen II
Jigme Phuntsok Jungne
1824–1863
Minyak Kunzang
Sönam
1823–1901
Jamgön Kongtrul
Lodrö Thaye
1813–1899
MuraTulku
Pema Dechen
Zangpo
19th c.
TerchenChokgyur
Dechen Lingpa
1829–1870
Jamyang Khyentse Wangpo
1820–1892
(Body Incarnation)
Khenchen
Tashi Özer
1836–1910
Lama Mipham
Jamyang Namgyal
1846–1912
Adzom Drukpa
1842–1924
Karmai Khenpo
Rinchen Dargye
ca.1823–?
Wangchok Dorje
1860/2–1886
Önpo Orgyen
Tendzin Norbu
1851–1910
Nyoshul Lungtok
Tenpai Nyima
1829–1901
Dodrupchen III
Tenpai Nyima
1865–1926
Trama Tulku
Kunzang Dechen Dorje
19th c.
Khenpo Shenga
(Shenphen Chöky Nangwa)
1871–1927
Khenpo Kunzang Palden
1862–1943
Dzogchen V
Thubten Chökyi Dorje
1872–1935
Shechen Gyaltsap
Pema Namgyal
1871–1926
Khenpo Yönten Gyatso
19th–20th c.
Khenpo Ngawang Palzang
1879–1941
Dzongsar Khyentse
Chökyi Lodrö
1893–1959
(Body Incarnation)
Khenpo Thubga
(Thubten Chöphel)
1886–1956
Nyoshul Tulku
Shedrup Tenpai Nyima
20th c.
Dilgo Khyentse Rinpoche
1910–1991
(Mind Incarnation)
Khenpo Palga
(Palden Dorje)
b.1933
Pöpa Tulku Do-ngak
Tenpai Nyima
1900/7–1959
Khenpo Jigme
Phuntsok
1933–2004
Chatral Sangye Dorje
1913–2015
Nyoshul Khenpo
Jamyang Dorje
1932–1999
Khenpo Shönri
(Shönnu Dondrup)
1938–2015
Khenpo Wanglo
(Trinley Wangyal)
1927–1992
Tulku Urgyen
(Tsewang Chokdrup Pelbar)
1919–1996
Khenpo Pema Wangyal
b.1929

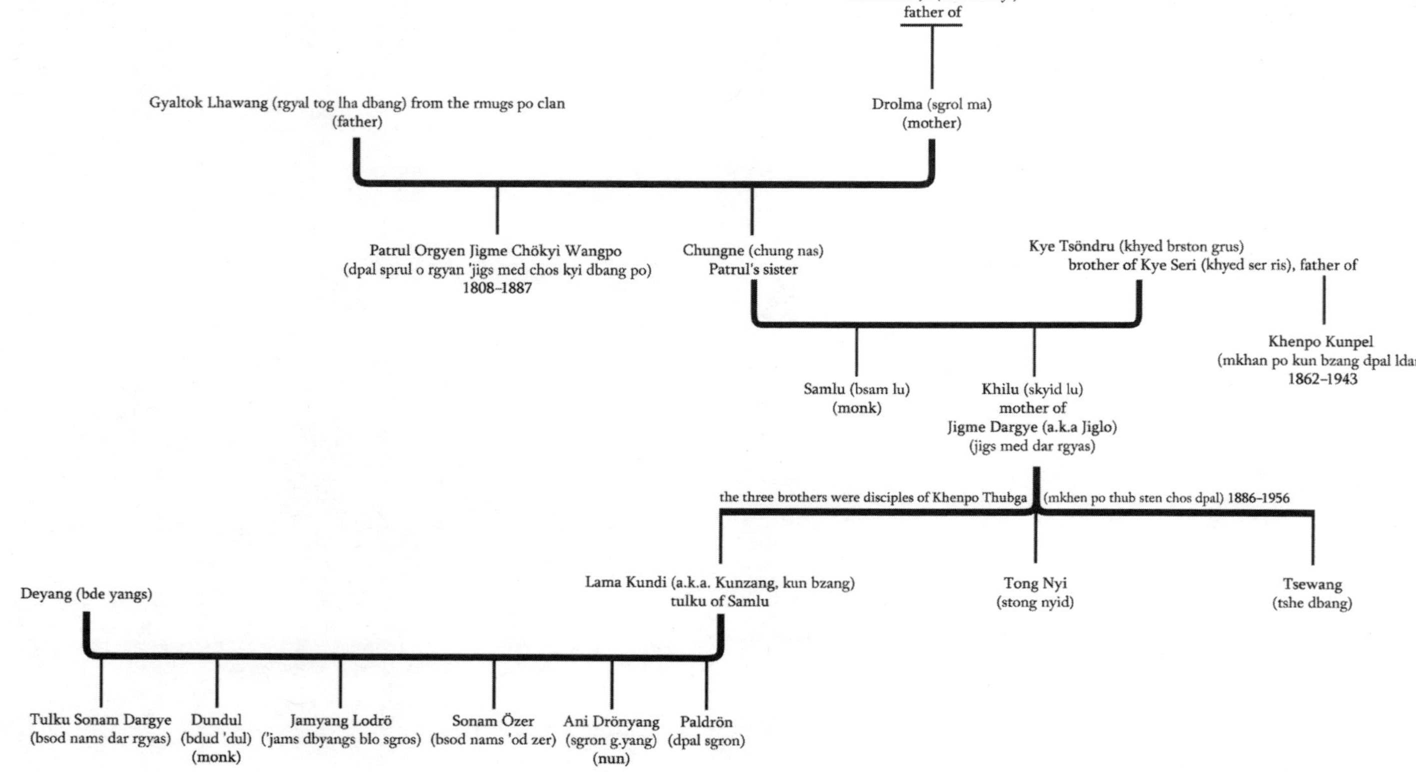

Patrul Rinpoche's Family Tree
(up to the present)
Khrom Za Je (krom za rje)
father of
Gyaltok Lhawang (rgyal tog lha dbang) from the rmugs po clan
(father)
Drolma (sgrol ma)
(mother)
Patrul Orgyen Jigme Chökyi Wangpo
(dpal sprul o rgyan 'jigs med chos kyi dbang po)
1808–1887
Chungne (chung nas)
Patrul's sister
Kye Tsöndru (khyed brston grus)
brother of Kye Seri (khyed ser ris), father of
Khenpo Kunpel
(mkhan po kun bzang dpal ldan)
1862–1943
Samlu (bsam lu)
(monk)
Khilu (skyid lu)
mother of
Jigme Dargye (a.k.a Jiglo)
(jigs med dar rgyas)
the three brothers were disciples of Khenpo Thubga
(mkhen po thub sten chos dpal) 1886–1956
Lama Kundi (a.k.a. Kunzang, kun bzang)
tulku of Samlu
Tong Nyi
(stong nyid)
Tsewang
(tshe dbang)
Deyang (bde yangs)
Tulku Sonam Dargye
(bsod nams dar rgyas)
Dundul
(bdud 'dul)
(monk)
Jamyang Lodrö
('jams dbyangs blo sgros)
Sonam Özer
(bsod nams 'od zer)
Ani Drönyang
(sgron g.yang)
(nun)
Paldrön
(dpal sgron)

BIOGRAPHICAL NOTES

INFLUENTIAL FIGURES, MASTERS, AND DISCIPLES

The following brief biographies are presented to enhance the portrait of Patrul Rinpoche by highlighting some of the notable masters and disciples associated with him. Some of these masters had a major influence on Patrul Rinpoche's life (such as Gyalwa Longchenpa and Rigdzin Jigme Lingpa) even though Patrul Rinpoche did not meet them; some taught and inspired him (such as Jigme Gyalwai Nyugo and Do Khyentse Yeshe Dorje); and some had close spiritual relationships with him (such as Jamyang Khyentse Wangpo). We have also included biographies of some of Patrul Rinpoche's disciples who figure preeminently in the two written biographies or in the oral stories. For the sake of brevity, we did not include biographies of Patrul Rinpoche's many other disciples who are mentioned in passing or who were very young when they met Patrul.

Foremost among Patrul Rinpoche's teachers were Jigme Gyalwai Nyugu and Do Khyentse Yeshe Dorje. Other important teachers were Dola Jigme Kalzang, Kilung Jigme Ngotsar, Gyalse Shenphen Thaye, Mingyur Namkhai Dorje (4th Dzogchen), Shechen Öntrul (Shechen Mahapandita Öntrul Thuthop Namgyal), Drupwang Rogza Palge, and Chokgyur Dechen Lingpa.

Among Patrul Rinpoche's many students, the most outstanding were Nyoshul Lungtok Tenpai Nyima, Önpo Tenga (Orgyen Tendzin Norbu), Minyak Kunzang Sönam, Jamgön Lama Mipham, and Khenpo Kunzang Palden. Other important disciples were Jigme Phuntsok Jungne (2nd Dodrupchen), Jigme Tenpai Nyima (3rd Dodrupchen), Dzogchen Khenchen Pema Dorje, Mura Tulku Pema Dechen Zangpo, Gemang Khenchen Yönten Gyatso, Trama Tulku Kunzang Dechen Dorje, and Adzom Drukpa Drodul Pawo Dorje.

Other disciples were Chökyi Lodrö (1st Kathok Situ), Drime Shingkyong, Kushog Gemang Tenpe Nyima (the tulku of Gyalse Shenphen Thaye), Khenpo Shenga (Khenpo Shenphen Chökyi Nangwa), Gyarong Namtrul Kunzang Thekchog Dorje, Lingtrul Thubten Gyaltsen, Khenpo Könchog Özer, Pema Thekchog Tenpai Gyaltsen (5th Shechen Rabjam), Gyurme Pema Namgyal (3rd Shechen Gyaltsap), and the 45th King of Derge, Chime Takpai Dorje ('chi med rtag pa'i rdo rje, 1840–1896) and his family.

Among Patrul's students from the Kagyu school were Karmai Khenpo Rinchen Dargye and Khenchen Tashi Özer. Among students from the Geluk school were Minyak Kunzang Sönam, Alak Do-ngak Gyatso, Hor Khangsar Khyabgön, and Sershul Larampa Thubten.

Adzom Drukpa (1842–1924)

Adzom Drukpa, Drodul Pawo Dorje Natshok Rangdröl (a 'dzom 'brug pa 'gro 'dul dpa' bo rdo rje sna tshogs rang grol) was born in the Tromtar region of Kham. He was an incarnation of the great translator Ma Rinchen Chok (ma rin chen mchog, 8th c.), one of twenty-five chief disciples of Padmasambhava, and the immediate reincarnation of Adzom Rigdzin Sangye Tashi (a 'dzom rig 'dzin sangs rgyas bkra shis, d.u.). Others considered him to be the embodiment of the great Drukpa Kagyu master Pema Karpo ('brug chen padma dkar po, 1527–1592).

Among his main teachers, in addition to Patrul Rinpoche, were Shechen Öntrul Gyurme Thutop Namgyal (zhe chen dbon sprul 'gyur med mthu stobs rnam rgyal, 1787–1854); Kathok Situ Chökyi Lodrö, whom he met at the age of twelve; Nyagla Pema Dudul (nyag bla padma bdud 'dul, 1816–1872), who advised him to remain a layman and let his hair grow long in the style of a *ngakpa* (Sanskrit *mantrika*), a nonmonastic practitioner of the tantras; Jamyang Khyentse Wangpo; Jamgön Kongtrul Lodrö Thaye; and Dzogchen Khenpo Pema Dorje. From the age of thirteen, he devoted himself to quintessential unelaborate meditation practices.

Patrul Rinpoche gave him instructions on the preliminary practices according to his text *The Words of My Perfect Teacher*. He also bestowed on him empowerments and transmissions. Khyentse Wangpo gave him transmissions of Longchen Nyingthig and other Terma lineages, making him one of the spiritual heirs of the Chetsun Nyingthig (lce btsun snying thig) Dzogchen teachings. He also studied with Lama Mipham, Khenchen Tashi Özer (mkhan chen bkra shis 'od zer, 1836–1910), and the 4th

Dzogchen Mingyur Namkhai Dorje (rdzogs chen mi 'gyur nam mkha'i rdo rje, 1793–1870).

In 1886, Adzom Drukpa established Adzom Gar, his main seat in Tromtar. He traveled widely throughout Kham, giving teachings to numerous disciples from all traditions of Tibetan Buddhism.

His son, Adzom Gyalse Gyurme Dorje (a 'dzom rgyal sras 'gyur med rdo rje, 1895–ca. 1959), became a renowned master in his own right.

Among his main disciples were Khenpo Kunzang Palden (see biographical note below), Tertön Sogyal Lerab Lingpa (gter ston bsod rgyal las rab gling pa, 1856–1926), the 3rd Katok Situ Orgyen Chökyi Gyatso, Dzongsar Khyentse Chökyi Lodrö (rdzong sar chos kyi blo gros, 1893–1959), Yukhok Chatralwa Chöying Rangdröl (g.yu khog bya bral ba chos dbyings rang grol, 1872–1952), and Kunu Rinpoche Tendzin Gyaltsen (khu nu rin po che bstan 'dzin rgyal mtshan, ca. 1894–1977).

When the young tulku Dilgo Khyentse Tashi Paljor (dil mgo mkhyen brtse bkra shis dpal 'byor, 1910–1991) and family came to visit him, Adzom Drukpa took the boy under his protection, administering novice vows and clearing away obstacles that might hamper his longevity.

Alak Do-ngak Gyatso (1824–1902)

Japa Do-ngak Gyatso ('ja' pa mdo sngags rgya mtsho), commonly known as Alak Do-ngak, was considered by some to be an incarnation of the great Geluk scholar Gungthang Könchog Tenpai Drönme (gung thang dkon mchog bstan pa'i sgron me, 1762–1823), the abbot of Labrang Monastery in Amdo.

Foremost among his many teachers were Shabkar Tsogdruk Rangdröl and Patrul Rinpoche.

Alak Do-ngak was well versed in Sutra and Tantra teachings of both the Geluk and Nyingma traditions. His writings have been lost.

Alak Do-ngak's students included the 3rd Dodrupchen, Jigme Tenpai Nyima, and the four main Khenpos of Dodrupchen Monastery: Garwa Khenpo Jigme Ösel (mgar ba mkhan po 'jigs med 'od gsal, ?–1926); Khenpo Könchog Drönme (mkhan po dkon mchog sgron me, 1859–1936), a.k.a. Lushul Khenpo Lobsang Kunkhyab (klu shul mkhan po blo bzang kun khyab); Amye Khenpo Damchö (a mye mkhan po dam chos, d.u.); and Sershul Khenpo Ngawang (ser shul mkhan po ngag dbang, d.u.). In addition, Alak Do-ngak was both a teacher and a disciple of Lingtrul Pema Lungtok Gyatso (gling sprul padma lung rtogs rgya mtsho, 1852–?).

Alak Do-ngak spent twelve years meditating on bodhichitta in a hermitage at Drakkar Gephel Ling in Amdo. He then spent a further six years in retreat focused on the developing stage (*kyerim* / bskyed rim) and the perfection or completion stage (*dzogrim* / rdzogs rim) of Mantrayana practice.

Chokgyur Dechen Lingpa (1829–1870)

Chokgyur Dechen Lingpa (mchog gyur bde chen gling pa), also known as Shikpo Lingpa (zhig po gling pa) and as Chokling for short, was born in Nangchen province in Kham. He was said to be the reincarnation of Murub Tsenpo, King Trisong Detsen's second son.

When he was a boy, as he was herding cattle, Guru Rinpoche appeared to him in person, in the form of an Indian yogi.

One day he found a small *tsa tsa,* a miniature stupa containing a scroll of paper with the list of all the termas he was meant to reveal in his life.[229]

He first stayed as a monk at Parmi, a monastery of the Drigung Kagyu school, then at Nangchen Gar, a Nyingma monastery. By then, he had already revealed several termas, but he kept them secret.

At Nangchen Gar he was made the leader of the sacred dances. Once, while leading one of these dances, he had a vision of Guru Rinpoche with his twenty-five main disciples performing a completely different dance. He joined in it, causing the other dancers to make mistakes. This was considered to be unacceptable behavior, and he was expelled from the monastery.

He then went to Derge area and stayed at Jamgön Kongtrul's monastery in Palpung. When he told some people that he was a tertön, he was mocked by everyone.

At twenty-five, Chokgyur Lingpa met the 9th Palpung Situ, Padma Nyinche Wangpo (si tu padma nyin byed dbang po, 1774–1853), who acknowledged him as a genuine tertön. He then returned to Jamgön Kongtrul, who was very sick and who asked him to perform long-life ceremonies for him.

Chokling had a strong wish to meet Jamyang Khyentse Wangpo and went to Dzongsar. Khyentse Wangpo immediately said that Chokling was no different from Guru Rinpoche himself, adding, "For thirteen lifetimes, we have been connected like father and son."

Khyentse Wangpo gave many transmissions to Chokling, and during the empowerment of the Lama Yangthig cycle of Longchen Rabjam, Chokling saw Jamyang Khyentse as the Indian *mahapandita* Vimalamitra in person.

When Chokling showed Khyentse Wangpo the yellow parchment scroll for the terma of the *Heart Practice That Dispels All Obstacles* (*thugs sgrub bar chad kun bsal*), the latter said that he had an almost identical terma, which he had not yet written down. He added that they should merge these two termas into one.

Khyentse Wangpo also helped Chokling put into writing many of the termas that he had not yet written down, transcribing them with his own hand. He then requested Chokling to give him the transmission for all these teachings.

Chokling subsequently returned to his native Nangchen province, where he revealed thirty-six important termas.

When discovering the Vajrakilaya cycle known as Zabdun Phurba, Chokling dug a hole in a rock and saw seventy-five *kilaya* daggers emitting sparks of fire. He took the main phurba, which was made of agate *zi* stone. The dakini script for this cycle of teachings was written on yellow parchment tied to the central hub of the phurba.

Following this, Chokling returned to Dzongsar, where at the Lotus Crystal Cave (Pema Shelphuk), together with Jamyang Khyentse and Jamgön Kongtrul, he revealed a terma in front of a large crowd. As the three lamas were performing some ceremonies inside the cave, at one point Chokgyur Lingpa flew up to reach the ceiling of the cave, from which he extracted the "treasure box" containing the yellow parchment for the Three Sections of the Great Perfection (*rdzogs chen sde gsum*). Everyone present was amazed.

Chokgyur Lingpa then went to Central Tibet to fulfill an earlier invitation by the 14th Karmapa, Thekchog Dorje (theg mchog rdo rje, 1798–1868). As Samye Monastery, he met Guru Rinpoche in person and revealed a precious terma. During his life, Chokling visited the Zangdokpalri (Glorious Copper-Colored Mountain), Guru Rinpoche's pure land, three times. He had many other visions of Guru Rinpoche.

Having returned to Kham, at Yegyal Namkhadzö in Nangchen he founded Neten Monastery. He then revealed many termas throughout Kham.

After Chokgyur Lingpa passed away, Jamyang Khyentse saw him in a vision in a buddhafield, a vision during which he received many teachings from him.

Chöying Rangdröl (1777–1853)

Tsopu Drupchen Gyurme Chöying Rangdröl (mtsho phu grub chen 'gyur med chos dbyings rang grol) was born in Lower Sam, an area between

Nyakrong and Tromtar. He was the rebirth of Druptop Drungpa Namkha Gyatso (grub thob drung pa nam mkha' rgya mtsho, 17th–18th century), an accomplished yogi from Kathok Monastery who had taught the great Kathok Rigdzin Tsewang Norbu (rig 'dzin tshe dbang nor bu, 1698–1755).

Chöying Rangdröl had strong predispositions toward the dharma. Once, for instance, when receiving and empowerment from the tertön Rinchen Lingpa, he kept hearing dharma teachings within the sound of the bell that the tertön was ringing during the rituals. But as he was unable to fully comprehend the meaning of the sentences he heard, he felt a strong urge to study and practice the dharma.

Yet he first had to become a shepherd for a while. Even at a young age, he sometimes displayed unusual powers. Once, after he had crossed a river, his companions noticed that his boots, which he had kept on, were not wet at all.

Mainly, he studied and practiced the termas of Rigdzin Longsal Nyingpo (rig 'dzin klong gsal snying po, 1625–1692). Among his teachers were Tromge Kundun Rinpoche Sönam Rinchen (khrom dge sku mdun rin po che bsod nams rin chen, d.u.), the famed scholar Getse Mahapandita, Gyurme Tsewang Chokdrup (dge rtse maha pandita 'gyur med mchog grub, 1761–1829), and the hermit Nyingön Chatralwa Namkha Dorje (nyin dgon bya bral ba nam mkha' rdo rje, d.u.), who gave him the name Gyurme Chöying Rangdröl.

After completing his studies, he spent most of his life in retreat in various places, including many years at Tram Tsopu; hence he became known as Tsopu Drupchen (mtsho phu sgrub chen), meaning the "greatly accomplished one of Tsopu." (He was also known as the Mahasiddha of Trom.)

He chiefly taught the Longsal Dorje Nyingpo (klong gsal rdo rje snying po) cycle revealed by Tertön Longsal Nyingpo (klong gsal snying po, 1625–1692). Among his many students were his nephew the 2nd Kathok Situ, Chökyi Lodrö Orgyen Tenpa Namgyal; Rigdzin Sönam Palden (rig 'dzin bsod nams dpal ldan), who lived at the seat of Longsal Nyingpo; Drupchen Nyida Kundze (grub chen nyi zla kun mdzes); the great yogi and tertön Nyakla Pema Dudul (nyag bla padma bdud 'dul, 1816–1872); and the 3rd Shingkyong, Jigme Yönten Gönpo (dri med zhing skyong 'jigs med yon tan mgon po, 1837–1898).

Do Khyentse Yeshe Dorje (1800–1866)

Do Khyentse Yeshe Dorje (mdo mkhyen brtse ye shes rdo rje) was born into the Akyong bandit tribe of Golok in eastern Tibet. When he was a year old, he began saying to his mother and father that unless he met a lama called Sönam Choden, he would die.

When the 1st Dodrupchen came to that part of Golok, Do Khyentse's father made it a point to meet him. His father asked if the 1st Dodrupchen knew a lama called Sönam Choden.

Dodrupchen replied that yes, he did know Sönam Choden, and he arranged to go meet little Do Khyentse.

When the two met, Dodrupchen asked little Do Khyentse, "Do you know me?" (Only one or two people in the whole world knew that Dodrupchen had ever been known by the name Sönam Choden.)

The baby replied, "Yes, you are Sönam Choden. Did you desert me?"

With tears in his eyes, Dodrupchen took the child into his arms, saying, "Until just now, I couldn't find you! Now I'll look after you."

Dodrupchen recognized Do Khyentse, the mind-incarnation of his teacher Jigme Lingpa, but this recognition was kept secret until it could be confirmed. Later, in the presence of Dodrupchen, the queen regent, the crown prince, lamas, officials, and sons of Jigme Lingpa, Do Khyentse passed all formal tests, recognizing the personal effects of his predecessor with such unfailing accuracy that everyone present was moved to joy and devotion. Dodrupchen brought Do Khyentse to Shukchen Tago, the monastery he had founded in Dokhok.

When he was ten, Do Khyentse had to be taken to Central Tibet to be enthroned formally as the mind-incarnation of Jigme Lingpa. The young boy was inconsolable at having to part from his teacher.

At Yangri Gar, in Drigung, he met the son of Jigme Lingpa, Jigme Lingpa's consort, and his nephew. He also visited Jigme Lingpa's seat at Tsering Jong. He went to Yarlung Sheldrak, a cave that is one of five main sites sacred to Padmasambhava, where there was a statue of Padmasambhava called "Looks Like Me." People saw a beam of light emanate from the statue's heart and stream into the heart of the little boy. Later, Do Khyentse said that he'd had a profound experience of pure awareness and of the primordial purity of all phenomena.

When he was twelve, he returned to Kham. Staying at the monastery of Yarlung Pemakö, he received extensive transmissions from the 1st Dodrupchen, including those of Longchenpa's Nyingthig Yazhi.[230] When he was fifteen, he met Jigme Gyalwai Nyugu and Kilung Jigme Ngotsar, two other eminent disciples of Jigme Lingpa.

From the first, Do Khyentse regarded Dodrupchen as Padmasambhava himself, and saw him surrounded by miraculous beings no one else was able to see. Once, in the presence of Jigme Gyalwai Nyugu, he seemed to have fallen asleep and remained so for three whole days. When the young tulku awoke, he said he had been experiencing a profound vision of Guru Padmasambhava in a crystal palace and had received empowerment from Guru Rinpoche's consorts, Yeshe Tsogyal and Mandarava.

When Do Khyentse was twenty, while staying at the court of the King of Derge, he decided he wanted to renounce the complicated life of a tulku, so full of obligations, aristocrats, and attendants. To the King of Derge, Do Khyentse announced his intention: he wished to become a wandering yogi.

"If you won't let me," Do Khyentse told the king, "you'll just have to lock me up!"

The King of Derge was shocked, as was everyone else.

They decided to consult Do Khyentse's teacher, Dodrupchen, to whom they sent a formal letter asking for advice.

The response from Dodrupchen was that Do Khyentse should leave the king's court at once and spend a year living near Dodrupchen and receiving teachings.

In this way, Do Khyentse was allowed to leave the king's court.

When Do Khyentse arrived, Dodrupchen told his student that he did not expect to be alive much longer. He told Do Khyentse to remain with him for one year; after that, he could do whatever he wished.

Do Khyentse offered his teacher all his possessions, and Dodrupchen bestowed on him the white felt robes of a yogi and blessed Do Khyentse's hair, which, from that moment on, he would never again cut.

Over the course of this year, Dodrupchen bestowed upon his student the transmission and instruction on important Dzogchen teachings such as the Khandro Nyingthig and the *Yeshe Lama*.[231] Do Khyentse dreamed that Longchenpa gave him further detailed instructions on the Khandro Nyingthig.

After the year ended, Do Khyentse told Dodrupchen that his wish was still to become a wandering practitioner, renouncing home and possessions. Thus, after taking leave from his root master with great sadness, Do Khyentse went on his way. First he traveled to Amdo with Rogza Palge.

Some months later, Do Khyentse experienced a vision of Dodrupchen: he was sitting in the sky, a radiant body amid rainbow lights, singing his spiritual testament. Rays of light emerged from Dodrupchen and dissolved into Do

Khyentse's heart. Do Khyentse fainted. When he regained consciousness, he realized that Dodrupchen must have passed away.

After his teacher's death, Do Khyentse stopped wearing the white felt robes of a yogi, and put on the ordinary black garments worn by nomads. This drew criticism from many people, not the least of whom was the King of Derge.

Do Khyentse began wandering around the wildest areas of Golok, his unconventional behavior making him appear like a hunter—but if so, it would be one who would hunt animals down, kill them, and then bring them back to life.

Once, seeing Do Khyentse kill a little marmot, his uncle scolded him, saying, "How can a tulku kill animals just like a sinner?" Do Khyentse struck the rodent's corpse with his whip. At once, the little marmot sprang back to life and scrambled off into the forest. That wasn't enough for his uncle, who remarked sarcastically, "*Oho,* so now you're doing magic tricks, too?"[232]

After spending time teaching in Nyarong, Do Khyentse began to live mainly in Dartsedo, often referred to as "Do"; thus, he became known as "Khyentse of Do."

His revealed treasures and teachings, including the *Chö Dzinpa Rangdröl* (*gcod 'dzin pa rang grol,* Spontaneous Liberation of Grasping), which is still widely practiced, filling nine volumes of the modern edition. He had countless disciples.

Do Khyentse returned to Dartsedo for the last years of his life. When he passed away in 1866, people said that he'd dissolved into Jigme Lingpa's body-incarnation, Jamyang Khyentse Wangpo, making that great lama even more radiant than before. He remarked, "Now this mad yogi has come to me."

Dola Jigme Kalzang (early 19th c.)

Dola Jigme Kalzang (rdo bla 'jigs med skal bzang), was a close disciple of the 1st Dodrupchen, Jigme Trinley Özer. He became an accomplished master in his own right and one of the main holders of the Longchen Nyingthig lineage.

Once, just as he was starting a three-year retreat in a cave by the Machu River (Yellow River), he heard a pilgrim chanting, with an incredibly moving melody, the *chö* offering revealed as a terma by Jigme Lingpa. Dola Jigme could not resist coming out of his retreat and asking the pilgrim about this particular liturgy. The pilgrim answered that Jigme Lingpa had passed away but that his chief disciple, Jigme Trinley Özer, was living in Golok. Upon hearing Trinley Özer's name, Dola Jigme felt boundless devotion. Driven by a deep yearning, he left his retreat and found his way into the presence of the one who was to become his root master.

Dola Jigme was a teacher to Jigme Gyalwai Nyugu (who received teachings from him in 1815/16 and1820) and to Patrul Rinpoche, whom he recognized as being the rebirth of Palge Samten Phuntsok. He widely taught in major Nyingma monasteries such as Dzogchen, Shechen, and Kathok.

In the latter part of his life, he spent much time in Amdo, in the areas around Lake Kokonor, giving teachings to Tibetan and Mongolian disciples.

Dilgo Khyentse Rinpoche related the following story about Dola Jigme Kalzang's death: "One day, while on pilgrimage to China, Dola Jigme came to the central square of a small town where a crowd had gathered. As he approached, he found that a thief was about to be put to death in a particularly cruel fashion: he was to be forced to straddle an iron horse that had been made red-hot from within. Dola Jigme pushed his way through the crowd and proclaimed: 'I am the thief!' A great silence fell. The presiding mandarin turned impassively to the newcomer and asked, 'Are you ready to assume the consequences of what you have just told us?' Dola Jigme nodded. He died on the horse, and the thief was spared."

He thus acted out of unconditional benevolence to save the life of a stranger, even a stranger who happened to be a thief. It is hard for ordinary people to fathom the depth of a bodhisattva's wisdom and compassion, but it is clear that Dola Jigme saw more benefit for sentient beings in doing this than in simply going his own way.

Gyalse Shenphen Thaye (1800–1865/66)[233]

Gyalse Shenphen Thaye (rgyal sras gzhan phan mtha' yas) was born in the Gemang area of Dzachukha province in Kham. From an early age he felt a strong feeling of renunciation and devoted himself with great perseverance to the study and practice of the dharma. His root master was Dola Jigme Kalzang, and he studied as well with many teachers from all schools, without any sectarian bias. These included the 1st Dodrupchen, Trinley Özer, whom he regarded as the Buddha in person; Jigme Gyalwai Nyugu; the 4th Dzogchen, Mingyur Namkhai Dorje; Sengdruk Pema Tashi; and the two main masters of Mindrolling Monastery, Minling Trichen[234] and Minling Khen Rinpoche. He was considered to be an incarnation of Minling Terchen Gyurme Dorje (1646–1714).

Shenphen Thaye practiced in many sacred places, from Mount Kailash in far western Tibet to Mount Emei (Lanchen Gying Ri) in China.

He became so learned and compassionate that at some point there was hardly any lama or practitioner in Kham, from both the Old Translation (Nyingma) and the New Translation traditions, who did not consider himself his disciple.

After the death of the 1st Dodrupchen, Shenphen Thaye served as the Regent of Dodrupchen Monastery for some years and initiated an annual forty-five-day teaching and practice of the *Guhyagarbha Tantra*, thus reviving the transmission of this most important tantra of the Nyingma tradition. Patrul Rinpoche acted as his assistant for the first year and then officiated himself for the next two years.

In 1842, Shenphen Thaye became the abbot of Dzogchen Monastery after it had been almost totally destroyed in an earthquake. He rebuilt the monastery and, in 1848, started the Shri Singha Philosophical College, where he initated a tradition of giving extensive commentaries[235] upon the *Thirteen Great Treatises* from the Sutra tradition.

He also began gathering the collection of the Nyingma Kahma, the major texts of the Nyingma traditions that have been passed from master to disciple in an uninterrupted transmission since Guru Padmasambhava's time. According to Kyabje Dudjom Rinpoche (1904–1987), "Gyalse Shenphen Thaye's kindness and legacy to the Buddha's teachings surpass the imagination."

His foremost students were Patrul Rinpoche, Khenpo Pema Dorje, and Shechen Öntrul Thuthop Namgyal, who were his heart-disciples, and Dagpo Thupden Yondzin in Central Tibet. He was also a teacher to Do Khyentse Yeshe Dorje, Jamyang Khyentse Wangpo, and the 7th Minling Trichen, Sangye Kunga Do-ngak Tendzin Norbu.

Gyurme Pema Namgyal, 3rd Shechen Gyaltsap (1871–1926)

The 3rd Shechen Gyaltsap, Gyurme Pema Namgyal (zhe chen rgyal tshab 'gyur med padma rnam rgyal), was one of the main spiritual teachers and writers of the late nineteenth and early twentieth centuries. He is considered to be the chief disciple of Lama Mipham Rinpoche.

He was also a disciple of Patrul Rinpoche, Jamyang Khyentse Wangpo, Jamgön Kongtrul Lodrö Thaye, Gyurme Kunzang Tenpai Nyima (5th Shechen Rabjam, zhe chen rab 'byams 'gyur med kun bzang bstan pa'i nyi ma, 1864–1909), Khenchen Tashi Özer, and Jamyang Loter Wangpo (ngor dpon slob 'jam dbyangs blo gter dbang po, 1847–1914).

He was the master of eminent twentieth-century teachers such as Dilgo Khyentse Rinpoche, Jamyang Khyentse Chökyi Lodrö ('jam dbyangs mkhyen brtse chos kyi blo gros, 1893–1959), and the 6th Shechen Rabjam, Nandze Drupai Dorje (zhe chen rab 'byams snang mdzad grub pa'i rdo rje, 1910–1959).

He spent most of his life in the Pema Ösel Ling hermitage above Shechen monastery in eastern Tibet. Once, after announcing that he would spend three years in continued retreat, he came out after six months, without giving any specific explanation. The same day, people could see a footprint clearly imprinted in the large stone that was at his doorstep. This footprint is now kept at Shechen Monastery in Kham. This was indeed an extraordinary sign that he had accomplished all that needed to be done during that particular retreat. (A photograph of it can be seen in Matthieu Ricard, *Journey to Enlightenment* [New York: Aperture, 1996].)

His collected works fill thirteen large volumes, which constitute one of the richest and most diverse collections of writings in Tibetan literature, and include lucid and profound commentaries on various aspects of Buddhist philosophy and practice.

Jamgön Kongtrul Lodrö Thaye (1813–1899)

Jamgön Kongtrul Lodrö Thaye ('jam mgon kong sprul blo gros mtha' yas), also known as Kongtrul Yönten Gyatso (kong sprul yon tan rgya mtsho), was born in Kham into a family of the Bön tradition and was named Tendzin Yungdrung (bstan 'dzin g.yung drung). From an early age, he showed signs of having extraordinary capacities. He subsequently received a Buddhist education and studied four years at Shechen Monastery under Shechen Mahapandita Öntrul Thuthop Namgyal. He also took monastic vows at Shechen at age twenty.

His mentor and benefactor, Tsephel, the governor from Chöde Phodrang (who was also a Drukpa Kagyu monk), then took Kongtrul to Palpung

Monastery. There he met one of his main teachers, the 9th Tai Situ, Pema Nyingje Wangpo (ta'i si tu padma nyin rje dbang po, 1775–1853). Kongtrul had such a bright intelligence that Tai Situ feared he was going to be recruited to serve at the court of the King of Derge. To avoid this, knowing that incarnate lamas were excused from performing such duties, Tai Situ recognized the young man as the incarnation of one of his late students, Kongpo Bamteng Tulku (kong po bam steng sprul sku), hence the name Kongtrul (kong sprul). He received the bodhisattva vows, and the name Lodrö Thaye, from the 14th Karmapa, Thekchog Dorje (karma pa theg mchog rdo rje, 1798–1868), at Karma Gön Monastery. He then received the transmission of the Shangpa Kagyu lineage from Karma Norbu (karma nor bu), as well as many teachings from the Nyingma tradition from Dzogchen Mingyur Namkhai Dorje and other masters.

But his main spiritual master was Jamyang Khyentse Wangpo, whom he referred to as the "Omniscient Precious Master" (Kunkhyen Lama Rinpoche). Much of Jamgön Kongtrul's activity and writings during the remaining sixty years of his life was either inspired by or done in concert with Khyentse Wangpo. They would work together to open sacred sites, reveal treasures, compose and edit compilations of texts, and spearhead the Rime nonsectarian movement that greatly contributed to the revival of Tibetan Buddhism in East Tibet.

Jamgön Kongtrul also became very close to Chokgyur Dechen Lingpa. These three lamas became widely known as "Jam-Kong-Chok-Sum" (mkhyen kong mchog gsum), the "trio of Khyen, Kong, and Chok."

One of the matchless contributions of Jamgön Kongtrul to Tibetan Buddhism was the compilation of the *Five Great Treasuries* (*mdzod chen rnam pa lnga*), a vast collection of teachings, sadhanas, texts for empowerments, practice manuals, and explanations of Buddhist philosophy and practice. In his autobiography, Jamgön Kongtrul says that the thought of creating these collections never even crossed his mind, and that he compiled them at the behest of his precious master Jamyang Khyentse Wangpo.

While he was bestowing teaching upon Jamgön Kongtrul, Khyentse Wangpo had a prophetic dream in which he saw a huge, magnificent stupa with five doors, one in each cardinal direction and one in the upper vase of the stupa. Inside the stupa were beautiful statues and precious texts. When Khyentse asked about the nature of those texts, someone answered that they were *Five Great Treasuries*. Khyentse Wangpo told Kongtrul that this dream indicated that he, Kongtrul, was the one destined to bring those *Five Treasuries* to reality. He also gave Kongtrul indications of the content of each treasury.

Accordingly, over many years, Jamgön Kongtrul collected, edited, or wrote (1) the *Mantra Treasury of the Kagyu Tradition* (*bka' brgyud sngags mdzod*, 3 to 8 vols., depending on the editions); (2) the *Great Treasury of Precious Rediscovered Teachings* (*rin chen gter mdzod chen mo*, 63 to 71 vols.), which gathers the most important rediscovered teachings (termas) of the Nyingma tradition and which includes the *Extraordinary Treasury* (*thun mong ma yin pa'i mdzod*), Jamgön Kongtrul's own termas; (3) the *All-Encompassing Treasury of Knowledge* (*shes bya kun la khyab pa'i mdzod*, 4 vols.), an encyclopedia of Buddhist knowledge and traditional sciences; (4) the *Vast Treasury of Teachings* (*rgya chen bka'i mdzod*, 16 vols.), which gathers the remaining writings of Jamgön Kongtrul himself; and (5) the *Treasury of Precious Instructions* (*gdams ngag mdzod*, 13 or 18 vols.), which gathers the pith instructions of the eight main "chariots" of the practice lineages (*sgrub brgyud shing rta brgyad*, 13 to 18 vols.).

It is thanks to these five collections (which have been reedited and printed in the twentieth century under the direction of Dilgo Khyentse Rinpoche) that countless major and rare transmissions are still extant in our day.

Jamgön Kongtrul also spent many years in retreat in two hermitages, Tsadra Rinchen Trak (tsa 'dra rin chen brag), above Palpung Monastery, and Dzongshö Deshek Dupa (rdzong shod bde gshegs 'dus pa), a complex of rocky caves located between Dzongsar and Kathok. At Dzongshö, in 1867, Khyentse Wangpo and Chokgyur Lingpa formally enthroned Jamgön Kongtrul as a tertön under the name of Chime Tennyi Yungdrung Lingpa ('chi med bstan gnyis g.yung drung gling pa) and urged him to reveal the termas entrusted to him by Guru Padmasambhava, which he did in the following years.

Jamgön Kongtrul had countless disciples, including Jamyang Loter Wangpo ('jam dbyangs blo gter dbang po, 1847–1914), Lama Mipham, Tokden Shakya Shri (rtogs ldan shakya shri, 1853–1919), Jigme Tenpai Nyima (3rd Dodrupchen), Thubten Chökyi Dorje, the 5th Dzogchen (rdzogs chen thub bstan chos kyi rdo rje, 1872–1935), Pema Thekchog Tenpai Gyaltsen, 5th Shechen Rabjam (zhe chen rab 'byams padma theg mchog bstan pa'i rgyal mtshan, 1864–1909), and the female master Ayu Khandro Dorje Paldrön (a g.yu mkha' 'gro rdo rje dpal sgron, 1839–1953). Five reincarnations of Jamgön Kongtrul were identified.

Jamyang Khyentse Wangpo (1820–1892)

Jamyang Khyentse Wangpo ('jam dbyangs mkhyen brtse'i dbang po) was born in the Dilgo family in the Terlung (gter lung) Valley, west of Dzongsar (rdzong sar) Monastery, in the Derge province of Kham. He was given the name Khyentse Wangpo Kunga Tenpai Gyaltsen (mkhyen brtse' dbang po kun dga' bstan pa'i rgyal mtshan) by the Sakya master Tartse Khenchen Jampa Kunga Tendzin (thar rtse mkhan chen byams pa kun dga' bstan 'dzin, 1776–1862), who recognized him as the incarnation of Tartse Khenchen Jampa Namkha Chime (thar rtse mkhan chen byams pa nam mkha' 'chi med, 1765–1820).

In the Sakya tradition, he received teachings from Sakya Trichen Pema Dundul Wangchok (sa skya khri chen padma bdud 'dul dbang phyug, 1792–1853), Zhalu Losel Tenkyong (zhwa lu blo gsal bstan skyong, b. 1804), and Ngor Khenchen Jampa Kunga Tendzin (ngor mkhan chen byams pa kun dga' bstan 'dzin, 1776–1862).

In the Nyingma tradition, when he was eighteen he studied with Shechen Öntrul Thuthop Namgyal. He also studied at Dzogchen Monastery with Mingyur Namkhai Dorje and Khenpo Pema Dorje.

But the one whom he considered to be his most precious master was Jigme Gyalwai Nyugu, who came to Terlung, Khyentse Wangpo's birthplace, when the latter was nineteen. It is said that it was like a reunion between father and son. Gyalwai Nyugu imparted many teachings to Khyentse Wangpo, including those of the Longchen Nyingthig, from the preliminaries up to the most profound Dzogchen teachings of *trekchö* and *thögal.*

According to the oral tradition told by Dilgo Khyentse Rinpoche, Khyentse Wangpo achieved full understanding of the nature of samsara and nirvana and of all subsequent practices when contemplating the "four thoughts that turn the mind to dharma," which is the first step of the so-called "preliminary" (but actually quite profound) practices (*ngöndro*). When receiving the Dzogchen teachings from Gyalwai Nyugu, he realized all things as being the manifestation of pure awareness.

Gyalwai Nyugu recognized Khyentse Wangpo as being the body-incarnation of Rigzin Jigme Lingpa and acknowledged him as being his spiritual or dharma heir.

He had countless pure visions. When he was fifteen, for instance, he had a vision of being transported to Bodhgaya and receiving teaching from Jampel

Shenyen (Manjushrimitra), one of the eight Great Vidyadharas of India, who eventually dissolved into him. When climbing down from the eighth floor of the stupa where he had received the teachings, he saw a burning fire and was irrestibly drawn to jump into it, whereby all the defilements of his gross body were burnt out. He then turned into a body of light and thought, "I am Vimalamitra."

When he was sixteen, he traveled in a vision to the pure land of Zangdokpalri, where Guru Padmasambhava prophesied that Khyentse Wangpo would be the holder of the seven modes of transmission (*kabap dun* / bka' babs bdun).

When he was twenty-four, at Oyuk in Central Tibet, he clearly remembered having been Chetsun Senge Wangchok in a former life, and consequently revealed and put into writing the Dzogchen cycle of the Chetsun Nyingthig (lce btsun snying thig).

In fact, Khyentse Wangpo is said to be the only master who received these seven transmissions: (1) teachings transmitted from master to disciple through an unbroken oral lineage (Kahma), (2) earth treasures (*sa gter*), (3) mind treasures (*dgongs gter*), (4) re-extracted treasures (*yang gter*), (5) teachings recollected from a previous life (*rje dran*), (6) teachings received during "pure visions" (*dag snang*), and (7) teachings heard from Padmasambhava and other masters appearing in person to the tertön (*snyan brgyud*).

He traveled twice to Central Tibet. At Mindrolling Monastery, at the age of twenty-one, he received full monastic ordination and the name Kunga Tenpai Gyaltsen (kun dga' bstan pa'i rgyal mtshan) from Khenchen Gyurme Rigdzin Zangpo (smin gling mkhan chen 'gyur med rig dzin bzang po, d.u.), and the bodhisattva vows from the 7th Minling Trichen, Sangye Kunga Dongak Tendzin Norbu (smin gling khri chen sangs rgyas kun dga' mdo sngags bstan 'dzin nor bu). There he also studied with the great female master Jetsun Trinley Chödrön (rje btsun 'phrin las chos sgron, early 19th c.).

Over thirteen years, he traveled widely on foot, like a simple pilgrim, visiting hundreds of holy places, monasteries, temples, caves, and hermitages, collecting empowerments (*wang*/dbang), scriptural transmissions (*lung*), and explanations (*tri*/khrid) wherever he went. He thus received teachings from more than 150 masters.

Being an incarnation of King Trisong Detsen, he revealed many treasures and is considered to be the "seal of all tertöns." His collected works fill thirteen volumes. His tertön names were Pema Ösel Do-ngak Lingpa (padma 'od gsal mdo sngags gling pa) and Ösel Trulpai Dorje ('od gsal sprul pa'i rdo rje). His other names, found in his writings, included Dorje Ziji (rdo rje gzi brjid) and Manjugosha. Together with Jamgön Kongtrul, Patrul Rinpoche, and Lama Mipham, he was the guiding light of the nonsectarian Rime movement.

Khyentse Wangpo was very close to Jamgön Kongtrul and Terchen Chokgyur Lingpa, with whom he exchanged teachings and shared several rediscovered treasures.

At the age of twenty-four, he established his main residence at Dzongsar Monastery, in Menshö Valley (sman shod). From age thirty-seven, he decided to devote himself to contemplative practice and vowed to never cross the threshold of his living quarters.

He had countless visions of deities and masters of the past, some of them blending with reality. Once, for instance, as he was in strict retreat, his attendant heard someone else talking in the innermost room. Wondering who could thus have penetrated unnoticed inside his master's retreat, he peeped through the doorway curtain and saw Khyentse Wangpo in conversation with an old lama. After a while, when the attendant returned to take care of his master's needs, he asked him, "Who was that person who came into your retreat?" Khyentse Wangpo replied, "You saw him? That means you have quite a pure karma. This was Vimalamitra."

Khyentse Wangpo compiled and edited a fourteen-volume compendium of sadhanas known as Druptap Kuntu (sgrub thabs kun btus) and inspired Jamyang Loter to do the same with the thirty-two volumes of the *Gyude Kuntu* (*rgyud sde kun btus*), a collection of sadhanas and empowerments chiefly practiced in the Sakya tradition.

Following a visionary dream he had in 1861, Khyentse Wangpo inspired Jamgön Kongtrul to undertake redaction of the *Five Great Treasuries* (see the biographical note on Jamgön Kongtrul).

Khyentse Wangpo had numberless disciples and was probably the most influential teacher in Kham in his day.

Before he passed away in 1892, he prophesied that he would reappear in five incarnations (body, speech, mind, qualities, and activities). Among these, two became eminent: Dzongsar Khyentse Chökyi Lodrö (1894–1959), the activity incarnation, and Dilgo Khyentse Rinpoche (1910–1991), the mind incarnation.

Jigme Gyalwai Nyugu (1765–1842)

Jigme Gyalwai Nyugu ('jigs med rgyal ba'i myu gu) was born in Kham in the Dzagyal Valley of Dzachukha province. As a child, he showed no interest in worldly activities but felt a strong urge to devote himself to spiritual practice. As he grew up, he was pressured by some of his family to marry and become a householder.

His mother, however, advised him to avoid such a life, as it would have created a powerful obstacle to his desire to devote himself to the dharma. She gave him a piece of silver and some provisions and so he could leave secretly. Gyalwai Nyugu thus went to meet the 3rd Dzogchen Rinpoche (nges don bstan 'dzin bzang po, 1759–1792), before traveling on foot to Central Tibet, a journey that takes several months.

At Samye Monastery in Central Tibet—the first Buddhist monastery in Tibet, built at the time of Guru Padmasambhava—he met the 1st Dodrupchen Rinpoche, Jigme Trinley Özer. Dodrupchen Rinpoche invited him to practice with him at the Chimphu hermitage above Samye. He advised him first to go to Tsering Jong Monastery and meet Dodrupchen Rinpoche's own teacher, Rigdzin Jigme Lingpa, to receive instruction.

When Gyalwai Nyugu met Jigme Lingpa for the first time, all ordinary appearances of this life vanished and he experienced an indescribable joy. At Tsering Jong, he received teachings and transmissions that included the empowerment for the Rigdzin Dupa practice (taken from Jigme Lingpa's own mind treasures, the Longchen Nyingthig), the oral transmission of the *Treasury of Precious Qualities,* written by Jigme Lingpa, and some profound instructions on the Great Perfection.

Gyalwai Nyugu returned to Samye to practice near Dodrupchen Rinpoche. Later, while they were traveling to Lhasa, Dodrupchen fell seriously ill. He accepted his illness with great joy, an attitude that inspired Gyalwai Nyugu. While Dodrupchen was ill, Gyalwai Nyugu often would carry him on his back over long distances. Following this, Gyalwai Nyugu went into retreat for three years in the Tsang area of western Tibet.

Later, he returned to Tsering Jong to receive additional teachings from Jigme Lingpa, including the dakini empowerment, Queen of Great Bliss. He then went on pilgrimage to Tsari, a sacred place in southern Tibet. On his way to Tsari, after having given his shoes to a beggar, he walked a long way barefoot, even on snow. He circumambulated the Tsari Ravines (which takes several weeks), going through the lowland jungle near India as well as over the highlands and snow mountains.

At one point, risking his own life, he rescued some pilgrims who had gotten buried in the snow. During this pilgrimage, he continuously experienced all appearances as the display of the infinite purity of all phenomena.

After finishing this long and dangerous circumambulation, he practiced in solitude in the higher grounds of Tsari, near its central Pure Crystal Mountain. He remained there, practicing, for nine months. When he ran out of food, he lived on boiled nettles and other wild plants.

Once, when he was in retreat in Central Tibet, he went outside and looked in the direction of his beloved teacher Jigme Lingpa. A strong sense of devotion arose in him. He felt an unprecedented sense of renunciation for samsara and wept for a long time.

He contemplated the ultimate nature of mind and at one point lost consciousness. When he revived, all his preconceptions about the view and meditation had vanished. He reported his experience to Dodrupchen Rinpoche and Jigme Lingpa. The latter was very pleased that Gyalwai Nyugu had realized the ultimate nature of mind.

After going back to Kham and spending more time in retreat, Gyalwai Nyugu traveled a second time to Central Tibet, where he was able once again to see his master, Jigme Lingpa.

After this final meeting, he returned to his native Dzachukha. He spent twenty years in extremely austere conditions, in caves and wild places, mostly in the Trama Valley in Upper Dzachukha. He became known as the Hermit of Dzachukha (Dza Tsampa) and as Dza Trama Lama. (His reincarnation was known as Trama Tulku: Dza Trama Tulku Kunzang Dechen Dorje.)

Gradually, disciples gathered around him, living in tents on the windswept hillside. Fulfilling the command of his master, in the later part of his life he tirelessly taught all earnest students who requested teachings. During this time, he gave Patrul teachings on the preliminary practices (*ngöndro*) of Jigme Lingpa's Longchen Nyingthig, no fewer than twenty-five times. He also gave teachings on yoga (*tsalung*) and on the Great Perfection (Dzogchen). His *ngöndro* teachings were written down by Patrul Rinpoche as *The Words of My Perfect Teacher*.

Jigme Gyalwai Nyugu become known as one of the four "fearless" sons of Jigme Lingpa, all of whom bore the name Jigme (fearless), the others being Jigme Trinley Özer, Barjung Jigme Gocha ('bar chung 'jigs med go cha, 1763–?), and the Bhutanese Jigme Kundröl ('jigs med kun grol).

After he passed away in 1842, his preserved body was enshrined as a precious relic at Dzagyal Monastery. Patrul Rinpoche often said that any prayer made in the presence of this relic would be fulfilled. The relic was destroyed during the Chinese invasion of Tibet, though a piece of Gyalwai Nyugu's mummified heart was saved; it is now enshrined in a Guru Rinpoche statue in the main temple at Dzagyal.

The author of Jigme Gyalwai Nyugu's *namtar* (rnam thar, traditional spiritual biography), in 160 folios (*'gro mgon bla ma rje'i gsang gsum rnam thar rgya mtsho las thun mong phyi'i mngon rtogs rgyal sras lam bzang*), is unknown. A digital version was typed at Shechen Monastery in Nepal from a manuscript in dbu med (handwriting) that was offered to Kyabje Dilgo Khyentse Rinpoche when he returned to Kham in 1985; it has been published by Shechen Publications.

According to the oral tradition passed on by Khenpo Pema Wangyal of Gemang Monastery and by the late Khenpo Bumther of Dzagyal, Patrul Rinpoche wrote the initial and concluding verses of his biography, while a scholarly monk from Dzagyal, who chose to remain anonymous, compiled the main section. According to Khenpo Yegyam of Barjung in Dzachukha, some autobiographical notes written by Gyalwai Nyugu himself have been incorporated into this biography by the anonymous scholar.

Jigme Lingpa (1729–1798)

Rigdzin Jigme Lingpa (rig 'dzin 'jigs med gling pa) was considered to be an incarnation of Avalokiteshvara as well as of Vimalamitra and King Trisong Detsen. At the age of six he entered the monastery of Palgi Riwo, the "Glorious Mountain," and received the name Pema Khyentse Öser. At the age of thirteen he met his root guru, Rigdzin Thekchog Dorje. He also received instructions on the Kahma and Terma traditions from many other teachers. Without arduous study he was able, due to his inner realization, to assimilate and express the whole of the Buddhist doctrine. At the age of twenty-eight he did a three-year retreat in the hermitage near Palri Monastery and had many signs of accomplishment. He had visions of Guru Padmasambhava and his consort Khandro Yeshe Tsogyal in which the terma cycle known as the Longchen Nyingthig was revealed to him. He did another three-year retreat in the Metok Phuk (Flower Cave) at Chimphu above Samye. He had three visions of Gyalwa Longchen Rabjam, thus receiving the blessings of Longchenpa's body, speech, and mind. In the second vision, Longchenpa handed over to Jigme Lingpa a book, saying, "Here is a text in which are explained all the profound meanings that I did not reveal in my *Trilogy of Resting at Ease.*" This blessing of Longchenpa's speech, was permission for Jigme Lingpa to compose the *Treasury of Precious Qualities* (*Yönten Rinpoche Dzö / yon tan rin po che'i mdzod,* also known as *Yönten Dzö*). In thirteen chapters written in verse, Jigme Lingpa gave a masterful description of the nine vehicles of the Buddhist path, beginning from the foundation of the sutras and culminating in the Great Perfection, or Dzogpa Chenpo (rdzogs pa chen po), Dzogchen for short.

Because of the terseness and depth of this poetic text, several exegeses of it were soon composed. Jigme Lingpa himself wrote a two-volume autocommentary known as the *Two Chariots* (*shing rta rnam gnyis*): one volume, dedicated to the sutra section, and one to the tantra section. Patrul Rinpoche wrote a guide for teaching the *Yönten Dzö;* a short, a medium, and a detailed outline; and a clarification of the difficult points. In continuation of Patrul Rinpoche's works, Khenpo Yönten Gyatso of Gemang (see biographical note below) wrote a two-volume commentary famed for its clarity and thoroughness, which has become widely used. Among the several other existing commentaries, the one written by Kangyur Rinpoche Longchen Yeshe Dorje (bka' gyur rin po che klong chen ye shes rdo rje, 1897–1975) has been translated into English by the Padmakara Translation Group, under the title *Treasury of Precious Qualities* (Boston: Shambhala Publications, 2001).

At Tsering Jong in Southern Tibet, Jigme Lingpa established the hermitage of Pema Ösel Thekchog Chöling, where countless disciples were to come from all over Tibet and the neighboring countries.

Jigme Lingpa's immediate incarnations were Jamyang Khyentse Wangpo (1820–1892), body-incarnation; Patrul Rinpoche (1808–1887), speech-incarnation; and Do Khyentse Yeshe Dorje (1800–1866), mind-incarnation.

Jigme Ngotsar Gyatso (18th–19th c.)

Jigme Ngotsar Gyatso ('jigs med ngo mtshar rgya mtsho), also known as Getse Lama Sönam Tendzin (dge rtse bla ma bsod nam bstan 'dzin), was one the earliest important disciples of Rigdzin Jigme Lingpa. His master instructed him to build a monastery in Kham, which became known as Kilung Monastery, located in Dzachukha. Jigme Lingpa named the monastery Ömin Rigdzin Pelgye Ling.

Jigme Ngotsar succeeded Jigme Lingpa as a teacher to the King and Queen of Derge. He had many disciples, including Patrul Rinpoche. Some of his relics were incorporated in the Mani Wall built by Mura Tulku in Dzachukha.

Jigme Phuntsok Jungne, 2nd Dodrupchen (1824–1863)

Before passing away, the 1st Dodrupchen, Jigme Trinley Özer, gave a clear prediction about his next rebirth. Accordingly, the young incarnation Jigme Phuntsok Jungne (rdo grub chen 'jigs med phun tshogs 'byung gnas) was recognized by Do Khyentse Yeshe Dorje and confirmed by Sakya Trinzin, the head of the Sakya lineage.[236]

Phuntsok Jungne was an exceptionally gifted child of beautiful physical appearance and was renowned for his miraculous powers, which he displayed on many occasions, knowing people's minds and bringing dead animals back to life.

He received the main transmissions for the Longchen Nyingthig tradition from Jigme Gyalwai Nyugu and from Do Khyentse Yeshe Dorje, whom he often accompanied during his short life. He was also a student of Patrul Rinpoche. He stayed for a while at Yarlung Pemakö, the seat of his predecessor in Serta. As the area was about to be invaded by the bloody chieftain from Nyakrong, Gonpo Namgyal, at the request of his followers, Phuntsok Jungne left for Dokhok, where he established Dodrupchen Monastery, now a large monastic estate.

He then went to Dartsedo, where Do Khyentse often resided. There an epidemic of smallpox broke out. It is said that, by the strength of his boundless compassion, Phuntsok Jungne took the epidemic upon himself. Soon after he passed away, the epidemic subsided.

The oral tradition says that before dying he stated that "a real yogi should die like a stray dog." Accordingly he laid down in a street and died right there. Soon after, Do Khyentse arrived on the scene and kicked the body, shouting, "Why are you dying like a dog?" Dodrupchen then sat in meditation posture and remained in postmortem meditation (*thukdam*) for a whole week. When Do Khyentse's young son, Rigpai Raltri, saw this, he felt a great shock as well as boundless devotion that made him realize the ultimate nature of mind. He later said that even though he had not met Phuntsok Jungne while he was alive, he considered him to be his root teacher.

Jigme Tenpai Nyima, 3rd Dodrupchen (1865–1926)

Dodrupchen Jigme Tenpai Nyima (rdo grub chen 'jigs med bstan pa'i nyi ma)—referred to for short as Dodrup Tenpai Nyima—was the son of the great tertön Dudjom Lingpa (sgas gter chen bdud 'joms gling pa, 1835–1903). He was recognized by Dzogchen Mingyur Namkhai Dorje and enthroned at the age of five at Yarlung Pemakö, the seat of his predecessors.

He began his studies at a very early age at Dzogchen Monastery with Khenpo Pema Dorje but soon became desperate about his inability to understand the meaning of philosophical texts. Such desperation in itself seems quite remarkable for a seven-year-old child! Then, one night, he had a dream of three lamas. The lama sitting in the middle was holding a book.

"Who are you? What is this book?" asked young Tenpai Nyima.

The lama answered, "I am Do Khyentse Yeshe Dorje. This volume is for helping people who cannot learn their lessons."

Tenpai Nyima asked Do Khyentse to give him the book and felt extremely happy when the master did so. After this dream, he had no difficulty in understanding the most profound texts, which amazed everyone, including Patrul Rinpoche, when, at his request, Tenpai Nyima, then eight years old, taught *The Way of the Bodhisattva* to a large crowd in Dzachukha.

Even though he spoke of it only occasionally, throughout his life he had countless visions of previous masters and wisdom deities.

Tenpai Nyima studied with the greatest masters of his time, in addition to Patrul Rinpoche: Jamyang Khyentse Wangpo, Jamgön Kongtrul, Trama Tulku, Shechen Öntrul Thuthop Namgyal, and Tertön Sogyal Lerab Lingpa. He spent extended periods of times near Lama Mipham at Dzongsar Monastery.

From the age of twenty-one, he began composing many profound treatises, which fill the five (or seven, depending on the edition) volumes of his collected works.

From Dzogchen Monastery, Tenpai Nyima went to Dodrupchen Monastery, which had become his main seat, where he had the main temple rebuilt and a large stupa erected. There he taught continually for many years. In particular, he taught *The Way of the Bodhisattva* one hundred times, as he had promised Patrul Rinpoche, and the *Guhyagarbha Tantra* forty times.

Suffering from poor health, he spent the latter part of his life in retreat at Gephel Ritrö, a secluded place in what he would call the "Forest of Many

Birds," two miles above Dodrupchen Monastery. There he practiced, studied, and composed treatises praised by eminent scholars, meeting only a few people from time to time. His brother, noticing his relentless efforts, once asked him when he was ever going to stop. He replied, "When I have reached perfect enlightenment."

Many great masters came to see him and receive teachings, while he was in retreat, including Tertön Sögyal, who was a frequent visitor. In 1920, Dzongsar Khyentse Chökyi Lodrö came to receive teaching for several months. One day, as Chökyi Lodrö was alone with his teacher, receiving the empowerment of the Rigdzin Dupa ("Gathering of Vidyadharas," from the Longchen Nyingthig tradition), light rays began to shine forth from the main vase placed at the center of the mandala, and the room became filled with red light to such an extent that Chökyi Lodrö could hardly see Tenpai Nyima anymore. When the light subsided, Chökyi Lodrö realized that there was now a beautiful woman bedecked with ornaments, acting as a ritual attendant to Dodrupchen during the empowerment. Later, Tenpai Nyima told Chökyi Lodrö that the lady was none other than the protrectress of the Longchen Nyingthing teachings, Dorje Yudrönma. When receiving the Guru Yoga practice of the Tigle Gyachen,[237] Chökyi Lodrö saw Tenpai Nyima as Longchen Rabjam himself.

His contemporaries have described him as being almost childlike, very easygoing, without any pride. But the depth of his realization was such that even the most haughty person felt humbled in his presence. When he died, extraordinary signs appeared, including earth tremors and rainbows.

Jigme Trinley Özer, 1st Dodrupchen (1745–1821)

Born in the Do Valley of Golok, Jigme Trinley Özer ('jigs med phrin las 'od zer) was the foremost disciple of Rigdzin Jigme Lingpa and thus was the main holder of the Longchen Nyingthig lineage. He had been recognized by Jigme Lingpa as the mind-incarnation of Murum Tsenpo (one of King Trisong Detsen's sons) and given the name Jigme Trinley Özer. He took his refuge vow with the 2nd Shechen Rabjam, Gyurme Kunzang Namgyal (zhe chen rab 'jams 'gyur med kun bzang rnam rgyal, 1713–1769), who gave him the name Kunzang Shenphen (kun bzang gzhan phan).

He traveled four times to Central Tibet, meeting various eminent masters during his peregrinations. During his first journey, beginning at age twenty-one, he received teachings from Situ Chökyi Jungne (si tu chos kyi 'byung gnas) and the 5th embodiment of Gampopa, Jampel Trinley Wangpo (sgam po pa 'jam dpal 'phrin las dbang po).

After returning to Kham, he studied with Shechen Rabjam (founder of Shechen Monastery) and the 2nd Dzogchen Pönlop, Pema Sang-ngak Tendzin (rdzogs chen dpon slob padma gsang sngags bstan 'dzin, 1731–1805).

During his second pilgrimage to Central Tibet, he met the 13th Karmapa, Dundul Dorje (karma pa bdud 'dul rdo rje). Back at Kham, Trinley Özer spent four years in retreat in Tsering Phuk (Long-Life Cave), in the forest above Dzogchen Monastery. There, living in a very austere way, he practiced the Könchog Chidu (dkon mchog phyi 'dus) cycle of Rigdzin Jatshön Nyingpo. The cave earned its name from the fact that the protectress of long life, Tseringma (tshe ring ma), used to appear to Trinley Özer and bring him curd to sustain him. In that cave, Trinley Özer had many visions. He subsequently moved down to the Yamantaka Cave, where he practiced Chögyal Ratna Lingpa's Vajrakilaya rediscovered treasure[238] and Chakrasamvara according to the Dagpo tradition. This cave earned its name due to a vision Trinley Özer had of the wrathful deity Yamantaka, and his drawing of the Yamantaka mantra in the stone wall of the cave.

Trinley Özer felt boundless devotion toward Jigme Lingpa and decided to go to meet him. Thus, during his third journey to Central Tibet, he met his root master.

Jigme Lingpa immediately identified the new disciple as the principal heir for his Longchen Nyingthig mind treasures. He also gave him the transmission of his various writings and numerous other transmissions, such as that of the Lama Gongdu cycle of Sangye Lingpa.

Trinley Özer fell seriously ill in Central Tibet and was attended by Jigme Gyalwai Nyugu, who even carried him on his back for many days. After recovering, he returned to Kham and began to spread the Longchen Nyingthig teachings. He also started to build a small monastery at Shukchen Tago, also known as Drodön Lhundrup Ling, a few miles away from what would later become the main Dodrupchen Monastery.

On his fourth and last journey to Central Tibet, Jigme Trinley Özer traveled with another of Jigme Lingpa's close students, Kilung Jigme Ngotsar (who would become one of Patrul's teachers), and received many more teachings from their root master.

Another of his students was an Amdo king of Mongolian descent, Chinwang Ngawang Dargye (ching wang ngag dbang dar rgyas), who was the root teacher of the great yogi Shabkar Tsogdruk Rangdröl.

Jigme Trinley Özer established three main centers. The first was Shukchen Tago Drodön Lhundrup at his birthplace in the Dokhok Valley. In 1810, he established a second monastery-cum-retreat-center, Yarlung Pemakö Tsasum Khandro Ling at Drakchen Yarlung in Serta. It is in this third place that he lived during the later part of his life, and this was also to become the seat of the 3rd Dodrupchen, Tenpai Nyima. The third center was Arik Ragya Monastery on the banks of the Yellow River.

Jigme Trinley Özer was himself a tertön. Among his revelations is the mind treasure known as *The Supreme Path of Great Bliss* (*dam chos bde chen lam mchog*). He also wrote a concise commentary on Jigme Lingpa's *Treasury of Precious Qualities.*

The 1st Dodrupchen passed away amid many wondrous signs. Do Khyentse Yeshe Dorje identified the reincarnation of Jigme Trinley Özer as Jigme Phuntsok Jungne.

Karmai Khenpo Rinchen Dargye (ca. 1823–?)

Karmai Khenpo Rinchen Dargye (kar ma'i mkhan po rin chen dar rgyas) was recognized as the reincarnation of the great abbot Shantarakshita, who, together with Guru Padmasambhava and King Trisong Detsen, established Buddhism in Tibet. He was a disciple of the tertön Chokgyur Dechen Lingpa and was the abbot of Karma Gön Monastery in Kham.An exemplary holder of the Vinaya lineage, he was also an influential teacher and writer, with many commentaries on the New Treasures of Chokgyur Lingpa and collected works filling four volumes.

Kathok Situ (2nd), Chökyi Lodrö Orgyen Tenpa Namgyal (1820–1879?)

The 2nd Kathok Situ, Chökyi Lodrö Orgyen Tenpa Namgyal (ka thog si tu chos kyi blo gros bstan pa rnam rgyal), was the reincarnation of the 1st Kathok Situ, Orgyen Samdrup Jigme Chökyi Senge (o rgyan bsam grub jigs med chos kyi seng ge, mid-18th c.–early 19th c.), who had received teachings from Rigdzin Jigme Lingpa. He studied with Moktsa Tulku Chöying Dorje, Shechen Öntrul, Patrul Rinpoche, Jamyang Khyentse Wangpo, and many other masters. He was followed by the 3rd Kathok Situ, Chökyi Gyatso (si tu chos kyi rgya mtsho, 1880–1925).

After holding the throne of Kathok for a while, following Patrul Rinpoche's example he became a wandering hermit and did extensive retreats around the snow mountain range of Shar Shingo in Tromgo and, futher away, on the Kawa Karpo Mountain in Yunnan.

A story is told that one day a pilgrim came to Kathok Situ's cave along with the young niece of Jamyang Khyentse Wangpo. After receiving the lama's blessing, the girl offered him some tsampa.

Kathok Situ, now a hermit, said, "Well, I have nothing to put it in. Just put it here in a heap on this flat stone."

"Please accept the tsampa and the bag that contains it," she said.

In front of Situ there happened to be a special offering someone had just made to him. It was a rare kind of onyx marked with lines and eyes, called a *zi* (gzi)—a stone highly treasured in Tibet. Situ handed the young girl the *zi* stone, telling her she should wear it around her neck for protection and blessings.

At first, she refused to accept such a valuable gift, but Situ was adamant.

"You must keep it," he insisted. "It has great meaning."

After the young girl finished her pilgrimage, she went home. Not long after that, she heard that Kathok Situ had passed away. Later, that young woman's son was identified as the rebirth of Kathok Situ.

Khenchen Tashi Özer (1836–1910)

Khenchen Tashi Özer (mkhan chen bkra shis 'od zer) displayed natural compassion from an early age. He received his lay vows at Palpung Monastery from Jamgön Kongtrul Lodrö Thaye and, later, novice (*shramanera*) monastic vows from Khenchen Dawa Zangpo. He studied for a long time with Jamgön Kongtrul, receiving teachings on all the major and minor Tibetan traditions. At age twenty-four, he did a three-year retreat at Palpung under the guidance of Karma Ngedön Nyingpo, a great retreat master and scholar who was a close disciple of Jamgön Kongtrul.

After completing his retreat, he went to Patrul Rinpoche and received extensive instructions on *The Way of the Bodhisattva*. In particular, he received the explanations on the wisdom chapter seven times. At age twenty-seven he received full monastic vows (*gelong*) from Khenchen Dawa Zangpo. He then studied further with the 14th Karmapa, Thekchog Dorje (1798–1868), Jamyang Khyentse Wangpo, and Chokgyur Dechen Lingpa. After Khenchen

Dawa Zangpo passed away, Khenchen Tashi Özer became the main Khenpo of Palpung Monastery. He was an exemplary holder of the monastic tradition and ordained thousands of monks and nuns.

Khenchen Tashi Özer became the tutor of the 11th Tai Situ, Pema Wangchok Gyalpo (1886–1952), and a teacher to many masters of the late nineteenth and early twentieth centuries in Kham.

In his old age, Khenchen Tashi Özer retired to the Palpung retreat center, Tsadra Rinchen Drak, where Jamgön Kongtrul had spend a great part of his life.

Khenpo Kunzang Palden (Khenpo Kunpel, ca. 1862–1943)

Khenpo Kunzang Palden (mkhan po kun bzang dpal ldan), also known as Khenpo Kunpel, was born to a family at Gegong in Upper Getse, in the Dzachukha Valley, a few kilometers away from Patrul Rinpoche's birthplace.

He was distantly related to Patrul Rinpoche[239] and became one of his closest disciples from an early age. He was also a devoted student to Lama Mipham. Though Kunzang Palden was not from a poor family—his parents owned many sheep and yaks—his father was rather stingy and did not provide him with much sustenance once he became a monk. Kunzang Palden thus underwent great hardship in pursuit of his studies, often studying by moonlight or by the light of an incense stick due to his inability to afford oil for his lamp. In admiration, some of his fellow students would tease him, saying, "Normal people tend sheep under the sunlight. Kunzang Palden tends books under the moonlight."

He received his monastic vows from Önpo Tendzin Norbu (Gyalse Shenphen Thaye's nephew Önpo Tenga). He also studied at Shri Singha Philosophical College at Dzogchen Monastery, and with many great masters, including the 5th Dzogchen Rinpoche, Thubten Chökyi Dorje (rdzogs chen thub bstan chos kyi rdo rje, 1872–1935); Khenpo Pema Dorje, the 8th Abbot of Shri Singha (rdzogs chen mkhan chen padma badzra, 1807–1884); Jamyang Khyentse Wangpo ('jam dbyangs mkhyen brtse'i dbang po, 1820–1892); the 3rd Dodrupchen, Jigme Tenpai Nyima ('jigs med bstan pa'i nyi ma, 1865–1926); Mura Tulku Pema Dechen Zangpo (mu ra padma bde chen bzang po, d.u.); and Khenpo Shenga (Khenpo Shenphen Chökyi Nangwa, mkhan po gzhan phan chos kyi snang ba, 1871–1927).

Above all, Khenpo Kunpel accompanied Patrul Rinpoche for many years and received from him teachings and instructions on many texts, such as the *Guhyagarbha Tantra*. Having received many times detailed explanations upon *The Way of the Bodhisattva* from Patrul Rinpoche, Lama Mipham, and Önpo Tendzin Norbu, at the request of the 3rd Kathok Situ Chökyi Gyatso he composed an extensive commentary on Shantideva's text (*jam dbyangs bla ma'i zhal lung bdud rtsi'i thig pa*). This work has been translated into Western languages and was published in English as *The Nectar of Manjushri's Speech: A Detailed Commentary on Shantideva's Way of the Bodhisattva,* translated by the Padmakara Translation Group (Boston: Shambhala Publications, 2010). A manuscript of notes he took while receiving teaching from Patrul Rinpoche has also survived and is now kept at Shechen Monastery in Nepal in Dilgo Khyentse Rinpoche's library.

He was as determined to teach as he had been at first to study, and would say, "I promised Abu [Patrul Rinpoche] that I would teach continuously and that I would teach even to a pillar if no one happened to be around."

Khenpo Kunpel also wrote short biographies of Patrul Rinpoche (*Elixir of Faith;* see Sources section) and Lama Mipham, as well as a commentary on Mipham's *Beacon of Certainty* (*nges shes rin po che'i sgron me rtsa 'grel*) and *Account of the Origin of the Vinaya Rules* (*so thar 'dul ba'i gleng gzhi*).

In 1906, at the 3rd Kathok Situ's request and following the advice of Lama Mipham, he became the head of the newly founded philosophical college of Kathok Monastery, where he was assisted by Khenpo Ngawang Palzang (mkhan po ngag dbang dpal bzang, 1879–1941), also known as Khenpo Ngakchung. After spending three years in Kathok, he returned to Dzachukha, where he taught until his death.

Among his main students were the 3rd Kathok Situ, Chökyi Gyatso; the 3rd Shechen Gyaltsap, Pema Namgyal (zhe chen rgyal tshab padma rnam rgyal, 1871–1926); Dzongsar Khyentse Chökyi Lodrö (mkhyen brtse chos kyi blo gros, 1893–1959); Pöpa Tulku Do-ngak Tenpai Nyima (bod pa sprul sku mdo sngags bstan pa'i nyi ma, 1900/7–1959); and Kunu Rinpoche Tendzin Gyaltsen (khu nu rin po che bstan 'dzin rgyal mtshan, ca. 1894–1977).

Khenpo Pema Dorje (ca. 1807–1884)

Khenpo Pema Dorje (mkhan po padma rdo rje), also known as Khenpo Pedor and Khenpo Padma Vajra, was born in the Rudam area of Dzogchen.

He became a student of Dzogchen Mingyur Namkhai Dorje, Jigme Gyalwai Nyugu, Gyalse Shenphen Thaye, Patrul Rinpoche, and Sengtruk Pema Tashi (seng phrug padma bkra shis, d.u.). He was considered to be an incarnation of the great holder of the Kahma tradition Zurchen Chöying Rangdröl (zur chen chos dbyings rang grol, 1604–1669).

Khenpo Pema Dorje became abbot of the Shri Singha Philosophical College. Among his students were Önpo Tendzin Norbu, Lama Mipham, Jamyang Khyentse Wangpo, Adzom Drukpa, Tertön Sogyal Lerab Lingpa, Jigme Tenpai Nyima (3rd Dodrupchen), and Gyurme Pema Namgyal, the 3rd Shechen Gyaltsap (zhe chen rgyal tshab gyur med padma rnam rgyal, 1871–1926), who was Dilgo Khyentse Rinpoche's root teacher.

Khenpo Shenphen Chökyi Nangwa (Khenpo Shenga, 1871–1927)

Khenpo Shenphen Chökyi Nangwa (mkhan po gzhan phan chos kyi snang ba), widely known as Khenpo Shenga (mkhan po gzhan dga'), was born to the Gya Dema (rgya sde ma) family in Kham near Yongsar, a nomadic area between Dzachu and Jekundo. He was related to Ayang Thubten (a yang thub bstan), a tulku connected with Drubju Gön (sgrub brgyud mgon), a monastery of the Drigung Kagyu ('bri gung bka' brgyud) school.

The oral tradition recounts that Shenga was a hunter in his youth. He once wounded a pregnant doe, and as he was approaching her to give the final blow, his glance met the doe's eyes, filled with the fear of death. Suddenly great compassion and regret welled up in his mind. Realizing his wrongdoings, he renounced hunting and decided to practice the dharma. He went to the Dzogchen Monastery to study under Önpo Tendzin Norbu, himself a disciple of Patrul Rinpoche, whom Khenpo Shenga also met at a young age.

Blessed by a vision of the goddess Sarasvati, Shenga soon became one of the most learned teachers of his time. His collection of commentaries and subcommentaries, known as the *Thirteen Great Treatises,* relies entirely upon Indian commentaries and are renowned for their clarity. An exception among Nyingma masters, Khenpo Shenga was an exclusive defender of the view of "intrinsic emptiness" (rang stong), which can also be translated as "emptiness of self-nature" or "emptiness of its own essence." It is contrasted with the view of "extrinsic-emptiness" (gzan stong), which contends that ultimate reality is empty of all obscurations—empty of anything that is relative, conditioned, and conceptually fabricated—but that it is endowed with the qualities of the buddha nature (*tathagatagarbha*)

Teaching for many years at Dzogchen Shri Singha Philosophical College,

Khenpo Shenga had disciples belonging to all schools of Tibetan Buddhism. They included, among the Sakyapas, Dzongsar Ontö Khyenrab (rdzong gsar dbon stod mkhyen rab); among the Kagyupas, Pema Wangchok Gyalpo (11th Tai Situ, si tu padma dbang mchog rgyal po, 1886–1952); and among the Nyingmapas, Khenpo Lhagyal (mkhan po lha rgyal), Pema Thekchog Loden (padma theg mchog blo ldan), Thubten Nyendrak (thub bstan snyan grags) of Dzogchen Monastery, and Serkha Thubten Chödrak (gser kha thub bstan chos grags), who was said to have become even more learned than his teacher.

Khenpo Yönten Gyatso (Khenpo Yonga, 19th–20th c.)

Khenpo Yönten Gyatso (mkhan po yon tan rgya mtsho) of Gemang Monastery, also known as Khenpo Yonga, was a student of Patrul Rinpoche and Önpo Orgyen Tendzin Norbu of Gemang. He studied at Dzogchen and Shechen monasteries. Among his own students were Khenpo Thubga (Bathur Khenpo Thubten Chöphel, ba thur mkhan po thub sten chos dpal, 1886–1956), who was himself a teacher to Dilgo Khyentse Rinpoche, Khenpo Pema Wangyal, Khenpo Wangdi, Khenpo Wanglo (all three from Gemang), Khenpo Jigme Phuntsok, and many other eminent contemporary scholars. Khenpo Wanglo of Gemang (whose full name is Trinley Wangyal) was said to be his reincarnation. Khenpo Yonga wrote commentaries on the *Three Vows* of Ngari Panchen, and on the *Guhyagarbha Tantra,* and, in particular, a very clear and detailed two-volume commentary on Jigme Lingpa's *Treasury of Precious Qualities.*

Lama Mipham Rinpoche (1846–1912)

Lama Mipham (Mipham Jamyang Namgyal Gyatso, mi pham 'jam dbyangs rnam rgyal rgya mtsho)—also known as Jamgön Ju Mipham and Jampel Gyepai Dorje ('jam dpal gyes pa'i rdo rje)—was born in Dzachukha province of East Tibet on the banks of the Mekong River (Tib. Dzachu). He was gifted with exceptional intelligence, and it is said that at around the age of seven he memorized the root text of Ngari Penchen Pema Wangyal's commentary *Ascertaining the Three Vows* (*sdom gsum rnam nges*) simply by hearing a lama explain it in detail.

From the age of ten, Mipham began to compose texts on a variety of topics, including some of the most complex points of Buddhist philosophy. This earned him the nickname Little Scholar.

At the age of twelve, he joined Juniong Monastery in Dzachukha, a branch of Shechen Monastery. At fifteen, he met his first important spiritual master, Mingyur Namkhai Dorje, who predicted that he would become a highly accomplished practitioner.

Mipham then spent a year and a half in retreat in a hermitage above Juniong Monastery, where he had a vision of Manjushri, the Buddha of wisdom. Today, in Juniong, one can still see an image of Manjushri as well as Manjushri's mantra carved on two large flat stones by Mipham himself.

From the 5th Shechen Rabjam, Gyurme Kunzang Tenpai Nyima ('gyur med kun bzang bstan pa'i nyi ma, 1864–1909), at Shechen Monastery, Lama Mipham received the transmission for the practice of Amitayus, the Buddha of Boundless Life, according to the rediscovered treasure *Tsedrup Sangdu* (*tshe sgrub gsang 'dus*) of the tertön Ratna Lingpa. Later, he did a six-month retreat on each of the four main sadhana practices found in this terma. On this occasion, nectar spontaneously overflowed from the main vase containing the life substances at the center of the mandala, and many signs of accomplishment occurred.

At the retreat center above Shechen Monastery, while circumambulating the mani wall erected by the great siddha Sherab Yarphel (shes rab yar 'phel, d.u.), Lama Mipham recited one hundred thousand times an essential form of *Chanting the Names of Manjushri* in seven verse lines, revealed as a terma by Guru Chökyi Wangchuk (guru chos kyi dbang phyug, 1212–1273).

At eighteen, he made a pilgrimage to Central Tibet, where he had deep spiritual experiences. Upon returning to Kham, he received teaching from Patrul Rinpoche on *The Way of the Bodhisattva* for five days and fully mastered the deeper meaning of the text.

He then spent years in the presence of Jamyang Khyentse Wangpo, whom he considered to be his root master, and received countless empowerments and teachings from him. He also studied with Jamgön Kongtrul Lodrö Thaye, Khenpo Pema Dorje, Jamyang Loter Wangpo (who later also became Mipham's student), and other teachers from all schools.

Lama Mipham's connection with Jamyang Khyentse Wangpo extended to many past lives. When Khyentse Wangpo was Jigme Lingpa, Lama Mipham was his disciple Chöje Drakphugpa, a great scholar from Tsang Lathö who requested Jigme Lingpa to compose an extensive commentary on his

Treasury of Precious Qualities. He stayed for three years in retreat under Jigme Lingpa's guidance at Tsering Jong.

At the entreaties of Khyentse Wangpo, Mipham began composing large commentaries on some of the major Buddhist philosophical treatises emphasizing the view of the Nyingma school. Khyentse Wangpo once said, "In our time, there is no one on this earth more learned than Lama Mipham." The current edition of Mipham Rinpoche's collected works fills twenty-seven large volumes.[240]

In Palpung, Lama Mipham met Khenchen Tashi Özer, one of the most learned scholars of his time and they became close spiritual friends.

Lama Mipham was also a greatly accomplished practitioner. He had many visions of wisdom deities, displayed miraculous powers on many occasions, and had an ultimate realization of the Great Perfection.

Once, while traveling through Kham, he happened to walk alongside a learned Geshe. At some point the Geshe told Mipham teasingly, "You Nyingma tantric practitioners boast about the power of mantra recitation. You even claim that by reciting a certain mantra, you can make an eagle come to you. *Ha ha!*"

Mipham said nothing, but a few moments later, he blew some mantras on his thumb and raised it in the air. Within no time, an eagle swooped down and picked up the Geshe's hat in his claws.

One another occasion, Mipham remained thirteen years in retreat at Karmo Taktsang—the White Den of the Tigress, a place sacred to Dorje Drolö, one of Padmasambhava's Eight Manifestations—in a valley near Dzongsar Monastery. There, he accomplished the practices of Vajrakilaya, Hayagriva, and, in particular, Yamantaka, a wrathful aspect of Manjushri, according to the rediscovered terma of the twelfth-century master Gya Zhangtrom.[241]

One day, as Lama Mipham was performing a ceremony to remove obstacles, focused on the Black Hayagriva, someone told him, "It is said that the practice of Hayagriva is particularly powerful. The text of the practice itself describes the many signs of accomplishment that come from it." Mipham Rinpoche said nothing. At the end of the ceremonies, when the tormas were thrown at a rocky hillside across Karmo Taktsang, Lama Mipham gazed intensely at the hill and made a symbolic gesture (*mudra*) while reciting loudly the deity's mantra. The next morning the whole hill had collapsed.

While composing philosophical treatises, Mipham always kept in front of him a small statue of Manjushri. On other occasions, when the subject was particularly difficult, light rays would beam from the heart of the statue to Mipham's heart. After this, any hesitation he had would be clarified.

At Gothi hermitage above Sakar,[242] as well as in Chamdo Dzong, Lama Mipham also practiced extensively the tantra of the Kalachakra. Once, during a cold winter, while being in Gothi hermitage, Lama Mipham returned from a short walk with a beautiful, fresh blue flower in his hand. There are indeed no flowers in this area in the dead of the winter. The few people who were living at the hermitage were puzzled and asked Lama Mipham how could he have found a flower at this time of the year. After pausing for a while, Mipham answered, "It was given to me by Rigden, the King of Shambhala." Lama Mipham was an accomplished practitioner of the Kalachakra, and he told the people that he had experienced some kind of vision in which he visited the hidden land of Shambhala. But obviously, this was more than a mere vision.[243] A few years later, Mipham Rinpoche passed away at Gothi hermitage, sitting in a meditative posture, gazing into space.

Among Lama Mipham's many disciples, some of the most eminent were the 3rd Shechen Gyaltsap, Gyurme Pema Namgyal (Dilgo Khyentse Rinpoche's root teacher), to whom Mipham Rinpoche left all this books; his heart-disciple and close attendant, Lama Ösel (dbang phyug 'od gsal 'ja lus rdo rje); Khenpo Kunzang Palden; Önpo Tendzin Norbu; Jigme Tenpai Nyima (3rd Dodrupchen); Tertön Sogyal Lerab Lingpa (gter ston bsod rgyal las rab gling pa, 1856–1926); Thubten Chökyi Dorje (5th Dzogchen Rinpoche, thub bstan chos kyi rdo rje, 1872–1935); Pema Thekchog Tenpai Gyaltsen (5th Shechen Rabjam); Chökyi Gyatso (3rd Kathok Situ, ka thog si tu chos kyi rgya mtsho, 1880–1925); Adzom Drukpa; Tokden Shakya Shri; Jamyang Loter Wangpo; and Geshe Bari Lobsang Rabsel (dpa' ris blo bzang rab gsal, 1840–?), who first debated with Mipham Rinpoche on his interpretation of the ninth (wisdom) chapter of the *Bodhicharyavatara,* and then displayed deep admiration for his wisdom.

Longchen Rabjam (Longchenpa, 1308–1364)

The "omniscient" (*kunkhyen/kun mkhyen*) Longchen Rabjam, known as Longchenpa, is considered to have been the main exponent of the Nyingma tradition in all of history, since Guru Padmasambhava.

He was born in Central Tibet as the son of the tantric yogi Tenpa Sung. At the time of his conception, his mother dreamed of a sun placed on the head of a lion illuminating the entire world. At his birth, the dharma protectress Remati appeared in the form of a black woman. Holding the baby in her arms, she said, "I will protect him," handed him back to his mother, and disappeared. He was named Dorje Gyaltsen.

Longchen Rabjam is said to be the incarnation of Lhacham Pemasel, a daughter of King Trisong Detsen to whom Guru Padmasambhava had entrusted the teachings of the Khandro Nyingthig, the Heart Essence of the Dakinis.

His mother died when he was nine years old, and his father died when he was twelve. Dorje Gyaltsen went to Samye Monastery, where he received the novice vows from Khenpo Samdrup Rinchen, and was named Tsultrim Lodrö.

At sixteen, he had a vision of the goddess of learning, Sarasvati, who prophesied that he would effortlessly master all the teachings of the Buddha.

At nineteen, he entered the philosophical college of Sangpu Neutok where he became learned in Buddhist philosophy, logic, grammar, and poetry, as well as in Sanskrit.

He received countless empowerments and instructions upon the outer and inner tantras from various eminent masters, including Shönnu Gyalpo, Shönnu Dorje, Lama Dampa Sönam Gyaltsen (the throne holder of Sakya, bla ma dam pa bsod nams rgyal mtshan, 1312–1375), and the 3rd Karmapa, Rangjung Dorje (karma pa rang byung rdo rje, 1284–1339).

After some years, having become disgusted with the rude behavior of some scholars from Kham, Longchenpa decided to leave for solitary places, to the great dismay of some of his fellow students and teachers. He then spent five months in "dark retreat" (done in complete darkness) in a cave above Cha Valley in Uru. At the end of his retreat, he had the vision of a dakini who prophesied that he would soon meet his root master, Rigdzin Kumaradza (rig 'dzin kumaraja, also known as ye shes gzhon nu, 1266–1343).

At twenty-seven years of age, at the very moment Longchenpa met Rigdzin Kumaradza in the highlands of Yartökyam above Samye, he felt boundless devotion and gained inner certainty that he had finally met his root guru. He perceived Kumaradza as being the great pandita Vimalamitra in person.

Kumaradza was a disciple of the mahasiddha Melong Dorje and the lineage holder of the Vima Nyingthig teachings, the Heart Essence of Vimalamitra.

The night before Longchenpa arrived, Kumaradza dreamed that a divine bird came with a large flock that carried away Kumaradza's books in all directions. Kumaradza felt that this dream was announcing someone who was destined to hold his lineage. Later, in a dream, Vimalamitra told him that Longchenpa would become the main holder of his teachings.

Together with the Karmapa, Longchenpa accompanied Kumaradza and his other disciples for two years, receiving all the pith instructions of the Great Perfection. They lived in harsh and ascetic ways, as Kumaradza kept on moving from place to place to avoid becoming attached to any particular location. Longchenpa had very little food and used a ragged bag as both mattress and blanket to protect himself from the cold winter. Eventually, Kumaradza having bestowed all the Nyingthig teachings upon Longchen Rabjam, he proclaimed him his spiritual successor.

For the six following years, Longchenpa remained in retreat in various caves around Chimphu, above Samye Monastery. He had many visions and meditative experiences, and went back regularly to Kumaradza to seek his guidance. On five occasions, even though he owned very few possessions, Longchenpa offered all of them to his master as a sign of utter renunciation and devotion.

At thirty-one, while still in retreat, Longchenpa began bestowing empowerment and instructions on the Vima Nyingthig to his own disciples.

Soon after, his close disciple Özer Gocha found a copy of the Khandro Nyingthig, the Dzogchen cycle transmitted by Guru Rinpoche to Yeshe Tsogyal in Drigung Titro cave. The Khandro Nyingthig had been revealed as terma by Longchenpa's previous incarnation, Pema Ledrel Tsel (padma las 'brel rtsal, 1291–1315). Longchenpa was also presented the same text by the dharma protectress Shenpo Sodrupma. To stress the importance of receiving teachings through an unbroken transmission, Longchenpa also went to receive the transmission of the Khandro Nyingthig from Gyalse Lekpai Gyaltsen, a disciple of Pema Ledrel Tsel.

Then, at thirty-three, as he gave the transmission of the Khandro Nyingthig, some of the disciples saw Longchen Rabjam appearing in a sambhogakaya form, amid a rain of flowers, while beams and circles of lights were seen all over the mountain. Longchenpa himself had a vision of Guru Padmasambhava and his consort Yeshe Tsogyal giving him empowerments and entrusting him once more with the lineage of the Khandro Nyingthig. Guru Rinpoche gave Longchenpa the initiation name Orgyen Drime Özer (o rgyan dri med 'od zer), and Yeshe Tsogyal gave him the name Dorje Ziji (rdo rje gzi brjid).

Then, following the entreaty of the dharma protectress Yudrönma, Longchenpa went to stay in a cave at Kangri Thökar, high above the Kyichu River, south of Lhasa. There he achieved the ultimate realization of the Great Perfection and composed many of his most important treatises, including some of his famed *Seven Treasuries.*

He also had visions of the primordial Buddha Samantabhadra and of Vimalamitra. The latter urged him to extract the quintessence of the Vima Nyingthig teachings. Accordingly, Longchenpa wrote the Lama Yangthig. Vimalamitra also asked Longchenpa to restore the Uru Shayi Lhakhang temple that was built by Nyang Tingdzin Zangpo, one of the main disciples of both Guru Rinpoche and Vimalamitra.

Nearby, at Drigung, there was a powerful leader, Gompa Kunrin, who was threatening the authority of Tai Situ Changchup Gyaltsen (1302–1371), who was then ruling Central Tibet. There was a prediction that a son of demons, with a body mark resembling a sword, was going to go to hell unless an emanation of Manjushri would subjugate him. Gompa Kunrin recognized himself in this prediction and came to think that Longchenpa was this emanation. He invited him and became his disciple. Soon, thanks to Longchenpa's influence, Gompa Kunrin gave up his intention to wage war against Changchup Gyaltsen. But this did not prevent Changchup Gyaltsen from suspecting that Longchenpa was taking sides against him, and he sent troops to kill him.

Longchen Rabjam decided to seek refuge in Bhutan. There he had countless disciples and established eight hermitages and monasteries throughout the country. At his main seat, Tharpa Ling Monastery in Bumthang province, he wrote part of the *Seven Treasuries.* There, Longchenpa had a daughter and a son with his spiritual consort, the Bhutanese Kyipala. His son, Gyalse Tulku Trakpa Özer (rgyal sras sprul sku grags pa 'od zer, 1356–1409?), better known as Thugse Dawa (thugs sras zla ba), became a great scholar and one the main holders of Longchenpa's teachings.

Later, Tai Situ realized that Longchen Rabjam had done the right thing by dissuading Gompa Kunrin to wage war. He apologized, requested Longchen Rabjam to return to Tibet, and became his devoted disciple.

On one occasion, Longchenpa spent two weeks in Lhasa, where he was received with great pomp. He gave bodhisattva vows and many teachings to huge gatherings of devotees. He then gave extensive teachings on the Great Perfection in various places to thousands of disciples.

At the age of fifty-six, Longchenpa dictated his spiritual testament, entitled *Trima Mepai Ö* (Immaculate Radiance), which is included in the Khandro Yangthig.

He then went to Chimphu hermitage and was soon asked to come down to Samye Monastery, where he gave extensive empowerments on the Great Perfection. During that time he became increasingly ill and announced that he was going to pass away. On the 18th day of the 12th lunar month of the Female Water Hare Year (January 24, 1364, according to the calendar system quoted in the texts, and not 1363 as often given), Longchenpa sat in a meditation posture and his mind dissolved into absolute space. While his body was being preserved for twenty-five days, many miraculous signs occurred. When his body relic was finally cremated, the earth trembled three times and a loud sound was heard seven times. In the ashes, his heart, eyes, and brain were found together, unburned by the fierce fire of the cremation.

Various catalogues of Longchen Rabjam's writings list up to three hundred texts. His main writings are gathered into several collections: the *Seven Treasuries* (*mdzod bdun*), which present the whole scope of Buddhist philosophy and practice; the *Trilogy of Resting at Ease* (*ngal gso skor gsum*), which presents the graded path of practice; the *Trilogy of Natural Liberation* (*rang grol skor gsum*), focused on the practice of the Great Perfection; the *Trilogy of Dispelling Darkness* (*mun sel skor gsum*), consisting of commentaries on the *Guhyagarbha Tantra;* and the *Heart Essence in Four Parts* (*snying thig ya bzhi*), a most profound and complete presentation of the Great Perfection practice. The four parts of the Nyingthig Yazhi comprise (1) the *Khandro Nyingthig* (*mkha' 'gro snying thig*) given by Guru Rinpoche to Yeshe Tsogyal and found as a terma by Pema Ledrel Tsel; (2) the essence of the former, condensed by Longchenpa as the Khandro Yangthig (mkha' 'gro yang tig); (3) the Vima Nyingthig (bi ma snying thig) of Vimalamitra, received in a vision by Chetsun Senge Wangchok (lce btsun seng ge dbang phyug, 11th–12th c.); and (4) the Lama Yangthig (bla ma yang tig), which is the essence of the Vima Nyingthig written by Longchenpa. Finally, there is the Zabmo Yangthig (zab mo yang tig), in which Longchenpa wrote down the quintessence of all, so that it is not counted as a fifth part. Two volumes of miscellaneous writings (*gsung thor bu*) have also survived.

Longchenpa had countless disciples and is said to have reincarnated at various times in history, notably in Bhutan as the Bhutanese tertön Pema Lingpa (padma gling pa, 1450–1521).

Mingyur Namkhai Dorje (1793–1870)

Mingyur Namkhai Dorje (mi 'gyur nam mkha'i rdo rje) was the fourth incarnation of Dzogchen Pema Rigdzin, the founder of Dzogchen Monastery. He was enthroned as abbot by Namkha Tsewang Chokdrup, from whom he received numerous teachings.

At the age of seven, he manifested clear recollections of his past lives. From age twelve, for seven years in a row, he spent six months in retreat every year.

He was also a disciple of three of the main students of Jigme Lingpa: Dodrupchen Jigme Trinley Özer, Jigme Gyalwai Nyugu, and Jigme Gocha of Barjung.

Mingyur Dorje was also a student of the 3rd Rigdzin Nyima Trakpa, Mingyur Pende Gyatso (mi 'gyur phan bde rgya mtsho, 1772–1817); the 1st Shechen Gyaltsap, Pema Sang-gnak Tendzin Chögyal (rgyal tshab padma gsang sngags bstan 'dzin chos rgyal, 1760–1817); and the 3rd Shechen Rabjam, Rigdzin Paljor Gyatso Thubten Nyinche (rig 'dzin dpal 'byor rgya mtsho thub bstan nyin byed, 1771–1809).

He was introduced to the nature of mind by Do Khyentse Yeshe Dorje and thereafter became free of hope and fear, and ceased to discriminate between "good" and "bad" situations, feeling, and so forth, experiencing them in the state of "one taste."

He also became quite unpredictable and behaved in unconventional ways. He would sometimes teach with ease the most difficult texts, while at other times he explained the simplest texts in a way that seemed strange to some listeners because it had little to do with their meaning. Perhaps he was disconnecting from the text and teaching from his heart.

In 1842, an earthquake destroyed Dzogchen Monastery. Mingyur Dorje was in Derge and had a prophetic dream the same night. The next morning, he announced that he should return immediately to Dzogchen, for people needed him there. He was persuaded to stay in Derge to attend important ceremonies that had just begun. A few days later, the news of the earthquake finally reached Derge, and people realized why Mingyur Dorje had been in a hurry to return to the monastery. The King of Derge offered to sponsor the reconstruction of the monastery, which was carried out by Gyalse Shenphen Thaye.

When the bloodthirsty chieftain from Nyakrong, Gonpo Namgyal, arrived in Dzogchen with his troops, Pönlop Rinpoche—in an effort to prevent an attack on the monastery—urged Mingyur Dorje to praise the warlord and tell him how poor Dzogchen Monastery was, although that was not quite the case. When Gonpo Namgyal entered, Mingyur Dorje spoke as he had been instructed, and concluded by saying candidly, "This is what Dzogchen Pönlop told me to tell you."

Gonpo Namgyal asked him, "Where will I be reborn?" Mingyur Dorje replied without hesitation: "In hell." Impressed by the fearless straightforwardness of this master, Gonpo Namgyal, instead of confiscating the properties of Dzogchen Monastery and harming its people, offered a silver ingot to Mingyur Dorje and requested him to pray for him when died.

Since Mingyur Dorje did not worry much about anything, he found himself surrounded by notoriously careless attendants. When he became old, on a sunny winter afternoon, one of his attendants installed him on a chair on the terrace outside his residence. When the freezing night came, he forgot to bring the abbot back inside. The next morning, when it was realized that Mingyur Dorje was not in his room, his attendants found him still seated on the terrace, with numerous blisters on his forearm. Mingyur Dorje exclaimed to his attendants, "Look, look, some pink and blue flowers have blossomed on my arms. Isn't that peculiar?"

Among Mingyur Dorje's disciples were Patrul Rinpoche, Lama Mipham, Adzom Drukpa, Jamyang Khyentse Wangpo, Jamgön Kongtrul, and Chokgyur Dechen Lingpa.

After his passing, Gyalse Shenphen Thaye succeeded him as the abbot of Dzogchen Monastery.

Minyak Kunzang Sönam (1823–1901)

Minyak Kunzang Sönam (mi nyag kun bzang bsod nams), a.k.a. Thubten Chökyi Trakpa (thub bstan chos kyi grags pa), was a great Geluk scholar, and a very close disciple of Patrul Rinpoche, whom he accompanied in his travels for many years. Originally from Belo Hermitage (Belo Ritrö) in Garthar Dzong district, he was named after the Minyak area of Kham. After receiving the teachings on *The Way of the Bodhisattva* numerous times from Patrul Rinpoche, he wrote an extensive commentary upon it, as well as a commentary on *Thirty-seven Practices of a Bodhisattva* by Gyalse Ngulchu Thogme (rgyal sras rngul chu thogs med, 1295–1369).

Nyoshul Lungtok Tenpai Nyima (1829–1901)

Nyoshul Lungtok Tenpai Nyima (smyo shul lung rtogs bstan pa'i nyi ma) was born into the Nyoshul family of the Mukpo Dong line in the kingdom of Derge. From an early age he showed an exceptional inclination toward the Dharma. He first studied at Dzogchen Monastery with Gyalse Shenphen Thaye from whom he received monastic ordination and the name Lungtok Tenpai Nyima.

He spent twenty-eight years near Patrul Rinpoche, of whom he is considered to be the closest disciple, and received from him the teachings on the *Bodhicharyavatara* no fewer than eighty times. He was regarded as an incarnation of the great abbot Shantarakshita (725–788), who helped establish Buddhism in Tibet, together with Guru Padmasambhava and King Trisong Detsen.

Lungtok also received teachings from Jamyang Khyentse Wangpo, including Longchenpa's Nyingthig Yazhi. When Lungtok was at Dzongsar, he offered teachings on the *Yeshe Lama,* the main Dzogchen teaching of Jigme Lingpa, to a group of masters that included Jamyang Loter Wangpo and Lama Mipham.

When Lungtok turned fifty, in accordance with the instructions of Patrul Rinpoche, he returned to his homeland and settled in an encampment on the top of Pema Rito Mountain in the region of Tromtar.

In Tromtar he taught the young Khenpo Ngakchung and many other disciples. Patrul Rinpoche predicted that Nyoshul would meet an incarnation of Vimalamitra. This prediction turned out to refer to Khenpo Ngawang Palzang, also known as Khenpo Ngaga or Khenpo Ngakchung, who became his main student.

Later, he spent nine years at the dharma encampment of Nyakla Pema Dundul (nyag bla padma bdud 'dul, 1816–1872), where he taught some of the tertön's foremost disciples, including Nyakla Rangrik Dorje (nyag bla rang rig rdo rje, 1847–1903).

Önpo Orgyen Tendzin Norbu (Önpo Tenga, 1851–1910)

Önpo Orgyen Tendzin Norbu (o rgyan bstan 'dzin nor bu),[244] also known as Önpo Tenga, was the nephew (*önpo* / dbon po) of the great master Gyalse Shenphen Thaye, who took care of him from an early age. At age thirteen, he received from his uncle the novice monastic vows, instructions on the preliminary practice of the Longchen Nyingthig, and many other teachings. When Önpo Tenga was fifteen, Gyalse Shenphen Thaye passed away.[245] After he prayed with intense grief and devotion, Shenphen Thaye appeared to him in a vision, sitting radiantly upon a cloud, dressed as an Indian pandita. He uttered these words: "Don't grieve, my son! Even if I had stayed longer, I would not have had any deeper instructions to give you." He then gave Tendzin Norbu a most profound instruction on the view, meditation, practice, and fruit of Dzogchen. Önpo Tenga's spirits were greatly lifted.

At Dzogchen Monastery, he then received from Mingyur Namkhai Dorje the transmission of most of Gyalwa Longchenpa's writtings, including the *Seven Treasures* and the empowerments upon the Nyingthig Yazhi.

In 1868, when he turned seventeen, he met Patrul Rinpoche, who was to become his main teacher and whom he followed until the master's death in 1887.

He also received extensive teachings from Jamyang Khyentse Wangpo, Khenpo Pema Dorje, Terchen Chokgyur Dechen Lingpa, Drupchen Sönam Palge, Minyak Kunzang Sönam and others. He would say, with tears in his eyes, "Regarding their qualities, all my great teachers are indistinguishable, but as far as their kindness to me is concerned, no one in the three worlds of existence can be compared to the most kind Abu [Patrul Rinpoche]."

For many years, Önpo Tenga followed Patrul Rinpoche to various secluded places. He spent altogether twelve years in retreat. He had visions of Guru Padmasambhava and many wisdom deities, and attained the ultimate realization of the practice of the Great Perfection. He was also a living example of flawless monastic discipline.

Although he longed to spend the rest of his life as a wandering hermit like his teacher, Patrul Rinpoche instructed him to teach others. He did so tirelessly. Just to give a few examples from Khenpo Shenga, who wrote Önpo Tenga's biography, he taught no fewer than two hundred times *The Way of the Bodhisattva*, twenty-five times the *Root Verses on the Middle Way* (Skt. *Mulamadhyamakakarika;* Tib. *dbu ma tsa ba shes rab*), nineteen times Chandrakirti's *Entrance to the Middle Way* (Skt. *Madhyamakavatara-nama;* Tib. *dbu ma 'jug pa*), thirty-nine times the *Ornament of the Sutras* (*mdo sde rgyan*), thirty-eight times commentaries upon *The Three Vows* (*Domsum / sdom gsum*), twenty times the *Guhyagarbha Tantra*, nine times *The Wish-Fulfilling Treasury* (*Yishyin Dzö / yid bzhin mdzod*) by Longchenpa, thirteen times *Resting at Ease in the Nature of Mind* (*sems nyid ngal gso*) and no less than forty times the *Treasury of Precious Qualities.*

From 1883, Patrul Rinpoche stopped giving public teachings and referred people to receive instruction from Önpo Tenga.

After Patrul Rinpoche's death, Önpo Tenga compiled in six volumes all available writings of Patrul Rinpoche. He then entrusted Khenpo Shenga to have them carved on woodblocks at Shri Singha Philosophical College at Dzogchen Monastery. Khenpo Losel did the proofreading. Mipham Rinpoche wrote a detailed table of contents.[246]

Among Önpo Tenga's many disciples, we may mention his heart-disciple, the great yogi Kunga Palden, who spent most of his life in a cave-hermitage above the Middle Lake of Dzogchen Glacier Wilderness (Dzogchen Kangtrö), as well as Khenpo Trelo from Dzogchen.

In his sixtieth year, in 1910, he fell sick. Despite all supplications from his disciples and other masters to live longer, he told them, "My teachers prophesied that I would live to be sixty. Now that I have reached that age, all I can do is to prolong my life for one month."

Even though he was afflicted with intense pain, he told his disciples, "When the time to die comes, if you apply the pith instructions of the two omniscient masters [Gyalwa Longchenpa and Rigdzin Jigme Lingpa], it is certain that you will not be bothered at all by physical pain."

At that time, he had many visions and saw the space around him constantly filled with radiant forms of deities appearing in the midst of multicolored dots of light. He dreamed of messengers inviting him to come to Zandokpalri, the pure land of Guru Padmasambhava. Yet, he commented, "What's the point of trusting all these deluded perceptions?"

A few days before passing away, he said, "Throughout my life, all my activities have been dedicated to serving the Buddha dharma and helping others to transform themselves. Now I have understood that birth and death are nothing more than conventions and are devoid of true existence. Because of that, my mind is perfectly relaxed and at ease, and I am free from hopes and fears. But those whose minds are obscured and cling to the solidity of appearances, those who keep endeavoring in the affairs of this life, at the time of death they will carry a burden of negative actions as heavy as a mountain and will have to go without dharma, full of sadness and torments. When I think of them, I feel unbearable compassion."

At some point, he looked at the astrological calendar and said that for some days the celestial configuration was not auspicious, but that the fifth of the lunar calendar was a good date to pass away.

On that date, he sat upright in the meditation posture of the sages, with the right hand in the subduing *mudra* and the left hand resting in the equanimity *mudra* in his lap, in the way Guru Padmasambhava is depicted. He looked up, gazing into absolute space, and passed away.

On that day, though the blue sky was immaculate, domes of rainbow light were seen, and a rumbling sound was heard several times from the western direction.

The cremation and all related rituals were conducted by Mura Tulku. Thousands of disciples and devotees came to pay homage. Mipham Rinpoche advised that a stupa be made to shelter the master's relics. This was done, chiefly with the support of Jedrung Tulku from Lingtsang and the son of the Dilgo family from Sakar (Dilgo Khyentse Rinpoche's father).

Önpo Tenga used to say, "Because we don't have firm conviction in the karmic law of cause and effect, we don't meet with much success in our spiritual practice. If, however, we were to gain such conviction, we could become like our most kind teacher, Patrul Rinpoche."

Pema Dechen Zangpo, 3rd Mura Tulku (19th–20th c.)

Mura Tulku Pema Dechen Zangpo (mu ra sprul sku padma bde chen bzang po) was recognized by Dzogchen Mingyur Namkhai Dorje as the 3rd incarnation of Mura Rigdzin Gyatso, a master from the Dzachukha area, celebrated for his boundless compassion; he was said to have attained the ultimate realization of the Great Perfection. Dilgo Khyentse Rinpoche, who in his youth met Mura Tulku, recounted a few anecdotes about this great master.[247] Once, after having been first seized, then released, by ruthless bandits, he told his students, "In the *Yeshe Lama* [the famous Dzogchen teachings by Jigme Lingpa], it says that someone who has reached the culminating point of the 'exhaustion of phenomena in the absolute' would not experience any fear even when surrounded by a hundred mercenaries threatening him with death. You know, this is exactly what happened to me." Mura Tulku was very close to his spiritual consort, nicknamed "Apu" (an appellation normally used for a man), and used to say that without her he would not survive long. It so happened that she died while having gone a few hours away from Mura Tulku's residence. The disciples were very worried about breaking the news to Mura Tulku. Finally, a few close disciples came together and one of them said to their master, in a very somber tone, "We are sorry, but we have very bad news to tell you: Apu has passed away." Then they waited in silence. Mura Tulku looked at them and said, "Why are you looking so despondent as if something completely unthinkable and catastrophic has happened? Don't you remember the teachings on death and impermanence that I have been giving you time and time again? What kind of practitioners are you?"

Mura Tulku was a disciple of Patrul Rinpoche. He also extended the Mura Mani Wall, the construction of which was started by the Mura Rigdzin Gyatso. This wall was destroyed by the Communist Chinese but has now been rebuilt into a half-mile-long wall of stones carved with mantras and Buddhist scriptures.

Among Mura Tulku's disciples were Thupden Chökyi Dorje (5th Dzogchen Rinpoche), Lama Mipham Rinpoche, Gyurme Pema Namgyal (3rd Shechen Gyaltsap), Khenpo Yönten Gyatso, Khenpo Kunpel, Khenpo Thubga, and Dilgo Khyentse Rinpoche.

Rogza Sönam Palge (18th–19th c.)

Drupwang ("Powerful Siddha") Rogza Sönam Palge (grub dbang rog bza' bsod rnam dpal dge) was born in the district of Serta Rogza in Golok. His main teachers were Jigme Trinley Özer (1st Dodrupchen) and Do Khyentse Yeshe Dorje, who bestowed upon him the full transmission of the Longchen Nyingthig teachings. Rogza Palge became especially accomplished in the practices of *tsalung* (yogic practices on the prana and nadis) and the Great Perfection.

After the passing away of Trinley Özer, Rogza Palge followed Do Khyentse for many years, as the latter was moving around as a wandering yogi throughout Golok and Amdo, sometimes with Rogza Palge as his attendant and disciple. Do Khyentse considered Rogza Palge more like a dharma brother than a disciple, since they had the same root teacher.

It is said that, thanks to his capacity of swift running, Rogza Palge was able to catch deer and wild Tibetan asses (*kyang*) and mount them.

After leaving Do Khyentse, Drupwang Sönam Palge spent many years in retreat above Karchung Khormo Olu (Patrul Rinpoche's birthplace) and in other areas nearby, where he also taught some fortunate disciples, including Patrul Rinpoche, Dola Jigme Kalzang, and Önpo Tenga.

Sönam Palge spent the latter part of his life at the monastery of Rigdzin Chime Drupa Shedrub Gatsel in Upper Getse in Dzachukha.

Like Patrul Rinpoche, Sönam Palge adopted a very inconspicuous demeanor, dressing like a layperson and shunning honors and recognition.

Although there is no written biography of Sönam Palge, it is said that he passed away at eighty years of age at the village of Mamo Nakha in Doring Valley.

Shabkar Tsogdruk Rangdröl (1781–1851)

Shabkar Tsogdruk Rangdröl (zhabs dkar tshogs drug rang grol) was born among the Nyingma yogis of the Rekong region in Amdo. These yogis were renowned for their mastery of the Secret Mantrayana practices and gathered in the thousands to engage in meditations and rituals. They were much admired, and sometimes feared, for their magical powers. They were also famous for their hair, often six feet long, which they wore coiled on the top of their heads.

From a very early age, Shabkar showed a strong inclination toward the contemplative life. Even his childhood games were related to the teachings of Lord Buddha. By the age of six or seven, he had already developed a strong desire to practice. Visions, similar to those experienced in advanced Dzogchen practice, came to him naturally.

At fifteen years of age, Shabkar felt a strong desire to "pray to the precious master Guru Padmasambhava, the source of blessings." He recited one million Vajra Guru mantras and had auspicious dreams, such as of flying through the air, seeing the sun and moon rising simultaneously, and finding jewel-treasures. "From then on," he wrote, "by the grace of Guru Rinpoche I became filled with intense devotion to the Guru, affection toward my dharma friends, compassion for sentient beings, and pure perception toward the teachings. I had the good fortune to accomplish without obstacles whatever dharma practice I undertook."

Shabkar then met Jamyang Gyatso, a master whom he venerated greatly and of whom he later had visions and dreams.

Despite his deep affection for his mother and respect for his family, Shabkar managed to resist their repeated requests that he marry. He eventually left home in order to pursue his spiritual aims wholeheartedly. Determined to renounce worldly concerns, Shabkar received full monastic ordination at the age of twenty and entered a meditation retreat. He let his hair grow long again, as was customary for retreatants, who did not waste time in nonessential activities. As a sign of having accomplished certain yogic practices, he wore a white shawl rather than the traditional red shawl, although he continued to wear the patched lower robe characteristic of a fully ordained monk. This rather unconventional attire occasionally attracted sarcastic comments from strangers, to whom Shabkar would reply with humorous songs.

Shabkar left his native land behind and traveled south of Rekong to meet his main teacher, the Dharma King Chögyal Ngakyi Wangpo (chos rgyal ngag gi dbang po, 1736–1807). Ngakyi Wangpo was a learned and accomplished Mongolian king, said to be an incarnation of Marpa the Translator, who had renounced the remnants of the vast kingdom of Gushri Khan and become a prominent Nyingma master.

After receiving complete instructions from the Dharma King, Shabkar practiced for five years in the wilderness of Tseshung, where his meditation experiences and realization flourished. He then meditated for three years on a small island, Tsonying ("Heart of the Lake") in the Kokonor, the Blue Lake of Amdo. There he experienced numerous dreams and visions of gurus and deities.

His search for sacred places took him to many other solitary retreats: the glaciers of Machen, the sacred caves of the White Rock Monkey Fortress, the arduous pilgrimage of the Tsari Ravines, Mount Kailash, and the Lapchi Snow Range. He spent many years in the very caves where Milarepa and other saints had lived and meditated.

Shabkar's given names were Jampa Chödar (byams pa chos dar), "The Loving One Who Spreads the Dharma," and Tsogdruk Rangdröl (tshogs drug rang grol), "Self-Liberation of the Six Senses." He became renowned as Shabkar Lama, the "White Footprint Lama," because he spent years in meditation at Mount Kailash, below Milarepa's Cave of Miracles, near the famous White Footprint, one of the four footprints said to have been left by Buddha Sakyamuni when he traveled miraculously to Kailash. Shabkar was also called "White Foot" because wherever he set his feet, the land became "white with virtue," meaning that through his teachings the minds of the people would be turned toward the holy dharma.

Wandering as a homeless yogi, teaching all beings, from bandits to wild animals, Shabkar's pilgrimages brought him as far as Nepal, where, in the Kathmandu Valley, he covered the entire spire of the Bodhnath stupa with gold that his devotees had offered him.

In 1828, at the age of forty-seven, Shabkar returned to Amdo, where he tirelessly helped others through his extraordinary compassion. He spent the last twenty years of his life teaching disciples, promoting peace in the area, and practicing meditation in retreat at various sacred places, primarily at his hermitage in Tashikhyil.

Shechen Öntrul Gyurme Thuthop Namgyal (1787–1854)

Shechen Öntrul Gyurme Thuthop Namgyal (zhe chen dbon sprul 'gyur med mthu stobs rnam rgyal), a.k.a. Jamyang Gyepe Lodrö Tsokye Zhepe Drayang ('jam dbyangs dgyes pa'i blo gros mtsho skyes bzhad pa'i sgra dbyangs), also known as the Shechen Mahapandita (the Great Pandita of Shechen), was considered to be an incarnation of Songtsen Gampo's minister, Thumi Sambhota (thu mi sam bhota), of Yudra Nyingpo (g.yu sgra snying po), of Zurchung Sherab Trakpa, and of Minling Lochen Dharma Shri (lo chen dharma shri), among others. He was the immediate reincarnation of the great practitioner Tokden Sangye Rabten (rtogs ldan sangs rgyas rab brtan), who was himself the nephew (*önpo*) of the highly realized master Padma Gyaltsen (padma rgyal mtshan).

He was the heart-disciple of Dzogchen Mingyur Namkhai Dorje, Gyalse Shenphen Thaye, and the 1st Shechen Gyaltsap, Pema Sang-ngak Tendzin Chögyal (padma gsang sngags bstan 'dzin chos rgyal, 1760–1817). He was also a close disciple of the great Getse Mahapandita from Kathok, Gyurme Tsewang Chokdrup ('gyur med tshe dbang mchog grub, 1761–1829) as well as of the 6th Minling Trichen, Gyurme Pema Wangyal ('gyur med padma dbang rgyal, 18th c.). He attended altogether to fifty teachers. He spent six years in retreat at Shechen retreat center, Pema Ösel Ling.

Among his most eminent students were Jamgön Kongtrul, Jamyang Khyentse Wangpo, and Patrul Rinpoche, as well as the 5th Khamtrul, Drupgyu Nyima (khams sprul sgrub brgyud nyi ma, 1781–1847), and Kathok Situ.

NOTES

1. Sönam Tsering was constantly at Patrul Rinpoche's side after Patrul became seventy-one years old. See Khenpo Kunpel's biography in the Biographical Notes.
2. One of the most illustrious disciples of Khenpo Ngakchung, Chatral Sangye Dorje (bya bral sangs rgyas rdo rje, 1913–2015), passed away at the age of 102. When Matthieu visited Tibet in 1985, he was able to meet Tulku Urgyen Chemchog, a close disciple of Khenpo Ngakchung; in 2004, another disciple of Khenpo Ngakchung was still teaching in a mountain retreat at Nyarong, in Kham.
3. The full title of a collection of songs and words of advice, put together retrospectively by Khenpo Shenga Tenga, who arranged Patrul Rinpoche's collected works, can be translated roughly as "Authentic Pith Instructions, Spontaneous Vajra Songs, Melodies Free from Elaborations." It is a collection of written pieces of advice and instructions given or sent to students, poems, and songs of realization (vajra songs). This genre is widely found in Tibetan literature. The selections translated are not all literally songs, and Patrul Rinpoche was not known (unlike Milarepa and Shabkar, for instance) for actually singing such "songs."
4. A few of his personal possessions are preserved in the home of descendants of Patrul Rinpoche's sister: a small thangka of Jigme Gyalwai Nyugu (1765–1842), a hand-held prayer wheel, a monk's shawl (chos gos), a metal pot for boiling tea, and bellows for making a fire. There is also a woodblock print of Milarepa's biography and his *Hundred Thousand Songs,* given to Patrul Rinpoche by the Great Printing Press of Derge (Derge Parkhang). Patrul Rinpoche's begging bowl is now kept at Shechen Monastery in Nepal.
5. Collected in editions of six or eight volumes.
6. *tshig gsum gnad brdegs.* Patrul's commentary is titled *mkhas pa shri rgyal po'i khyad chos* (Special Teaching of the Wise and Glorious King).
7. *Dzö Dun* (*mdzod bdun*).
8. Patrul Rinpoche's birthplace is called Dru Karchung Khohor (gru dkar chung sko 'or) or more commonly Karchung Khormo Olu (dkar chung 'khor mo o lu).
9. The Dza River (rdza chu) becomes the Mekong after it leaves Tibet.

10. The Mukpo Dong ("Maroon-Faced") clan belongs to the Dongshakar (gdong zhwa dkar) family lineage that produced many ministers to the King of Derge.
11. The *Manjushrinamasangiti* (Tib. *Jampel Tsenjö; 'jam dpal mtshan brjod,* literally "Chanting the Names of Manjushri") is one of the most advanced teachings given by Buddha Shakyamuni, one of the few among the vast number of existing tantras that he taught. Numerous commentaries have been written on this profound text.
12. The Plain of the Mamos (*mamo tang;* ma mo thang) is not far from Patrul Rinpoche's birthplace. At the edge of the plain, in a small cliff, is the Cave of the White Mule (Drelkar Phuk / drel dkar phug). Jigme Gyalwai Nyugu and Patrul Rinpoche both practiced meditation in this cave, which has two small chamber caves within it. Jigme Gyalwai Nyugu stayed in the upper, smaller chamber and Patrul in the lower one. They both stayed there at different times.
13. *Labrang* refers to the residence of an important lama.
14. Some sections of the wall were made of stones carved with the entire 103 volumes of the Tripitaka.
15. The Palge Mani Wall (*palge mani dobum* / dpal dge ma ni rdo 'bum), located on the Plain of the Mamos, was dismantled during China's Cultural Revolution. Since it was located in a remote area and made out of heavy stones, the stones were not taken away but were scattered in the area. Khenpo Dönnyi of Gemang Monastery says that local people began to reassemble the wall during the mid-1980s, inspired by a lama called Gyaltsen Rabyang (Aku Rabyang). Once the wall was reassembled, it was gradually enlarged. Many stone carvers moved into the surrounding area, adding new stones when commissioned by others or simply out of personal devotion. In the 1990s, Akong Tulku commissioned the carving of the Kangyur, the 103 volumes of the Buddha's teachings. Later, a line of large stupas was erected halfway along the length of the wall by a faithful disciple from Hong Kong known by her Tibetan name, Kachö Wangmo. Then, a lama called Kunga Zangpo (acknowledged by Dilgo Khyentse Rinpoche as a possible incarnation of Patrul Rinpoche) added many more stupas. Many stones were carved and added through the work of Lama Gangshar of Dzagyal. Today, local authorities will not permit any further additions to the wall. At present, by our rough estimate, the wall is about 1.8 km (1.1 mi.) long, 4 m (4.4 yd.) high, and 18 m (19.7 yd.) wide. It takes forty-five to fifty minutes to complete one circumambulation, walking at a brisk pace. See the 2005 photograph of the wall on page 51.
16. This is most probably the 4th Taklung Matrul Rinpoche, Ngawang Tenpai Nyima (ngag dbang bstan pa'i nyi ma, also known as chos kyi 'byung gnas phrin las rnam par rgyal ba, 1788–?).
17. See Dilgo Khyentse Rinpoche, *The Heart Treasure of the Enlightened Ones: The Practice of View, Meditation, and Action* (Boston: Shambhala Publications, 1993, 2012).

18. "Orgyen" refers to the Kingdom of Oddiyana, the native land of Padmasambhava, who was born from a lotus on Lake Danakhosha, now tentatively identified as Lake Saiful Muluk in the Kaghan Valley of Pakistan.
19. In Kham and Amdo, *Aku* (Uncle) is an affectionate and respectful way to address monks and elder males.
20. Among Patrul's other teachers were Dola Jigme Kalzang, Jigme Ngotsar (one of four "fearless disciples" of Jigme Lingpa), and Gyalse Shenphen Thaye. From these masters, Patrul received the transmission of Longchenpa's *Trilogy of Resting at Ease,* Shantideva's *Way of the Bodhisattva,* and the *Guhyagarbha Tantra,* and instructions on the various traditional sciences.
21. Dzagyal Trama Lung (rdza rgyal khra ma lung). See the photo on page 123.
22. Dodrup Tenpai Nyima, *Dewdrop of Amrita;* Khenpo Kunpel, *Elixir of Faith.*
23. In Tibet, to this day, many dedicated practitioners renounce not only worldly affairs but, like Patrul, renounce involvement in monastery affairs as well. They give up all involvements, not wanting to "renounce a small home only to get caught up in a big one."
24. Excerpt translated from *gtam padma'i tshal gyi zlos gar* (The Lotus-Grove Play), Collected Works of Patrul Rinpoche, vol. 1 (2003), p. 351.
25. For more details on this topic, see Tulku Thondup, *Hidden Teachings of Tibet: An Explanation of the Terma Tradition of Tibetan Buddhism* (Boston: Wisdom Publications, 1986).
26. Tib. *byang chub sems dpa'i spyod pa la 'jug pa,* also known for short as *Chöjuk (spyod 'jug).*
27. Patrul received transmissions from the Longchen Nyingthig from Gyalse Shenphen Thaye. From Khenchen Sengtruk Pema Tashi, the first abbot of Shri Singha Philosophical College, he received teachings on much of the Nyingma Kahma.
28. Shechen Tennyi Dargyeling (zhe chen bstan gnyis dar rgyas gling) Monastery was destroyed during the Chinese Cultural Revolution. It was rebuilt in exile in the 1980s in Kathmandu, Nepal, and fully restored in Tibet in 2016.
29. *Thirteen Great Treatises* (*gzhung chen bcu gsum*) are thirteen commentaries on the Buddha's teachings and on the writings of the greatest Buddhist panditas of India (Aryadeva, Asanga, Chandrakirti, Nagarjuna, Shantideva, and Vasubhandu). The thirteen treatises are on Vinaya, Abhidharma, the path of the bodhisattva, prajnaparamita, and Madhyamaka. The well-known commentaries on these treatises by Khenpo Shenga (Shenphen Chökyi Nangwa), which are also titled *Thirteen Great Treatises,* revitalized scholarship on these topics; his approach is still widely used in Tibetan philosophical colleges. (See also note 235.) The collection also contains additional commentaries besides the thirteen.
30. When Rongzom Chökyi Zangpo (rong zom chos kyi bzang po, 1012–1088), known as Rongzom Mahapandita, was asked about the extent of his study of Buddhist scriptures, he answered, "I can't say I studied extensively, since most

of the texts I read only once. But I also can't say that I *didn't* study, since after reading them just once, I knew them almost by heart."

31. The Tibetan name of Long-Life Cave is Tsering Phuk (tshe rin phug).
32. Jigme Lingpa had three incarnations: Jamyang Khyentse Wangpo, his body-incarnation; Patrul, his speech-incarnation; Do Khyentse, his mind-incarnation. Thus these three were of the same wisdom-mindstream.
33. *Abu* is an intimate yet respectful way to address a male person.
34. People are often surprised to discover that not all Buddhists are vegetarians. Buddhists of China and Vietnam are usually strict vegetarians; most Japanese and Tibetan Buddhists eat meat. In Tibet, vegetarianism can be difficult, since altitude and harsh climate make growing crops impossible above 12,000 feet. Many Tibetans nonetheless regard eating meat as a regrettable practice. In India, where conditions are very different, most Tibetan monasteries have now adopted a vegetarian diet. A few eminent masters, such as Shabkar Tsogdruk Rangdröl (see Biographical Notes), have unambiguously promoted abstention from meat-eating, even in difficult environments. More recently, this has been the view of Khenpo Tsultrim Lodrö of Larung Gar (a monastic estate in Kham sheltering 20,000 nuns, monks, and lay practitioners) as well as of Tulku Pema Wangyal (Taklung Tsetrul Pema Wangyal Rinpoche) and many others.

    From a Buddhist point of view, it is unacceptable to live at the expense of the suffering and death of other beings. In the *Lankavatara Sutra,* it is said: "Alas, what sort of virtue do these beings practice? They fill their bellies with the flesh of animals, thus spreading fear among the beasts who live in the air, in the water, and on the earth! Practitioners of the Way should abstain from meat, because eating it is a source of terror for beings."

    Highly realized masters such as Do Khyentse Yeshe Dorje have the capacity to liberate the mindstream of an animal whose flesh they consume, such that it would not take rebirth in samsara but would be freed in the absolute expanse. Ordinary practitioners cannot do this. For a detailed explanation, see Shabkar Tsogdruk Rangdröl, *Food of Bodhisattvas: Buddhist Teachings on Abstaining from Meat,* trans. Padmakara Translation Group (Boston: Shambhala Publications, 2011).
35. The *Guhyagarbha Tantra* (*rgyud gsang ba snying po,* Secret Essence Tantra) is the main *mahayoga* tantra in the Nyingma tradition. Extensive commentaries on it have been written by luminaries such as Longchenpa, Minling Lochen Dharma Shri, and Lama Mipham Rinpoche.
36. The goal of the path, enlightenment.
37. Dilgo Khyentse Rinpoche's elder brother Shedrup said, "Patrul Rinpoche's students first gained a thorough understanding of a root text by using a word-by-word commentary. When beginners start by studying the detailed explanation of a text, their understanding is scattered. By memorizing the outline, one can understand the general meaning, and when reviewing the commentary from

there, one's study will be effective. These days there are too many annotated commentaries that lack an outline and so don't produce a good understanding." Dilgo Khyentse Rinpoche studied *The Way of the Bodhisattva* with Khenpo Shenga, a student of Patrul Rinpoche and Önpo Tendzin Norbu. Khenpo Shenga would teach one page a day of *The Way of the Bodhisattva;* Khyentse Rinpoche's tutor made him read the teaching a hundred times. See *Brilliant Moon,* pp. 31 and 33.

38. When there is not enough time to teach the whole text of *The Way of the Bodhisattva,* it is customary to teach chapters 1, 2, 3, and 10 (respectively on the benefits of bodhichitta, confessing one's faults, cultivating bodhichitta, and sharing accumulated merits).

39. *Chöjuk metok* (*spyod 'jug me tog*). In the fall of 1991, His Holiness the 14th Dalai Lama (Tenzin Gyatso, b. 1935) spent a week teaching *The Way of the Bodhisattva* in Dordogne in the southwest of France. A tent large enough to accommodate eight thousand people had been set up in a large meadow on the Côte de Jor near the Centre d'Études de Chanteloube, a Buddhist studies and retreat center. An apple tree grew in that meadow, just next to the teaching throne. Two weeks after the teachings had finished, that apple tree burst into full bloom. Normally, of course, apple trees bloom in the spring, not in the autumn. Matthieu, who at the time had been translating for H. H. Dalai Lama, has kept some of these apple blossoms.

40. According to Khenpo Kunpel's less-detailed version (*Elixir of Faith,* p. 391), this anecdote took place when Patrul Rinpoche came down from Dhichung Cave in Ari Forest.

41. Known as a *dotse* (rdo tshad), it was worth fifty *sang* (srang), a silver coin used prior to 1959. A *dotse* was about 4 pounds in weight of silver.

42. According to Do Khyentse's autobiography, *rig 'dzin 'jigs med gling p'ai yang srid sngags 'chang 'ja lus rdo rje'i rnam thar mkha' 'gro'i zhal lung* (Sichuan Minorities Press, 1997), and Tulku Thondup's *Masters of Meditation and Miracles* (p. 195), Do Khyentse was staying in Lauthang in 1836 when Patrul was twenty-eight years old. Lauthang is in the Gartar Dzong district west of Lhagong Monastery. In recent times, it was the residence of Lauthang Tulku Drachan, an incarnation of Dodrupchen, who died in 1958 or 1959.

43. Four demons (Skt. *mara;* Tib. *düzhi* / bdud bzhi): the demon of the aggregates (phung po'i bdud), embodied by the deity Brahma (tshang pa); the demon of obscuring emotions (nyon mong gi bdud), embodied by Indra (dbang phyug); the demon of Devaputra, "son of a god" (lha bu'i bdud), embodied by Devendra (lha dbang); and the demon of death ('chi bdag gi bdud), embodied by Vishnu (khyab 'jug).

44. Tibetan books are made of a collection of long, loose folios, which are wrapped in a cloth when one is not reading the book.

45. Patrul advised Nyoshul Lungtok: "Study all philosophical systems without bias.

Bias creates distorted understanding. When you study all teachings impartially, you will know what is true and what is not, you will know what is profound and what is not, you will know what accords with the buddhas' wisdom-mind, and so forth. From then on, understanding will come through your own insight." See Khenpo Ngawang Palzang, *Wondrous Dance of Illusion*, p. 102.

46. Krishnacharya (Skt.; Tib. Nakpo Chöpa / nag po spyod pa), one of the Eighty-four Mahasiddhas of India.

47. Some oral sources assert that Lungtok spent twenty-eight years with Patrul Rinpoche, leaving when he was fifty (1851–1879). Nyoshul Khen Rinpoche's *Marvelous Garland of Rare Gems* states that Patrul sent Lungtok home in 1869, when Lungtok was forty. Thus, Lungtok would have first met Patrul in 1848 at age nineteen.

48. Here, "gods" (Tib. *lha;* Skt. *deva*) refers to the beings of the realm of form (Skt. *rupadhatu*) and of the formless realms (*arupadhatu*), who can remain for a very long time in a state of absorption, in which all perceptions of the outer world stop. This state momentarily protects those gods from ordinary disturbing emotions but does not bring them to freedom from ignorance. Accordingly, they don't exhaust their negative karma and will eventually fall back in the lower realms of samsara.

49. *Shamatha* (Tib. *zhi gnas*), or "calm abiding" meditation, is a stage of concentration in which the mind remains unmoving on an object of concentration. Although this state is of great importance, it by itself cannot overcome ignorance and the conception of self. It must be associated with *vipashyana* (Tib. *lhag mthong*), or profound insight, which allows one to overcome the ignorant belief in the existence of the self and to realize the ultimate nature of the mind and of phenomena.

50. Nyoshul Khen Rinpoche places this episode at Changma Hermitage in Dzachukha. Khenpo Kunpel, in *Elixir of Faith,* places it at Dzogchen.

51. *Yeshe Lama* (*gdod ma'i mgon po'i lam gyi rim pa'i khrid yig ye shes bla*) is a teaching by Rigdzin Jigme Lingpa on the practice of Dzogchen, which Patrul frequently taught. It is found in volume 3 of the five-volume *Longchen Nyingthig Tsapö* (*klong chen snying thig rtsa pod*) (New Delhi and Kathmandu: Shechen Publications, 1994).

52. Threefold sky practice (ngam mkha' gsum phrug) is an advanced meditation practice of the Great Perfection. As the practitioner gazes into a cloudless blue sky, the immaculate outer sky, one's inner sky (the luminous crystal central channel, rtsa ka ti shel sgi bu gu), and one's secret sky (the nature of pure awareness, rig pa'i ngo bo) all merge inseparably as uncompounded appearance-emptiness, indivisibly united, free from all elaborations.

53. *Tegchog Dzö* (*theg mchog rin po chen mdzod*). I am not aware of whether the seven volumes of the collection, owned by Nyoshul Lungtok, are still extant at Shugu Shar, where they were preserved until the Communist invasion of Tibet.

54. *Chulen* (bcud len; Skt. *rasayana*), or "extracting the essence," is a means of extracting through deep meditation the quintessence of (depending on the object of concentration) small pebbles, flowers, or space, and subsisting upon it. This is said to be one of the eight common *siddhis*, or accomplishments (thun mong gi dngos grub), the supreme siddhi being enlightenment.
55. Shri Singha was the chief disciple and successor of Manjushrimitra in the lineage of the Dzogchen teachings, and a master to Guru Padmasambhava.
56. The symbolism of tormas is complex; generally speaking, white tormas are offered to peaceful deities and red tormas to wrathful ones.
57. See note 37.
58. *Dzakhok* refers to the remote inner reaches or back country of Dzachukha.
59. A similar story comes from Dilgo Khyentse Rinpoche. He was attending a picnic in the presence of his second main spiritual master, Jamyang Khyentse Chökyi Lodrö. Seeing that Dilgo Khyentse had forgotten to bring his own tea bowl, Jamyang Khyentse offered him his own. As in the story of Patrul and the little girl, to be offered the use of a high lama's own bowl was nearly unthinkable. Thus, out of respect, Dilgo Khyentse declined the great lama's offer.

    Jamyang Khyentse offered his tea bowl a second time, and again Dilgo Khyentse refused. Finally, appearing a bit exasperated, Jamyang Khyentse said, "Take it! It's not dirty!" When Dilgo Khyentse Rinpoche was telling this story and got to those words, "It's not dirty!" his eyes filled with tears. (From *Brilliant Moon*, p. xxxiii.)
60. *Lamtso Nam Sum (lam gyi gtso bo rnam gsum)*.
61. Je Tsongkhapa (rje tsong kha pa, 1357–1419).
62. See below an excerpt translated from the Prayer for the Swift Rebirth of Shabkar, in the Collected Works of Patrul Rinpoche (2003), vol. 8, pp. 80–83.

Protector, willingly, you displayed your form-body [*rupakaya*],
To benefit beings of this decadent age.
Yet, having taken care of your disciples, afflicted with bad karma,
For a short time, you went to rest in the absolute expanse.
How could this be right?

To benefit beings of this degenerate age,
You, Protector, willingly appeared in human form.
Yet, having cared for your bad-karma students for a while,
Now you've gone; you rest within the absolute expanse.
How can this be so?

Here, praying with both our eyes filled with tears,
Like children calling upon their mother,
We, your disciples, are left behind—
Suddenly, you went to sleep in dharmakaya.
Could this be really true?

We are here; tears well up,
Like those of children crying for their mother
As we make our supplications,
We, your students, left behind.
All at once, you're gone; you rest in dharmakaya.
How can this be so?

. . . .

I did not have the good fortune to behold your face:
What is the use for me now, to have two eyes in my forehead?
From now on, and for however long I may live,
I promise you that I shall endeavor in the essence of the practice.
O protector, in whichever pure buddhafield you abide now,
Gaze upon me with your compassionate eyes so that we both become indivisible.

With not enough merit to see your face in fact,
What's the use of my having eyesight?
From now on, for the rest of my life,
I vow to dedicate myself to practicing the very essence.
O protector, from whichever buddhafield you abide,
Look upon me with eyes of compassion,
So that we two are indivisible.

When I am overcome by demons of bad karma,
Lured off by distraction,
And the wrong views of ordinary life arise in mind,
Please show me your form—
In dreams, in meditation experiences, or in this life;
Help me be steadfast on the path that is immaculate and perfect.

Like a monkey who tries to imitate a man,
I try to ape your life-example of perfect liberation.
As I aspire to cultivate the two bodhichittas,
Keep me safely in the guard of your compassion,
Just as a mother keeps watch over her child.

63. Oral account of Dilgo Khyentse Rinpoche. See also Dilgo Khyentse, *Brilliant Moon*, p. 135. Several incarnations of Patrul Rinpoche became known in eastern Tibet. Tsö Patrul, in Amdo, was a well-respected lama who is said to have fulfilled a prediction made by Patrul Rinpoche (see the story "The Land of the Insect-Eaters," page 55, and the accompanying photo of Tsö Patrul). One of Tertön Dudjom Lingpa's sons became known as an incarnation of Patrul Rinpoche; he was called Patrul Namkha Jigme (his photo is shown alongside that of Tsö Patrul). Patrul Namkha Jigme was the brother of Dodrup Tenpai Nyima

and passed away in 1961. Khenpo Thubga (Bathur Khenpo Thubten Chöphel) was also considered by some to be an incarnation of Patrul Rinpoche. Since none of these masters was formally acknowledged as the 4th Palge (Patrul Rinpoche being the 3rd to bear the name), we have not included them in the Patrul Rinpoche Lineage Chart on pages 172–173.

64. *The Treatise on the Sublime Continuum* (Skt. *Uttaratantra-shastra;* Tib. *rgyud bla ma'i bstan bcos*) is a profound explanation of the buddha nature (*tathagatagarbha*) according to the teachings of the third turning of the wheel of dharma by Buddha Shakyamuni. It is one of the *Five Treatises* received by the great Indian pandita Asanga in visions from the bodhisattva Maitreya.

65. This Tibetan expression (*ey shi re*) indicates serious resolve or intent, as in the English phrases "Even if it kills me, I will do this!" or "Even at the cost of my own life, I won't do this!" Oral communication from Tulku Thondup.

66. Minling Lochen Dharma Shri, Chöphel Gyatso (smin gling lo chen gcung chos dpal rgya mtsho, 1654–1718), wrote two commentaries on the *Guhyagarbha Tantra,* known for short as *gsang bdag dgongs rgyan* (Ornament to the Wisdom Intention of the Lord of Secrets) and *gsang bdag zhal lung* (Oral Instructions of the Lord of Secrets).

67. Yarlung Pemakö is located 15 km (9.3 mi.) from Serta prefecture in Golok. It was a principal seat of the 1st Dodrupchen, Jigme Trinley Özer; the 3rd Dodrupchen, Jigme Tenpai Nyima; and the present 4th Dodrupchen. There are at present two incarnations of Dodrupchen Rinpoche: one who lives in Sikkim, who is well known around the world, and one who lives in Kham.

68. The *Mani Kahbum* (*ma ni bka' 'bum*) is a collection of teachings and practices focused on Avalokiteshvara, the Bodhisattva of Compassion, written by King Songtsen Gampo.

69. Shukchen Tago is located about 15 km (9.3 mi.) from Dodrupchen Monastery in Golok.

70. Jigme Trinley Özer had built there a small monastery, Drodön Lhundrup Ling. He lived there for a while but then moved his seat to Yarlung Pemakö in Serta Valley.

71. The Derge edition of the Kangyur, considered to be the most reliable, contains 103 volumes.

72. There are several species of *jolmo* ('jol mo, laughing thrush) in Tibet, belonging to the genus Garrulax. The onomatopoeic sounds of its call are rendered as *khyö kyi-hu, nga kyi-hu.*

73. "Penetrative insight" and "calm abiding" refer, respectively, to *vipashyana* and *shamatha.*

74. Shantideva, *The Way of the Bodhisattva*, rev. ed., trans. Padmakara Translation Group (Boston: Shambhala Publications, 2006), chap. 8, pp. 109–13. © 1997, 2006 by the Padmakara Translation Group.

75. Patrul's teacher Rogza Sönam Palge was a close spiritual friend of the 1st Dodrupchen, Jigme Trinley Özer and of Do Khyentse. It is said that he was able to sit

in the lotus position in space; he was able to run so swiftly that he could catch up with deer and wild Tibetan asses. In his old age, Patrul used to send some of his own students to learn the *tsalung* yogic practices from Rogza Sönam Palge, saying that he was one of the last authentic holders of these precious instructions.

76. Dhichung Phuk (dhi chung phug) in Dokhok (rdo khog), or Do Valley. Ari Forest is about five miles down the valley from the present Dodrupchen Monastery and about six miles up and across the Do River from Shukchen Tago.

77. Protection cords are thin strings, usually red or yellow, in the middle of which a spiritual master ties a double knot upon which he or she blows while reciting some mantras to protect the disciples from both outer obstacles (sicknesses and other adverse circumstances) and inner obstacles (difficulties in one's spiritual practices).

78. *Ngalso Kor Sum* (*ngal gso skor gsum*). For an introduction to this trilogy, see Tulku Thondup Rinpoche, *Buddha Mind: An Anthology of Longchen Rabjam's Writings on Dzogpa Chenpo,* new ed. (Ithaca, N.Y.: Snow Lion Publications, 1990).

79. *Semnyi Ngalso* (*sems nyid ngal gso*).

80. *Suru karpo,* or *surkar* (su ru dkar po; sur dkar), commonly known as balu, is a kind of wild white azalea.

81. Nomads might eat the meat from animals who died early in winter, ones who still had some fat on their bones. However, meat from animals who had died of starvation late in winter was regarded as not worth eating at all (except under dire circumstances).

82. *Samten Ngalso* (*bsam gtan ngal gso*).

83. *Gyuma Ngalso* (*sgyu ma ngal gso*).

84. The meeting between Do Khyentse and Patrul Rinpoche near Nyenpo Yutse happened in 1856/57 according to Tulku Thondup, *Masters of Meditation and Miracles,* and Do Khyentse's autobiography, *rig 'dzin 'jigs med gling p'ai yang srid sngags 'chang 'ja lus rdo rje'i rnam thar mkha' 'gro'i zhal lung* (Sichuan Minorities Press, 1997).

85. This is the Ngotsho Lake in front of the Nyenpo Yutse mountain range (gnyan po g.yu rtse). Nyenpo Yutse is the home of local deities and of a dharma protector belonging to the retinue of Amnye Machen, the powerful dharma protector residing in the mountain bearing his name. On the northern side of Nyenpo Yutse is a lake called Jara Yutso. Here, Do Khyentse and his disciples lived for many years in small hermitages. On the western side there are hundreds of hot springs; each one is reputed to cure a different illness.

86. Yumka Dechen Gyalmo (yum bka' 'gro bde chen rgyal mo), the dakini practice from the Longchen Nyingthig cycle of Jigme Lingpa.

87. The empowerment of manifestive power of awareness (rig pa'i rtsal dbang) guides the disciple toward recognizing that thoughts are, by their nature, nothing but the display of pure awareness.

88. A round hat of yellow felt with a fur brim was worn by some government officials at that time. Wild rhubarb (lcum) grows in some high-altitude meadows.
89. Because the butter was created with her son constantly in mind, out of her great love for him, Patrul felt he might be misusing the offering were he to accept it.
90. The exact date of Patrul's mother's death in relation to this account is uncertain. Although phowa is usually performed immediately after someone dies, it occasionally happens that people request a great lama to perform phowa years after the death of the person.
91. That is the tradition, or lineage, that came from Rigdzin Jigme Lingpa, and was transmitted through Jigme Trinley Özer (1st Dodrupchen) and Gegong Rogza Palge, as well as through Jigme Gyalwai Nyugu.
92. This is not a known buddhafield. Patrul Rinpoche was just making up this name to emphasize the opulence of the setting.
93. *Nadis* are the spiritual-energy channels of the physical body. *Prana* is the wind-energy that circulates through the nadis. *Bindu* (Skt.; Tib. *tigle*) is the essence-energy carried by prana as it flows through the nadis. By means of yogic practices involving visualizations and breath control, in various positions, these channels, winds, and energies are purified. These include meditations to develop inner heat (*tummo*) and various physical exercises.
94. Dodrup Tenpai Nyima said it was only the efforts of Patrul and Rogza Sönam Palge that enabled the yogic practices of the Longchen Nyingthig to be preserved and passed down to this day. Önpo Tenga in particular became one of the main holders of these teachings.
95. In this context, the "New Treasure" tradition most likely refers to Chokgyur Lingpa's termas, although it has been suggested that it may refer to the New Treasures discovered by the treasure revealer Rinchen Lingpa (rin chen gling pa, 1295–1375) of Yel-le Gar. In general, New Treasures, or Tersar (gter gsar), are termas found in recent or contemporary times. In the twentieth century, for instance, the treasures revealed by Dudjom Rinpoche, Jigdral Yeshe Dorje (bdud 'joms 'jigs bral ye shes rdo rje, 1904–1987), are known as Dudjom Tersar.
96. The descent of the actual wisdom deity (*jnanasattva*) into the visualized deity (*samayasattva*), which is the body of the recipient participating in the empowerment ceremony, is often said to induce spontaneous and effortless song and dance. Such events are mentioned in, for example, the biography of Longchen Rabjam. See Dudjom Rinpoche, *The Nyingma School of Tibetan Buddhism: Its Fundamentals and History* (Somerville, Mass.: Wisdom Publications, 2005).
97. Vajrakilaya (rdo rje phur ba) is one of the main wisdom deities practiced in the Nyingma tradition. Vajrakilaya is one of the Eight Herukas (bka' brgyad), who symbolize various aspects of enlightenment. The practice of Vajrakilaya, a wrathful deity associated with "enlightened activity," is considered to be one of the most powerful ways to dispel outer and inner obstacles on the path to enlightenment.
98. gter ston bsod rgyal las rab gling pa (1856–1926).

99. Treasure revealers (tertöns) may unearth spiritual revelations (terma) concealed in the form of ritual objects invisibly sealed within rocks or other objects by Padmasambhava and others, long ago.
100. Skt. Triyastrimsha, a celestial realm where many devas, or gods, live. Thirty-three is a symbolic number meaning "many."
101. Patrul always extolled monastic life, as he did in his "In Praise of the Vinaya" (*dam pa'i chos 'dul ba la bsngags pa me tog gi skyed mo'i tshal*), Collected Works of Patrul Rinpoche (2003), vol. 1.
102. The Buddha predicted that so long as the monastic tradition of the Vinaya remained in this world, the dharma would remain as well.
103. The extremely wrathful form of Hayagriva (yang khros rta nag) is part of the cycle of Tamdrin Sangdu (rta mgrin gsang 'dus) revealed by Chögyal Ratna Lingpa (chos rgyal ratna gling pa, 1403–1479).
104. In Tibetan traditional medical texts, leprosy is said to be caused by the negative influence of *nagas*, serpent spirits. The deity Hayagriva (here in a form that holds a sword) is the tamer of these nagas.
105. Demchok Sangye Nyamjor (bde mchog sangs rgyas mnyam spyor), one important cycle of Chokgyur Lingpa's revealed treasures. See vol. 4 of the new edition of the *Rinchen Terdzö* (*rin chen gter mdzod,* Treasury of Precious Termas) (Delhi and Kathmandu: Shechen Publications, 2004–2016).
106. This might have been the 4th Tertön Yonge Mingyur Dorje (gter ston yongs ge mi 'gyur rdo rje, 1628/41–1708), the present incarnation being the 7th.
107. Sangye Lingpa (sangs rgyas gling pa, 1340–1396) is one of the thirteen great *lingpas* (gling chen bcu gsum), or major tertöns. His Lama Gongdu (bla ma dgongs 'dus) cycle of rediscovered treasures fills thirteen volumes.
108. The *Jampal Dzogpa Chenpo* (*'jam dpal rdzogs pa chen po*) of the Rig Sum Nyingthig (rigs gsum snying thig cycle), which is found in vol. 23 of the *Collected Treasure Revelations* of Chokgyur Dechen Lingpa (Tsike redaction).
109. The quoted dialogue is a combination of the account by Tulku Urgyen Rinpoche, *Blazing Splendor,* p. 84, and an oral story told by Nyoshul Khen Rinpoche.
110. *Rigsum Nyingthig* (*rigs gsum snying thig*).
111. Chokgyur Lingpa's daughter, Könchog Paldrön (dkon mchog dpal sgron, 1858?–1939?), who was the grandmother of Tulku Urgyen Rinpoche (1919–1996).
112. This story was initially told by Chokgyur Lingpa's daughter, Könchog Paldrön, famed for her infallible memory; from her it was passed down to various people. The story was told to me by Nyoshul Khenpo. Tulku Urgyen also recounted the story with slightly different words. I used the version of Nyoshul Khenpo.
113. *Chang me ke mo* (chang med ke mo) is an expression in nomad dialect, meaning "nothing at all."
114. "Orgyen" is an epithet of Guru Padmasambhava. Orgyen is another name for the Kingdom of Oddiyana, where he was born.
115. *dam tshig thams cad kyi nyams chag skong ba'i lung bshags pa thams cad kyi rgyud*

dri ma med pa'i rgyal po. There are several editions, including in vol. 58 of the Nyingma Kama Gyepa (rnying ma bka' ma rgyas pa) (Kalimpong, India: Dupjung Lama, 1982–1987).

116. These are texts written in symbolic letters, said to be used by the dakinis, which can only be read by the treasure revealer to whom a particular spiritual treasure has been entrusted by Guru Padmasambhava in the past.
117. Childhood, adulthood, and old age.
118. Patrul Rinpoche here refers to himself. This verse alludes to an old Indian story that is found in the sutras. A jackal fell into a dyer's cauldron of indigo and came out dyed a beautiful blue color. When he came home all blue, the other animals did not recognize him and took him for a divine being; they made the blue jackal king of all the beasts. One night, while the blue king jackal was proudly overseeing his court, all the other jackals began to bay at the full moon. Unfortunately, the blue king jackal could not keep himself from baying at the moon along with the rest, proving he was not divine but was just another jackal. Unmasked, the impostor had to flee for his life.
119. Do and Mar are Dokhok and Markhok, two valleys in the Golok area of eastern Tibet.
120. From Tulku Urgyen Rinpoche, *Blazing Splendor,* p. 38.
121. King of Ghosts (gyal 'gong) is a kind of harmful spirit born of entertaining wrong views and produced from the union of two spirits, *gyalpo* (rgyal po) and *gongpo* ('gong po). They are said to often manifest in the guise of monks, hence Patrul's mischievous remark.
122. *Terchen* (gter chen) is a title for a major tertön.
123. *Kumbum* (sku 'bum) literally means "one hundred thousand bodies," referring to statues and images.
124. Kadampa Deshek, Sherab Senge (ka dam pa bde gshegs shes rab seng ge, 1122–1192), founder of Kathok Monastery.
125. Bumpa Namsum ('bum pa snams gsum): Yeshe Bum (ye shes 'bum), Dorje Bum (rdo rje 'bum), and Changchup Bum (byang chub 'bum).
126. The 2nd Kathok Situ, Chökyi Lodrö Orgyen Tenpa Namgyal (1820–1879?). See "Kathok Situ" in the Biographical Notes.
127. Dokham Kawa Karpo, one of the most sacred mountains of eastern Tibet, in the Chinese province of Yunnan.
128. In the 1980s, the Dzogchen master Khenpo Munsel told this story to Garchen Rinpoche, a Drigung Kagyu master. At once, Garchen Rinpoche said he wished to do likewise, making a vow to keep no possessions beyond a few basics. Garchen Rinpoche was born in 1949. By the time he finally left Tibet in the 1990s, he had spent twenty-three years in jail, imprisoned by the Chinese. Of his twenty-three years in prison, twenty years were spent in the company of his teacher, Khenpo Munsel.
129. Patrul Rinpoche most often taught straight from his heart, commenting

spontaneously based on his immense knowledge. When he did refer to written commentaries, he did so by school. In Sakya monasteries, he used the commentary of Jetsun Sönam Tsemo (rje btsun bsod nams rtse mo, 1142–1182). In Kagyu monasteries, he used the commentary of Pawo Tsuglak Trengwa (dpa' bo gtsug lag phreng ba, 1504–1566). In Geluk monasteries, he used the "Notes" (zin bris) and *Dar Tik* (commentary on *The Way of the Bodhisattva*) of Gyaltsab Dharma Rinchen (rgyal tshab darma rin chen, 1364–1432). In Nyingma monasteries, he used the commentary of the Indian pandita Prajnakaramati, known as Sherjung Lodrö in Tibetan (sher 'byung blo gros), or that of Gyalse Ngulchu Thogme (rgyal sras rngul chu thogs med, 1295–1369).

130. Dromtönpa Gyalwai Jungne ('brom ston pa rgyal ba'i 'byung gnas, 1005–1064), the chief disciple of the great Indian pandita Atisha Dipamkara, who began the Kadam lineage in Tibet.

131. The 84,000 sections refer to the four main categories of teachings contained in the Buddhist Canon: 21,000 sections are said to serve as antidotes to ignorance, 21,000 sections as antidotes to attachment, 21,000 as antidotes to hatred, and 21,000 as antidotes to the subtle aspects of the three poisons together. These three are the most afflictive mental states (Skt. *kleshas*) among what are known as the "five poisons," which also include pride and jealousy.

132. The nine vehicles (*yanas*) are the successive teachings that constitute the complete path of the dharma: the *shravaka-yana, pratyekabuddha-yana, bodhisattva-yana, kriyayoga-yana, upayoga-yana, yoga-yana, mahayoga-yana, anuyoga-yana,* and *atiyoga-yana.*

133. Longsal Nyingpo (klong gsal snying po, 1625–1692), a great tertön and a patriarch of Kathok Monastery.

134. The "exhaustion of phenomena in the absolute nature" (chos nyid zas sa) is the fourth and final stage of the Dzogchen practice of *thögal,* which is itself the pinnacle of the atiyoga path.

135. *Tsokchen dupa* (tshogs chen 'dus pa), an elaborate sadhana from the Nyingma Kahma that involves a detailed mandala comprising over 720 deities belonging to the nine vehicles (*yanas*).

136. Among Chöying Rangdröl's main disciples was Tertön Nyakla Pema Dudul and Drupchen Nyida Kundze (see biography of Chöying Rangdröl in Biographical Notes). He achieved the rainbow body, as did two of his own students, Ayu Khandro (a female master) and Nyalak Rigdzin Changchup Dorje.

137. According to Khenpo Kunpel's *Elixir of Faith.* Regarding the Chetsun Nyingthig, Dilgo Khyentse Rinpoche commented (orally) that Jamyang Khyentse Wangpo revealed two main cycles of Dzogchen teachings: (1) the Chetsun Nyingthig (lce btsun snying thig), based on a reminiscence from when Khyentse Wangpo was Chetsun Senge Wangchok (lce btsun seng ge dbang phyug, ca. 11th–12th c.), who had had a month-long vision of Vimalamitra appearing in space, and (2) the Vima Lhadrup (bi ma lha sgrub), a sadhana focused on three main enlightened

masters: Shri Singha, Vimalamitra, and Guru Padmasambhava. According to Dilgo Khyentse Rinpoche, these stand respectively for the "profound" and the "vast" aspects of the Great Perfection.

138. Six of these long-life prayers have survived and can be found in the *Collected Works of Patrul Rinpoche* (2003), vol. 8, pp. 108–9.

139. sman sgrub.

140. Shavaripa was one of the Eighty-four Mahasiddhas, or greatly realized beings, of India. Shavaripa was originally a hunter but gave up his nefarious activities to embrace the Dharma after meeting the bodhisattva Avalokiteshvara, who appeared to him in person. He became a disciple of the great pandita Nagarjuna and a teacher to Maitripa, two others among the Eighty-four Mahasiddhas.

141. Patrul's name, Jigme Chökyi Wangpo (Fearless Lord of Dharma).

142. Mipham expressed his profound admiration for Patrul's work after reading the latter's commentaries on the *Abhisamayalamkara Prajnaparamita* (Skt., Ornament of Clear Realization of the Perfection of Wisdom; Tib. *shes phyin mngon rtogs rgyan*), which condense the entire meaning of the long, medium, and short versions of the *Prajnaparamita Sutra.*

The text's full title is: *Abhisamayalankaranamaprajnaparamitopadesha-shastra* (Tib. *shes rap kyi pha rol tu phyin pa'i man ngag gi bstan bcos mngon par rtogs pa'i rgyan ces bya ba*), which means: *abhisamaya* (mngon par rtogs pa), "Realization(s)"; *alankara* (rgyan), "Ornament"; *nama* (zhes bya ba), "Called"; *prajnaparamita* (shes rap kyi pha rol tu phyin ba), "Perfection of Wisdom"; *upadesha* (man ngag), "Instructions" (lit. "an up-close look"); *shastra* (bstan bcos), "Treatise."

143. *Norbu Ketaka* (*nor bu ke ta ka*), lit. "Ketaka Gem." See *The Wisdom Chapter: Jamgön Mipham's Commentary on the Ninth Chapter of The Way of the Bodhisattva,* trans. Padmakara Translation Group (Boulder: Shambhala Publications, 2017).

144. snga 'gyur bstan pa rgyas pa'i smon lam chos rgyal dgyes pa'i zhal lung. Later, one of Mipham's foremost students, Shechen Gyaltsap Pema Namgyal, wrote an extensive commentary on this prayer.

145. One of Tibet's greatest translators, or Lotsawas, and one of the first seven monks to be ordained in Tibet. He was one of the main disciples of Guru Padmasambhava.

146. Jigme Chöying Ösel ('jigs med chos dbyings 'od gsal, ca. 1825–ca. 1897).

147. This stanza refers to the three consecutive ways of progressing toward wisdom: listening, reflecting, and meditating.

148. Before dawn, morning, afternoon, and evening (the traditional division of time when doing retreat).

149. This verse refers to the practice of *chö* (gcod), cutting through ego, in which one visualizes making an offering of one's material body, cut into pieces and transformed into nectar.

150. Trime Lodrö (dri med blo sgros), "Stainless Intelligence," is one of the several

names that Patrul Rinpoche received. It could refer, for instance, to the name he could have received when taking the bodhisattva vows or when being bestowed a Vajrayana empowerment.

151. Narak Dongtruk (na rak dong sprugs), a practice based on the Hundred Peaceful and Wrathful Deities, found in the collection of the Nyingma Kahma.
152. Longchenpa, *gsang snying gi 'grel pa phyogs bcu'i mun sel* (Paro, Bhutan: Shechen Publications, 1975), reproduced from a print from the a 'dzom 'brug pa chos sgar blocks.
153. *gsang bdag dgongs rgyan*, in the Collected Works (gsun 'bum) of Minling Lochen Dharma Shri (Dehra Dun: Khochen Tulku, 1999), vol. 8.
154. This 1.5-inch statue of Manjushri was Mipham's main support of meditation throughout his life. On other occasions as well, such as when Mipham was composing difficult treatises and had reached a point of confusion, light rays would beam from the heart of the statue to Mipham's heart. Following this, any confusion would be clarified. After Lama Mipham's death, the statue was enshrined within a much larger statue of Manjushri in the main temple of Shechen Monastery in Kham. During the Cultural Revolution, Shechen Monastery was razed to the ground, and all the large statues were destroyed. However, a local person managed to save the little statue; he took it away and kept it hidden. This man told his son that, should Dilgo Khyentse Rinpoche ever return to Tibet, the son should retrieve the statue and give it to Rinpoche. In 1987, the son met Khyentse Rinpoche in Derge and gave him Mipham's little statue as an offering. Khyentse Rinpoche was moved to tears. In gratitude, Rinpoche offered to the man's son every penny he had with him. This statue is now kept at Shechen Tennyi Dargyeling Monastery in Nepal in a golden stupa with Dilgo Khyentse Rinpoche's relics.
155. Verse translated by Adam S. Pearcey. Excerpted with kind permission from "Uniting Outer and Inner Solitude: Patrul Rinpoche's Advice for Alak Dongak Gyatso" (2014), https://adamspearcey.com/2014/12/21/solitude-patrul-rinpoches-advice-for-alak-dongak-gyatso/ (accessed October 2016).
156. Khenpo Ngakchung was considered to be an incarnation of Gyalwa Longchenpa, himself the incarnation of Vimalamitra.
157. Tertön Nyakla Pema Dudul (nyag bla padma bdud 'dul, 1816–1872).
158. This saying is quoted in Tulku Thondup, *Masters of Meditation and Miracles,* p. 222.
159. Changma Ritrö (lcang ma ri khrod) is named after the many small-sized mountain willow shrubs (*changma*) that grew there.
160. The three realms of existence are the desire realm (Skt. *kamadhatu*), the form realm (*rupadhatu*), and realm of formlessness (*arupadhatu*).
161. "Solitude of body, speech, and mind" is a formula often found in the teachings. It refers to ceasing physical activities, giving up idle speech (or all speech), and letting go the wandering stream of discursive thought until it exhausts itself completely.
162. Usually, Guru Dorje Drolö (gu ru rdo rje gro lod) is depicted as wearing, loose

around his neck, a long garland of fifty skulls, which symbolize (1) the fifty consonants and vowels of the Sanskrit alphabet, which stands for the purity of speech and the fifty kinds of purified winds (*vayu*), and (2) the death of the ego and the fifty kinds of deluded thoughts that reinforce mental delusion.

163. Padma Tötreng Tsal (padma thod phreng rtsal) is one of the secret names of Guru Rinpoche, meaning "Powerful Lotus of the Garland of Skulls."

164. Sacred substances from this very unique ganachakra were preserved and incorporated into special pills that are still in use to this day. (They were multiplied by mixing medicinal substances with a few of the original pills to make more pills.) These are given to people as blessings and placed inside statues along with other relics.

165. There are Eight Manifestations of Padmasambhava, different forms or aspects in which he appeared, as needed to benefit beings, during his life. Dorje Drolö is one of two wrathful manifestations. The eight aspects are Guru Tsokye Dorje (Lake-Born Vajra), Guru Shakya Senge (Lion of the Shakyas), Guru Nyima Özer (Rays of the Sun), Guru Pema Jungne (Lotus-Born), Guru Loden Choktse (Scholar Who Adores Intelligence), Guru Pema Gyalpo (Lotus King), Guru Senge Dradrok (Lion's Roar), and Guru Dorje Drolö (Vajra Loose-Hanging Belly).

166. It is said that there are two kinds of Dzogchen practitioners: (1) those capable of recognizing the manifestation of self-awareness (rig pa rang snang gi blo can), who realize that all appearances are manifestations of awareness alone; (2) those who still perceive appearances as external objects (snang ba yul gi blo can).

167. The 3rd Mura Tulku, Pema Dechen Zangpo (mu ra padma bde chen bzang po), reached a high level of accomplishment. He possessed unhindered clairvoyance, according to Dilgo Khyentse Rinpoche, who met him when the tulku was a child.

168. Today's Dzagyal Monastery is also the seat of the present incarnation of Jigme Gyalwai Nyugu.

169. The dharma of realization (rtogs pa'i chos) is contrasted with the dharma of the scriptural teachings (lung gi chos).

170. The Lotus Crystal Cave is Pema Shelphuk (padma shel phug), which is located near the top of Pema Ri Thang (padma ri thang), a sacred mountain above Denkhok ('dan khog).

171. *gtam pad ma tshal gyi zlos gar,* Collected Works of Patrul Rinpoche (2003), vol. 1, pp. 301–55. See Tulku Thondup's translation in *Enlightened Living*, pp. 44–97.

172. The actual names of real people and places referred to in the play have been cloaked in allegoric language. See Tulku Thondup, *Enlightened Living,* pp. 10–11; based on Tshega's *Sheche Zegma* (*shes bya'i zegs ma,* Drops of Knowledge), no. 35 (Beijing: Mirig Pedrun Khang), and on oral tradition told to Tulku Thondup by Dilgo Khyentse Rinpoche.

173. The suffix *-la* is a respectful honorific appended to names.

174. Khenpo Pema Wangyal of Gemang Monastery, a direct disciple of Khenpo Kunpel, who was eighty-eight at the time of the completion of the writing of this book, in 2016.

175. Patrul's collected works include a letter in which he reprimands a tantrika called Kune Phurli and all those tantric magicians who interfere with the natural course of the elements by preventing rain from falling during the rainy season (during festivals, for example): "dbyar kyi char gcod mkhan la spreng ba," in the Collected Works of Patrul Rinpoche (2003), vol. 1, pp. 520–21. What is quoted here is a summary of this letter made by Khenpo Kunpel in his biography *Elixir of Faith,* p. 451.

176. Collected Works of Patrul Rinpoche (2003), vol. 8, p. 146. The Tibetan text should read "*degs snying 'dod*" instead of "*. . . 'dor.*"

177. Ibid., p. 146. The Tibetan text should read *gnad med* instead of *gnang med.*

178. *Lima* is an alloy of five metals, including copper, tin, zinc, iron, lead, and sometimes silver. Statues and other objects made of this alloy are considered to be the best.

179. Others, such as the faithful Jamyang Lodrö from the noble Athub family, also urged Patrul to keep offerings and use them for virtuous purposes.

180. Patrul Rinpoche's words have proven to be true. See note 15.

181. Khenpo Kunpel, *Elixir of Faith,* pp. 406–9.

182. According to Chökyi Nyima Rinpoche, this story is well known in Tibet and many people still have keepsakes of this barley. Chökyi Nyima Rinpoche's father, Tulku Urgyen Rinpoche, had a few grains.

183. *Bumchen* (bum can), "vase breathing."

184. Clear light (*ösel* / 'od gsal) is one of the Six Yogas of Naropa. The clear light is a nonconceptual state, free of mental constructs, akin to the realization of dharmakaya. Highly experienced practitioners who have trained in this yoga are able to maintain a state of luminosity throughout the time of deep sleep.

185. In Nyoshul Khen Rinpoche's version of this story, the lama is named Nyukma Tulku. *Nyukma* (snyug ma) means "bamboo."

186. Dza Trama Tulku Kunzang Dechen Dorje (dza thra ma sprul sku kun bzang bde chen rdo rje, d.u.).

187. Jigme Tenpai Nyima, the 3rd Dodrupchen, was born in 1865, and Do Khyentse passed away in 1866.

188. Tsoknyi Rigdzin Chögyal Dorje of Nangchen (tshogs gnyis rig 'dzin chos rgyal rdo rje, 1789–1844).

189. See note 38.

190. Excerpt translated from *gtam padma'i tshal gyi zlos gar* (The Lotus-Grove Play), Collected Works of Patrul Rinpoche, vol. 1 (2003), p. 350.

191. See Tulku Thondup, *Masters of Meditation and Miracles,* p. 201.

192. Zurchungpa Sherab Trakpa (zur chung pa shes rab grags pa, 1014–1074) was

a very accomplished master who once spent thirteen years in strict meditative retreat. For a teaching by Sherab Trakpa, see Dilgo Khyentse Rinpoche, *Zurchungpa's Testament: A Commentary on Zurchung Sherab Trakpa's Eighty Chapters of Personal Advice,* trans. Padmakara Translation Group (Ithaca, N.Y.: Snow Lion Publications, 2006).

193. As both the son and lineage holder of Chokgyur Lingpa, Wangchok Dorje had been expected not to take a vow of celibacy but instead, for the sake of his family bloodline, to be a householder like his tertön father, with children to carry on his lineage.

194. See note 152.

195. To Önpo Tenga he gave teachings on the *Root Verses on the Middle Way* by Nagarjuna, and to others he taught as well the commentary on *The Three Vows* by Ngari Panchen Pema Wangyal (the commentary is titled *Ascertaining the Three Vows*), *The Way of the Bodhisattva,* the root text and commentary of *Resting at Ease in the Nature of Mind* by Longchenpa, and other teachings.

196. In addition to Pema Trinley's testimony: In 1980, after returning to Tibet, Tulku Orgyen Tobgyal met a nun at Neten Monastery (the traditional seat of Chokgyur Lingpa) who was more than a hundred years old. She had been in her twenties when she heard of the death of Wangchok Dorje.

197. This refers to the age of five degenerations (snyigs ma lnga). The "age of residues" (snyigs dus) is characterized by a degeneration in (1) life span (tshe), (2) general karma (las), (3) the view (lta ba), and (4) the faculties of beings (sems can), as well as by (5) an increase of the obscuring emotions (*nyonmong* / nyon mongs; Skt. *klesha*).

198. Dorje Phagmo of Yamdrok (yar 'brog rdo rje phag mo) was a daughter of a noble family. She had been one of the final candidates during the search for the reincarnation of the Samding Dorje Phagmo.

199. *Kudung* (sku gdung) is the "body relic" of a great master who has passed away, either before the cremation ceremony or in case it is embalmed and kept without being cremated.

200. The Jowo of Lhasa, a statue of Buddha Shakyamuni, is the most venerated statue in Tibet. It had been blessed by the Buddha himself, taken to China, and eventually brought to Tibet by Gyaza Konjo, the Chinese queen of King Songtsen Gampo. It is housed in the Jokhang Temple in Lhasa.

201. Khenpo Kunpel, *Elixir of Faith,* p. 437. Whenever Patrul himself went to pay homage to Gyalwai Nyugu's relic, he used this prayer:

> In all my future lives,
> May I never fall under the spell of bad companions;
> May I never harm even one hair of one sentient being;
> May I never be deprived of the light of the sublime dharma;
> May whoever has been connected with me in any conceivable way—

Through listening to my teachings,
Seeing me, hearing me, touching me, talking with me, or even thinking of me—
Be purified of even the most serious negative action.
May he or she find the doors to lower realms of existence shut
And take rebirth in the exalted pure land of the Potala Buddhafield of Avalokiteshvara, the Buddha of Compassion.

202. Lushul Khenpo Könchog Drönme (klu shul mkhan po dkon mchog sgron me, 1859–1936) from Dodrupchen Monastery, also known as Khenpo Könme.
203. This practice is known as Zhingdrup (zhing sgrub).
204. Rigdzin Dupa (rig 'dzin 'dus pa), the sadhana of the Longchen Nyingthig cycle, focused on the mandala of Guru Padmasambhava, his twenty-five disciples, and the Eight Vidyadharas.
205. Samye (bsam yas) was Tibet's first Buddhist monastery, built by Guru Padmasambhava under the patronage of King Trisong Detsen. Khangri Thökar (gangs ri thod dkar) is the famous hermitage of Longchen Rabjam in Central Tibet, where he composed many of his treatises, including the *Seven Treasuries.*
206. On one occasion, while teaching, Patrul said, "Regarding the infinite good qualities of a pure land and the ease with which one can be reborn there through supplication prayers, Vajrasattva's Eastern Buddhafield of Manifest Joy is peerless. Next, in the west, Sukhavati, Amitabha's Western Buddhafield of Great Bliss, is supreme."
207. Yanlagjung (yan lag 'byung) is the Tibetan name of the arhat Angaja (Skt.), one of the Sixteen Arhats at the time of the Buddha.
208. In fact, apart from the prediction of being reborn in Vajrasattva's buddhafield, a tulku of Patrul Rinpoche did appear in Tsö in Amdo. See page 56.
209. These are the first five of the twenty-one exercises in the Longchen Nyingthig *trulkhor.*
210. When great practitioners pass away, by snapping their fingers they request the wisdom deities who have been abiding in the mandala of their bodies to depart to their respective buddhafields. Likewise, a few days before passing away, Dilgo Khyentse Rinpoche was seen snapping his fingers near different parts of his body, thus requesting the peaceful and wrathful wisdom deities residing in the various places of the mandala of his body to leave his body, as it would soon be lifeless.
211. Dudjom Rinpoche, ri chos bslab bya nyams len dmar khrid go bder brjod pa grub pa'i bcud len, rendered in English as *Extracting the Quintessence of Accomplishment: Oral Instructions for the Practice of Mountain Retreat, Expounded Simply and Directly in Their Essential Nakedness,* translated and published by Konchog Tendzin [Matthieu Ricard] (Darjeeling: Ogyen Kunzang Chöling Monastery, 1976).

212. *Thukdam* (thugs dam), the meditative absorption of an advanced practitioner after death.
213. Palshu Lama Tseli was evidently one of Patrul's disciples, about whom no further information is available.
214. *Dakini* (Skt.; Tib. *khandroma* / mkha' 'gro ma, lit. "moving through space"). A dakini is the embodiment of wisdom in female form. There are several levels of dakini: wisdom dakinis, who have complete realization, and worldly dakinis, who possess various spiritual powers. The word *Dakini* is also used as a title for great women teachers and as a respectful form of address to the wives of spiritual masters.
215. The famous Indian Buddhist philosopher Nagarjuna (1st–2nd c.) wrote his *Letter to a Friend* in Sanskrit under the title *Suhrllekha* (Tib. *bshes pa'i spring yig*). It is advice written in the form of verse, addressed to Nagarjuna's friend King Gautamiputra. *Nagarjuna's Letter to a Friend: With Commentary by Kangyur Rinpoche*, trans. Padmakara Translation Group (Ithaca, N.Y: Snow Lion, 2005).
216. The *Five Treatises of Maitreya:* (1) Tib. *mngon rtogs rgyan* (Skt. *Abhisamayalamkara*), (2) *mdo sde'i rgyan* (*Mahayanasutralamkara*), (3) *rgyud bla ma* (*Uttaratantra*), (4) *chos dang chos nyid rnam 'byed* (*Dharmadharmatavibhaga*), (5) *dbus mtha' rnam 'byed* (*Madhyantavibhaga*).
217. "From his mind" refers to a spontaneous expression of his wisdom, a distillation of the essence of the teachings, and a commentary based on his vast knowledge, with excerpts drawn from his memory and explanations formulated in a way that is not just the repetition of written texts committed to memory.
218. *Nyingje* (snying rje), usually translated as "compassion," literally means "Lord of the Heart." The Sanskrit term for compassion is *karuna.*
219. The four powers (stobs bzhi): The power of regret for past misdeeds, the power of taking support of their teacher or a deity, the power of using a specific meditation as antidote for their negative actions, and the power of determination to henceforth stay aloof from such negative actions.
220. The Three Roots are three objects of reliance for Vajrayana practitioners: the Lama (or Guru), the Yidam (tutelary deity), and the Dakini (or dharma protector).
221. Drime Özer (dri me 'od zer), "Stainless Light," is one of Longchen Rabjam's names.
222. Khyentse Özer (mkhyen brtse 'od zer), "Light Rays of Wisdom and Kindness," is one of the main names of Jigme Lingpa.
223. Fearless (Jigme) bodhisattva, scion (Nyugu) of the Victorious Ones (Gyalwai), thus refers to Patrul Rinpoche's root teacher, to whom this supplication mostly refers.
224. The four immeasurables (tshad med bzhi) are loving-kindness, compassion, sympathetic joy, and impartiality.
225. Four ways of attracting disciples (bsdu ba'i dngos po bzhi): A teacher gathers

disciples by (1) his generosity, (2) the fact that his teachings are attuned to the minds of his disciples, (3) his ability to introduce disciples to the practice leading to liberation, and (4) the fact that he himself practices what he preaches.

226. The "twofold purity" refers to the fact that the buddha nature is both primordially pure and pure from adventitious stains, ephemeral veils that prevent ordinary beings from realizing it.

227. "Pristine simplicity that crushes delusion into dust": *Zang thal* is a synonym for *ma 'gags pa,* "unobstructed," but according to Tulku Pema Wangyal Rinpoche it can also be explained as *zang kha ma thal du 'byung. Zang kha ma,* "natural condition," refers to *ma bcos pa'i gdod ma'i gnas lugs,* the unmodified simplicity of the primordial nature; and *thal du 'byung,* "reduce to dust," refers to the annihilation of deluded thoughts, *'khrul pa'i rnam rtog.*

228. Literally "Samantabhadra activity." This term denotes boundless enlightened activity. Samantabhadra (Kuntu Zangpo; kun tu bzang po), one of the Eight Bodhisattvas (here we are not referring to the primordial Buddha of the same name) emanates countless rays of light. At the tip of every light ray is an emanation of himself, which in turn emanates countless rays of light, at the tip of each of which is yet another emanation, and so forth, thus filling the entire space with emanations that perform the buddha-activity.

229. *Tsa tsa* can also refer to a small clay figure of a deity made with a mold. These figures are used as objects of devotion (since they contain relics and written mantras) or as ways to mold the ashes of a deceased person into clay, to be placed in a sacred place or a pure natural setting, so as to dispose of the ashes in a meritorious way.

230. The Nyingthig Yazhi (snying thig ya bzhi, Fourfold Heart Essence) is a multi-volume collection of most profound teachings on the Great Perfection.

231. The *Yeshe Lama* is the main Great Perfection teaching of Jigme Lingpa (see note 51). The Khandro Nyingthig (Heart Essence of the Dakinis) is a cycle of teachings that is part of the Nyingthig Yazhi.

232. Tulku Thondup, *Masters of Meditation and Miracles,* p. 195.

233. In his biography of Önpo Orgyen Tendzin Norbu (Önpo Tenga), Khenpo Shenga mentions that Shenphen Thaye died when his nephew Önpo Tendzin Norbu was fifteen. If Shenga is correct, then Tendzin Norbu's dates are 1851–1910 (and not 1851–1900, as often quoted). This would put Shenphen Thaye's death in 1865/66. Some authors place it in 1855 or 1856, which seems incompatible with Tendzin Norbu's dates, or (according to the Tibetan scholar Karma Delek's biography of Shenphen Thaye) in 1869/70, in which case Önpo Tenga should have been eighteen or nineteen when his uncle passed away.

234. Probably the 6th Minling Trichen, Gyurme Pema Wangyal ('gyur med padma dbang rgyal).

235. Sometimes masters initiate a particular way of commenting upon an important text, for which there has been no such tradition. From then on, the disciples will

not explain these texts in their own ways but perpetuate as faithfully as they can the explanation given by their master. Sometimes they even made notes between the lines of texts, and these notes were copied from generation to generation.

236. Probably the 33rd throne holder of Sakya, Pema Dudul Wangchuk (pad ma bdud 'dul dbang phyug, 1806–1843).

237. Tigle Gyachen (thig le'i rgya can), the "Sealed Quintessence," a guru yoga focused on Longchen Rabjam, written by Jigme Lingpa.

238. On the meaning of "rediscovered," see the glossary entry for *terma.*

239. There are varied opinions regarding the family relations between Patrul Rinpoche and Khenpo Kunpel. This is due to the fact that when Tibetans speak of a "family member" (*punkyak* / spun kyag), they mean people related through blood. They use a different term for people related by marriage (*nyering* / nyes ring) and don't consider them real kin. According to various sources (including Khenpo Jampel Dorje from Ari Dza Monastery), Khenpo Kunpel was the son of Che Seri, who was a brother of Che Tsondru, himself the husband of Patrul Rinpoche's sister. So Khenpo Kunpel was not related to Patrul Rinpoche by blood, but through his sister's marriage.

240. The Expanded Redaction of the Complete Works of 'Ju Mi-pham Series, 27 vols. Published by Lama Ngondrup and Sherab Drimey (Paro, Bhutan, 1984–1993), now with Shechen Publications.

241. The *tshe bdag phyag rgya zil gnon* from the cycle of *'jam dpal khro chu dug gdong nag po'i sgrub skor,* a collection of spiritual treasures from the discoveries of Gya Zhangtrom (rgya zhang khrom).

242 A place in Denkhok Valley where Mipham Rinpoche spent many years in retreat and where he eventually passed away. This is also the place where Dilgo Khyentse Rinpoche was born and blessed by Mipham Rinpoche throughout the first year of his life. This story and the accompanying ones were told to Dilgo Khyentse Rinpoche by Lama Ösel, who was Mipham Rinpoche's faithful attendant and a great practitioner in his own right.

243. The *mala* (*phreng ba*) that Mipham Rinpoche used during that retreat, made of *rudraksha* beads, was kept by Khenpo Shönri of Juniong until he passed away in 2015. It is now with his niece.

244. The dates for Orgyen Tendzin Norbu are usually given as 1851–1900. However, in the biography of the master written by one of his closest disciples, Khenpo Shenga, it is said that Önpo Tenga passed away in the Male Earth Bird Year, which was 1910, and that he was then in his sixtieth year. Since Önpo Tenga himself is quoted saying that sixty was the life span predicted by his teachers, there can be little doubt about the year of his passing away, which is 1910.

245. Khenpo Shenga's biography says that Önpo Tenga met Patrul when he was seventeen, which fits well with the first mention of Önpo Tenga in Patrul Rinpoche's biography that can be estimated at around 1868. Shenga also writes that Önpo Tenga was Patrul's disciple for thirty years. Since Patrul Rinpoche

passed away in 1887, if all the above dates are correct it seems that this should be corrected to twenty years.

246. *dpal ldan bla ma dam pa shes bya kun mkhyen shrih nirma ka'i gsung 'bum gyi bzhugs byang 'dod 'byung rin po che'i za ma tog*. The Precious Vessel That Fulfills All Wishes, being the table of contents of the collected writings of the glorious, supreme, and omniscient Shri Nirmanakaya (Patrul). In the Collected Works of Patrul Rinpoche, vol. 1.

247. Told to Matthieu Ricard.

GLOSSARY

arhat (Skt.). One who has vanquished the enemies of afflictive emotion and realized the nonexistence of the personal self, and who is forever free from the sufferings of samsara. Arhatship is the goal of the teachings of the Root Vehicle, the Shravakayana or Hinayana.

auspicious coincidence (Tib. *tendrel* / rten 'brel, Skt. *pratitya-samutpada,* "dependent arising"). A coinciding of causes and conditions that creates a blessing or good fortune.

bhikshu (Skt.). A fully ordained monk.

bindu (Skt.; Tib. *tigle* / thig le). The essence-energy carried by prana as it flows through the nadis.

bodhichitta (Skt.). The wish to attain buddhahood, the enlightened state, for the sake of all sentient beings.

buddha nature (Skt. *tathagatagarbha*; Tib. de gshegs snying po). The essence of enlightenment present in all sentient beings.

buddhafield (Skt. *buddhakshetra*). See pure land.

dakini (Skt.; Tib. *khandro,* lit. "moving through space"). The representation of wisdom in female form. There are wisdom dakinis, who have complete realization, and worldly dakinis, who possess various spiritual powers.

dakini script. Text written in symbolic letters, said to be used by the dakinis, which can only be read by certain treasure revealers (tertöns).

dharma (Skt; Tib. *chö* / *chos*). The common term for Buddhist doctrine. It comes from the Sanksrit *dhr,* which means "holding," as the dharma can "hold" beings out of samsara and ignorance. Altogether, there are ten recognized meanings for this term. In its widest sense it means all that can be known. In this text, the term is used exclusively to indicate the teaching of the Buddha. It has two aspects: the dharma of transmission, namely the teachings that are actually given, and the dharma of realization, or the states of wisdom that are attained through the application of the teachings.

dharmakaya (Skt). One of the three bodies (*kayas*) of the Buddha, the dharmakaya is the formless body of enlightened qualities and the absolute dimension of enlightenment.

dri (Tib.). The female of the yak.

Dzogchen (Tib.; Skt. Atiyoga). The Great Perfection, the highest view according to the Nyingma tradition.

dzomo (Tib., sing., fem.). A cross between a yak and a cow .

five poisons. Five destructive emotions (Skt. *klesha*) that are the causes of suffering: ignorance (confusion), attachment, aversion (hatred, anger, etc.), jealousy, and pride.

four thoughts that turn the mind to dharma (Tib. lodok namshyi, blo ldog rnam bzhi). (1) contemplating the rarity and preciousness of human life, (2) impermanence and death, (3) karma, or cause and effect, and (4) the defects or shortcomings of samsara.

ganachakra (Skt.; Tib. tshogs). A sacred feast or ritual offering in tantric Buddhism in which oblations of food and drink are blessed as the elixir of wisdom and offered to the yidam deity as well as to the mandala of one's own body.

gelong (Tib. dge long; Skt. *bhikshu*). A fully ordained monk, who vows to abide by 253 rules of behavior. *See also* getsul.

Geluk (Tib. dge lugs). One of the four primary schools of Tibetan Buddhism. The Geluk school was founded by Je Tsongkhapa (1357–1419) as a reformation of the tradition of Atisha Dipamkara. Also spelled *Gelug*. An adherent of the Geluk school is called a Gelukpa.

Geshe (Tib. dge bshes). The title in the Geluk school for one who holds a high degree in Buddhist scholarship, comparable to a doctorate.

getsul (Tib. dge tshul; Skt. *shramanera*). A novice monk, who vows to abide by thirty-three basic rules of behavior, one of which is celibacy for life. *See also* gelong.

Great Perfection. *See* Dzogchen.

Guru Rinpoche. *See* Padmasambhava.

Guru Yoga. A practice consisting of visualizing the guru, making prayers and requests for blessing, receiving these blessings, and merging the mind in the guru's enlightened wisdom-mind. It is the final part of the preliminary practices (*ngöndro*) of the Vajrayana and is considered to be the quintessence of all subsequent practice.

hidden yogi. A realized being who assumes a modest appearances and who escapes the notice of most people. The term applies to both Patrul Rinpoche and Rogza Sönam Palge, among others. Hidden yogis can also be hermits who live in remote places and whose spiritual accomplishments remain unknown.

Kagyu (Tib. bka' brgyud). One of the four primary schools of Tibetan Buddhism. An adherent of the Kagyu school is called a Kagyupa.

Kahma (Tib. bka' ma; also spelled *Kama*). The long lineage of the scriptures that have been transmitted without interruption from master to disciple, from the primordial Buddha, Samantabhadra, through Guru Padmasambhava and other great Vidyadharas (Awareness Holders) up to our time.

Kangyur (Tib. bka' 'gyur, literally "translated words"). The Tibetan version of the Indian Buddhist canon (Skt. Tripitaka), that fills 103 volumes in the Derge edition, containing the Buddha's teachings in both sutras and tantras.

kaya (Skt., "body"). *See* dharmakaya; nirmanakaya; sambhogakaya.

Khenchen (Tib. mkhan chen, "great khenpo"). A title used for a particularly learned scholar.

Khenpo (Tib. mkhan po). A title for a person, mostly in the Nyingma, Sakya, and Kagyu traditions, who has completed the major course of nine to twelve years of studying traditional Buddhist philosophy, logic, Vinaya, and other subjects, and afterward has been authorized to teach. This title can also refer to the abbot of a monastery of any of the four traditions or the preceptor from whom one receives ordination.

lojong (Tib. blo sbyong). A practice of training (sbyong) the mind (*lo*/blo) and cultivating relative and absolute bodhichitta with the use of short phrases, or slogans, as taught by Atisha in his Seven-Point Mind Training and other eminent Kadam masters. Later, numerous *lojong* slogans were written by masters of all schools.

Longchen Nyingthig (klong chen snying thig, Heart Essence of the Great Expanse). An important cycle of teachings and practice in the Nyingma tradition that were rediscovered by Rigdzin Jigme Lingpa as a mind treasure.

Mahamudra (Skt., lit. "Great Seal"). The seal of the absolute nature of all phenomena. The term is used for the instructions and practice of the highest teachings of the Kagyu tradition

mahapandita (Skt.). *See* pandita.

mahasiddha (Skt.). A great *siddha*, an advanced practitioner who has attained the supreme accomplishment, which is enlightenment. A famous work by the 12th-c. Indian scholar Abhayadatta recounts the lives of eighty-four *mahasiddhas* of ancient India.

Mantrayana (Skt., mantra vehicle). *See* Vajrayana.

mind treasure. *See* terma.

nadi (Skt.; Tib. *tsa*-rtsa). The *nadis* are the spiritual-energy channels of the physical body.

nirmanakaya (Skt.; Tib. *tulku*). One of the three bodies (*kayas*) of the Buddha, the nirmanakaya ("manifestation body") is the manifestation in physical form.

Nyingma (Tib. rnying ma). One of the four primary schools of Tibetan Buddhism. The Nyingma school is the oldest. An adherent of the Nyingma school is called a Nyingmapa.

Om mani padme hung. The mantra of Avalokiteshvara, the Buddha of Compassion. The most popular mantra in Tibetan Buddhism, also known as the six-syllable mantra. *Hung* is the Tibetan pronunciation of Sanskrit *hum.*

Padmasambhava. The Indian master, known to Tibetans as Guru Rinpoche. Together with Shantarakshita, Padmasambhava brought the Buddha's teachings to Tibet in the ninth century at the invitation of King Trisong Detsen.

pandita (Skt.). A learned master, scholar, or professor of Buddhist philosophy; *mahapandita* means "great *pandita.*"

paramita (Skt.). The *paramitas,* or transcendent perfections, are six activities that form the practice of the bodhisattva path: generosity, ethical discipline, patience, diligence, concentration, and wisdom. It is said that the five first paramitas are all meant to accomplish the sixth, the perfection of wisdom. *Paramita* literally means "gone to the other shore," having transcended samsara and attained nirvana. Compared to ordinary "perfections," they are said to be transcendent inasmuch as their practice is free from grasping at the notions of subject, object, and action.

phowa (Tib. 'pho ba). A ritual performed at the moment of death, either by a lama or by a dying practitioner, for the transference of consciousness to a buddhafield where enlightenment will ultimately be attained. In its quintessential form, it consists in merging with the Guru's enlightened mind at the time of death. Phowa is also practiced during one's lifetime, combined with a longevity practice, as a training to be fully applied at the time of death.

phurba (Tib. phur ba; Skt. *kilaya*). A three-sided ritual dagger, such as that held by the deity Vajrakilaya. It symbolizes the transformation of the three main mental poisons (*kleshas*) into the three *kayas* (bodies or dimensions) of buddhahood and the cutting of all outer, inner, and secret obstacles on the path to enlightenment.

poison. *See* five poisons.

prajnaparamita (Skt.). The transcendent perfection of wisdom.

prana (Skt.; Tib. *lung*/rlung). The subtle "wind," or energy, that circulates through the spiritual channels, or *nadis.*

pure land (Tib. *zhingkham* / zhing khams). A world or dimension manifested by a buddha or great bodhisattva through the spontaneous qualities of his or her realization. In a pure land, beings can progress toward enlightenment without falling back into the lower realms of samsara. Also called a buddhafield.

rainbow body (Tib. 'ja' lus). When they die, accomplished practitioners of the Great Perfection sometimes gradually dissolve their body into rainbow light, leaving behind nothing but their hair and nails (which are considered to be "dead" parts of the body).

Rime (ris med) movement (Tib.). The nonsectarian approach to the study and practice of the Eight Chariots of the Practice Lineage of Tibetan Buddhism: Nyingma,

Kadam, Sakya, Kagyu, Shangpa, Chöd, Kalachakra, and Orgyen Nyendrub.

Sakya (Tib. sa skya). One of the four primary schools of Tibetan Buddhism. An adherent of the Sakya school is called a Sakyapa.

samadhi (Skt.). The word *samadhi* can be understood according the Buddhist interpretation as "concentration" or "unification of mind." The Tibetan translation, *ting gne dzin* (ting nges 'dzin), means "holding on to what is profound and certain," referring to a deep and perfectly focused meditation. One also speaks of *tsechik ting nge dzin* (rtse gcig ting nges 'dzin), or "single-pointed concentration."

samaya (Skt.; Tib. *damtsik* / dam tshig). A series of vows or pledges, related to body, speech, and mind. In the Vajrayana, samayas are sacred links between teacher and disciple, as well as among disciples. When these vows are kept, spiritual realization is assured. When they are broken, major obstacles and suffering obstruct further progress on the path.

sambhogakaya (Skt., "enjoyment body"). One of the three bodies (*kayas*) of the Buddha. Part of the sambhogakaya can only be apprehended by fully enlightened Buddhas, and part of it can be apprehended by highly realized practitioners still on the path.

shamatha (Skt.). A kind of meditation meant to achieve inner calm, through cultivating a mind that is stable, clear, and quiet.

shedra (Tib. bshad grwa). Philosophical college.

shingdrup (Tib. shing sgrub). Accomplishing the Pureland, a practice for taking rebirth in Sukhavati, Amitabha's Buddhafield of Great Bliss.

siddha (Skt.). An accomplished practitioner or adept who has attained the *siddhis,* or accomplishments. *See also* mahasiddha.

six paramitas. *See* paramita.

six realms (Tib. 'khor ba rigs drug). The six realms of existence in which one takes rebirth, until liberation from samsara is attained. The three higher realms are the long-life god (*deva*) realm, the jealous god (*asura*) realm, and the human realm. The three lower realms are the animal realm, the hungry ghost (*preta*) realm, and the hell realm.

stupa (Skt; Tib. *chörten* / mchod rten, lit. "support of offering"). A monument often containing relics of Buddhist saints, as well as mandalas, hundred of thousands of mantras, sacred books, and earth from various sacred places. Stupas symbolize the enlightened mind of the buddhas, while statues symbolize the enlightened body and books symbolize the enlightened speech. There are many kinds of stupas, which are all built according to well-defined proportions. It is said that they bring great benefit to the land where they are built and contribute to reducing conflicts, famines, and other causes of suffering throughout the world.

terma (Tib. gter ma). "Revealed treasure." (When capitalized, *Terma* refers to the tradition or the body of terma literature.) When Padmasambhava gave empowerments and teachings to his main disciples, he entrusted specific teachings to each one. These teachings were miraculously hidden in various places—temples, images, the sky (i.e., a parchment falls from the sky into the tertön's hand), rocks, and lakes. Those found in nature are called earth treasures (sa gter). He foretold that in future incarnations these disciples would reveal (find) these hidden teachings and share them for the benefit of beings. These incarnations are known as *tertöns.* In the case of "mind treasures" (dgongs gter), the hidden teachings are not physically unearthed but arise in the tertön's mind by the blessings of Padmasambhava. When a terma is called "rediscovered" (yang gter), this means it was first concealed by Guru Padmasambhava and then found by a tertön. When a terma is called "re-extracted," it means that it was (1) hidden by Padmasambhava and (2) rediscovered or revealed by a first tertön, who then realized that the time was not suitable and hid the treasure again; it was then (3) revealed a second time by a later tertön, who shared it with others. We could also call this a "twice-discovered" terma.

tertön (Tib. gter ston). "Treasure master," or revealer of terma. A tertön experiences visions or signs indicating how and where to discover his or her destined terma. Many such treasure masters have appeared throughout the centuries, down to the present day. *See also* terma.

thögal (Tip. thod rgal, "direct crossing"). A Dzogchen practice relating to the realization of spontaneous presence of pure awareness.

Three Jewels. The Buddha, the Dharma, and the Sangha. Taking refuge in the Three Jewels marks the entry into the Buddhist path and distinguishes one as a Buddhist.

torma (Tib. gtor ma). A ritual object composed of a variety of substances, such as flour, clay, or precious substances. Depending on the context, the torma is considered as an offering, a symbolic representation of a yidam deity, a vehicle of blessings, or a weapon for dispelling obstacles.

trekchö (Tib. khregs chod). A Dzogchen practice concerned with "cutting through" the solidity of clinging to reveal primordial purity.

Tripitaka (Skt., lit. "three baskets"). The three collections of the Buddha's teachings: the Vinaya, Sutra, and Abhidharma. These are the early teachings and dialogues of the Buddha, originally in the Pali language.

trulkhor (Tib. 'phrul 'khor). Physical yoga exercises combined with visualization focused on spiritual channels (Skt. *nadi*), winds (Skt. *prana* or *vayu*) and essences (Skt. *bindu;* Tib. *tigle* / tig le).

tsalung (Tib. rtsa rlung; Skt. *nadi-vayu*). Advanced yogic teachings including practice of the subtle channels, energies, and essences.

tulku (Tib. sprul sku). The Tibetan translation of the Sanskrit *nirmanakaya,* lit. "manifested body"; also called an emanation. A term and honorific title for a reincarnation of a recognized lama or deity. It is not uncommon that several tulkus of the same master may be recognized in the same time period, since reincarnation is not considered to be the incarnation of an autonomous, truly existing self, but rather the continuation of a stream of wisdom and compassion that can manifest in manifold ways to benefit beings as needed.

tummo (Tib. gtum mo, lit. "wild one," referring to the inner fire of wisdom; Skt. *chandali*). One of the Six Yogas of Naropa, *tummo* is the practice of the inner heat, and involves mastery of channels (Tib. *tsa*), prana (*lung*), and essences (*tigle*).

tutelary deity (Tib. *yidam* / yi dam; Skt. *ishtadevata*). The main deity upon which a Vajrayana practitioner focuses.

Vajrakilaya (Skt.; Tib. Dorje Phurba / rdo rje phur pa). Also known as Vajrakumara (Skt. Vajrakumāra; Tib. Dorje Shönnu / rdo rje gzhon nu). One of the main wisdom deities practiced in the Nyingma tradition. Vajrakilaya is one of the Eight Herukas (bka' brgyad), who symbolize various aspects of enlightenment. The practice of Vajrakilaya, a wrathful deity associated with "enlightened activity," is considered to be one of the most powerful ways to dispel outer and inner obstacles on the path to enlightenment.

Vajrasattva (Skt.). The buddha who is the "lord of all mandalas" and embodies the forty-two peaceful and fifty-eight wrathful deities. The sadhana of Vajrasattva and recitation of his mantra are practiced for the purification of negative thoughts, words, and actions.

Vajrayana (Skt., "diamond vehicle"). The teachings and practices based on the tantras. Also called Mantrayana. The Vajrayana is said to be meant for individuals of the sharpest faculties, since it is very profound, and to be endowed with many skillful means to reach enlightenment swiftly and with ease. It is also called the "resultant vehicle," since the result of the path (buddhahood) is already present in the ground as the buddha nature that dwells in every sentient being and is used on the path through recognizing the basic nature of mind.

Victorious One (Skt. Jina). An epithet of the Buddha. In the plural, buddhas.

vidyadhara (Skt., "awareness holder"; Tib. *rigdzin* / rig 'dzin). A master of high attainment in the Vajrayana. The Eight Great Vidyadharas were tantric siddhas from India.

Vimalamitra (Skt.). One of the eight vidyadharas and a great Indian master of the eighth century. He taught widely in Tibet and was the main Indian pandita who oversaw the translation of Buddhist texts from Sanskrit into Tibetan at Samye Monastery under the patronage of King Trisong Detsen. The particular Dzogchen lineage that he initiated is known as the Vima Nyingthig.

Vinaya (Skt.). The section of the Buddha's teaching (Tripitaka) that deals with discipline, and in particular with the vows of monastic ordination.

Yamantaka (Skt.; Tib. gshin rje gshed). A deity who is the wrathful form of Manjushri. *Yamantaka* means "destroyer of Yama," the embodiment of death.

yoga (Skt.; Tib. *naljor* / rnal 'byor). A term commonly used to refer to spiritual practice. *Yoga* literally means "joining" or "union" with the natural state of the mind.

yogi (Skt.; Tib. *naljorpa* / rnal 'byor pa). A tantric practitioner. In this book *yogi* refers to someone who has already attained stability in the natural state of mind and is proficient in the practices based on *nadis, pranas,* and *bindus.*

SOURCES

About the Contributors

DILGO KHYENTSE RINPOCHE (dil mgo mkhyen brtse rin po che bkra shis dpal 'byor, 1910–1991) was a foremost meditation master, poet, and scholar of the Mahayana and Dzogchen traditions of Vajrayana Buddhism. One of the principal holders of the Nyingma lineage of Tibetan Buddhism, he was as well a dedicated exponent of the nonsectarian movement. In addition to spending thirty years in contemplative retreat, he worked tirelessly to preserve the teachings of Tibetan Buddhism through the publication of texts, the building of monasteries and stupas, and instructions to thousands of practitioners throughout the world. His collected works in the Tibetan language fill twenty-five volumes.

DODRUP TENPAI NYIMA (Jigme Tenpai Nyima, 3rd Dodrupchen, 1865–1926) was the author of a spiritual biography of Patrul Rinpoche, *Dewdrop of Amrita.* See Biographical Notes, page 197.

GARCHEN RINPOCHE, KÖNCHOG GYALTSEN (mgar chen dkon mchog rgyal mtshan, b. 1949), is a master of the Drigung Kagyu tradition. By the time he finally left Tibet in the 1990s, he had spent twenty-three years imprisoned by the Chinese. Of his time in prison, twenty years were spent in the company of his teacher, Khenpo Munsel (mkhan po mun sel, 1916–1994). Since coming out of Tibet, he has been tirelessly teaching throughout the world.

KHENPO JAMPEL DORJE (mkhan po 'jam dpal rdo rje, b. ca. 1970) is a teacher at Ari Dza Monastery in Dzachukha, Kham.

KHENPO KÖNCHOG MÖNLAM (mkhan po dkon mchog smon lam, b. 1940) was born at Nangchen, in Kham. He studied in Drigung Kagyu monasteries in Tibet before seeking refuge in India, where he studied with Pomda Khenpo, Lama Wangdor, Khenchen Thupden Özer, Kunu Rinpoche, and many other teachers. He is currently teaching at his monastery in Manali, at the Drigung Kagyu Institute in India, and at the retreat center he established in Nepal.

Khenpo Kunpel (Khenpo Kunzang Palden, ca. 1862–1943) was the author of a spiritual biography of Patrul Rinpoche, *Elixir of Faith.* See Biographical Notes, page 202.

Khenpo Ngawang Palzang (mkhan po ngag dbang dpal bzang, 1879–1941), also known as Khenpo Ngakchung or Khenpo Ngaga (ngag dga'), was an influential Nyingma master regarded as an incarnation of Vimalamitra. His principal teacher was Nyoshul Lungtok, and his other teachers included Tertön Sogyal, Khenpo Shenga, Katok Situ Chökyi Gyatso, Khenpo Kunpel, and the 5th Dzogchen Rinpoche, Thubten Chökyi Dorje. Among his disciples were Chatral Rinpoche, Tulku Orgyen Chemchok, and Nyoshul Shedrup Tenpai Nyima. He left thirteen volumes of writings. His autobiography was translated as *Wondrous Dance of Illusion* (see Written Sources: Works in English).

Khenpo Palga, whose full name is Khenpo Palden Dorje (mkham po dpal ldan rdo rje, b. 1933), is one of the three known surviving students of Khenpo Thubga. For many years he has lived in semi-retreat in Gosa hermitage, about two hours' drive from Shechen Monastery.

Khenpo Pema Wangyal (mkhan po padma dbang rgyal, b. 1929) of Gemang Monastery is currently one of the most respected masters in Kham. He is among the very few surviving disciples of Khenpo Kunpel and of Khenpo Thubga. He also studied with Pema Siddhi and Dzogchen Khenpo Gönri, and was a close disciple of Dilgo Khyentse Rinpoche and Dodrupchen Rinpoche.

Khenpo Shönri (Shönu Dondrup, gzhon nu don grub, 1938–2015) of Juniong Monastery was a disciple of Khenpo Thubga (Khenpo Thubten Chöphel) and a custodian of many of Lama Mipham Rinpoche's and Patrul Rinpoche's relics.

Khenpo Tsering Gonpo (mkhan po tshe ring mgon po, b. ca. 1970) graduated from Larung Gar Philosophical College as a disciple of Khenpo Jigme Phuntsok. He currently resides at Dzagyal Trama Lung hermitages in Upper Dzachukha.

Kunu Rinpoche Tendzin Gyaltsen, also known as Kunu Lama Tendzin Gyaltsen (khu nu bla ma bstan 'dzin rgyal mtshan, ca. 1894–1977), was born in Kunu, Himachal Pradesh, India. He went to Sikkim at the age of twenty and from there to Central Tibet to study with a Buddhist master. At age twenty-seven he proceeded to Kham, where he studied with Kathok Situ Chökyi Gyatso, Khenpo Shenga, Dru Jamyang Trakpa (a direct disciple of Jamyang Khyentse Wangpo), Khenpo Kunpel, and Khenpo Ngawang Palzang. In 1938, he returned to India, where he did fifteen years of retreat in Kalimpong and Varanasi. After His Holiness the 14th Dalai Lama requested him to give teachings on the *Bodhicharyavatara,* he began teaching extensively, living mostly in Bodhgaya. He finally returned to Kunu, where he passed away.

NYOSHUL KHEN RINPOCHE, JAMYANG DORJE (myo shul mkhan po 'jam dbyangs rdo rje, 1932–1999), known as Nyoshul Khenpo, was an extremely learned Nyingma master. His root teacher was Nyoshul Shedrup Tenpai Nyima (known as Nyoshul Tulku), the reincarnation of Nyoshul Lungtok. Nyoshul Khenpo was a holder of the Longchen Nyingthig tradition and particularly of the Great Oral Lineage of Pith Instructions of the Great Perfection (Mengak Nyengyu Chenmo). He was also a disciple of Dudjom Rinpoche, Dilgo Khyentse Rinpoche, and the 16th Gyalwang Karmapa. He taught extensively in India and in France, where he spent seven years near the Chanteloube retreat center (Centre d'Études de Chanteloube). He traveled and taught widely at Buddhist centers in Europe and the United States. Nyoshul Khenpo is the author of a detailed history of the Nyingthig lineage in Tibetan, published in English under the title *A Marvelous Garland of Rare Gems.*

NYOSHUL LUNGTOK TENPAI NYIMA was a heart-disciple of Patrul Rinpoche. Many of the stories told by Khenpo Ngawang Palzang (author of *Wondrous Dance of Illusion*) were quoted verbatim from Nyoshul Lungtok. See Biographical Notes, page 215.

TROGAWA RINPOCHE, GYURME NGAWANG (khro dga' ba 'gyur med ngag dbang, 1931–2005) was an eminent practitioner and teacher of Tibetan medicine, who was trained at the famed Lhasa Chakpori medical college. He taught at the Tibetan Medical and Astrological Institute (Men-Tsee-Khang) in Dharamsala at the request of H. H. the Dalai Lama and then spent many years in Darjeeling, India, where he founded the Chagpori Institute in commemoration of the famous institute of the same name that existed in Lhasa. His main spiritual teacher was Dzongsar Jamyang Khyentse Chökyi Lodrö, and he was also a disciple of Dudjom Rinpoche, Kangyur Rinpoche, and Dilgo Khyentse Rinpoche.

TSOKNYI RINPOCHE (Ngawang Tsoknyi Gyatso, ngag dbang tshogs gnyis rgya mtsho, b. 1966), was recognized as the 3rd Tsoknyi Rinpoche by the 16th Gyalwang Karmapa. He has studied with great masters of the Drukpa Kagyu and Nyingma lineages, including Khamtrul Rinpoche Dongyu Nyima; his father, Tulku Urgyen Rinpoche; Dilgo Khyentse Rinpoche; Nyoshul Khen Rinpoche; and Nangchen Adeu Rinpoche. The author of *Fearless Simplicity* and other books, he teaches extensively around the world.

TULKU ORGYEN TOBGYAL RINPOCHE (o rgyan stobs rgyal rin po che, b. 1951) is the elder son of the 3rd Neten Chokling Rinpoche. He is considered to be an incarnation of Taksham Nuden Dorje. After the death of his father, he took care of Pema Ewam Chögar Gyurme Ling Monastery in Bir, India, for many years before handing it over to the 4th Neten Chokling Rinpoche. He is a disciple of Dzongsar Khyentse Chökyi Lodrö and Dilgo Khyentse Rinpoche. Renowned for his vast memory of the lives of past teachers, he recounted *The Life of Chokgyur Lingpa* to Erik Pema Kunsang.

TULKU PEMA WANGYAL is the informal name for Taklung Tsetrul Pema Wangyal Rinpoche (stag lung rtse sprul padma dbang rgyal, b. 1947). He is the eldest son of the great Nyingma master and tertön Kangyur Rinpoche, Longchen Yeshe Dorje (bka' 'gyur rin po che klong chen ye shes rdo rje, 1898–1975). Following the death of his father in Darjeeling, he has tirelessly worked to preserve and spread his father's lineage, taught as well as invited many great masters to teach at the Centre d'Études de Chanteloube in France, and directed the Padmakara Translation Group, which has published numerous translations of major Indian and Tibetan Buddhist texts.

TULKU THONDUP RINPOCHE was born in Golok in 1936 and trained from childhood at Dodrupchen Monastery, after having been recognized as the reincarnation of Khenpo Könchog Drönme (1859–1936). He lives in Cambridge, Massachusetts, where he writes and translates under the auspices of the Buddhayana Foundation. A few of his books in English are *Masters of Meditation and Miracles; Enlightened Living; The Healing Power of Mind; Peaceful Death, Joyful Rebirth;* and *The Heart of Unconditional Love.*

TULKU URGYEN CHEMCHOG (1915?–2003?) was one of the closest disciples of Khenpo Ngawang Palzang and a disciple of Dudjom Rinpoche, Jigdral Yeshe Dorje. He was able to teach quite a few disciples in secret while spending twenty years in Chinese labor camps in Tibet. After being freed, he lived and taught in Konjo province. After his passing away, his body shrank to the size of an arm's length, a phenomenon considered to be similar, though not identical, to the achievement of the rainbow body.

TULKU URGYEN RINPOCHE, TSEWANG CHOKDRUP PELBAR (sprul sku o rgyan tshe dbang mchog grub dpal 'bar (1919–1996), was born in Nangchen province, Kham. He began practicing at a very early age under his father, Chime Dorje, and subsequently studied with his uncle Samten Gyatso, his root master. He was very close with many other lamas of both the Kagyu and Nyingma schools, including the 16th Gyalwang Karmapa, Dudjom Rinpoche, and Dilgo Khyentse Rinpoche, with whom he exchanged many teachings. In his youth he stayed in retreat for twenty years and then spent thirty years in Nepal at Nagi Gonpa hermitage. He had many Western students, some of whom collected his teachings in numerous books, including his biography, *Blazing Splendor*, which also contains insights onto the lives of other masters.

YANTANG RINPOCHE (g.yang thang rin po che, 1929–2016) was born in Sikkim and traveled to Kham, since he was recognized as the reincarnation of Tertön Dorje Dechen Lingpa of Domang (mdo mang) Monastery. In 1959, even though he was an Indian citizen, he was imprisoned for twenty-two years in Chinese labor camps. After his release in 1981, he returned to Sikkim. In India, he received teachings from Dilgo Khyentse Rinpoche, Dodrupchen Rinpoche, and Penor Rinpoche. He gave extensive teachings and transmissions from the Nyingma tradition throughout the world.

Sources for Stories

This and the following section—"Sources for Stories" and "Sources for Biographical Notes"—use short forms of citation for published works. The full facts of publication for Tibetan and English sources appear in the section "Written Sources."

The titles of stories here (which include the Introduction and the excerpts from Patrul Rinpoche's writings) are listed in alphabetical order.

Advice for Alak Do-ngak: Oral account of Dilgo Khyentse Rinpoche, followed by excerpts from *Uniting Outer and Inner Solitude: Patrul Rinpoche's Advice for Alak Dongak Gyatso,* trans. Adam Pearcey. www.academia.edu/14932720/Uniting_Outer_and_Inner_Solitude_Patrul_Rinpoche_s_Advice_for_Alak_Dongak_Gyatso (accessed October 2016). Reproduced with permission.

Advice for Garwang from the Eastern Gorges of Gyalmo Rong: *Collected Works of Patrul Rinpoche* (2003), vol. 8, p. 317.

Advice to Myself: *Collected Works of Patrul Rinpoche* (2003), vol. 8, p. 286.

Adzom Drukpa's Dilemma: Oral account of Khenpo Pema Wangyal, with additional details from Adzom Gyalse Gyurme Dorje, Biography of Adzom Drukpa.

After Patrul's Death: Dodrup Tenpai Nyima, *Dewdrop of Amrita;* Khenpo Kunpel, *Elixir of Faith.*

Among You Three Great Masters: Oral account of Nyoshul Khen Rinpoche, with additional details from Tulku Urgyen Rinpoche, *Blazing Splendor,* pp. 51–52.

Animate and Inanimate Dances: Adapted from Khenpo Ngawang Palzang, *Wondrous Dance of Illusion,* pp. 30–31, with slight modifications.

Another Offering of Silver: Oral account of Nyoshul Khen Rinpoche.

Beggars and Mani-Stone Carvers: Khenpo Kunpel, *Elixir of Faith.*

Beginnings: Dodrup Tenpai Nyima, *Dewdrop of Amrita;* Khenpo Kunpel, *Elixir of Faith.*

The Boulder Reminder: Khenpo Kunpel, *Elixir of Faith.*

Calling the Lama from Afar: *Collected Works of Patrul Rinpoche* (2003), vol. 5, pp. 94–99.

Chöying Rangdröl Demonstrates Higher Perception: Oral account of Nyoshul Khen Rinpoche.

The Crucial Points of Practice: *Collected Works of Patrul Rinpoche* (2003), vol. 3, p. 127.

Developing Empathy, Understanding Emptiness: Oral account of Nyoshul Khen Rinpoche.

Do Khyentse Takes Patrul by Surprise: Dodrup Tenpai Nyima, *Dewdrop of Amrita;* oral accounts of Dilgo Khyentse Rinpoche and Nyoshul Khen Rinpoche.

Do Khyentse's Hospitality: Oral accounts of Dilgo Khyentse Rinpoche and Nyoshul Khen Rinpoche; Dodrup Tenpai Nyima, *Dewdrop of Amrita;* Khenpo Kunpel, *Elixir of Faith.*

Drive Them Off with Stones: *Collected Works of Patrul Rinpoche* (2003), vol. 8, p. 280.

Estimations and Rankings: Oral account of Dilgo Khyentse Rinpoche.

Far-Reaching Effects of Patrul's Teachings: Oral account of Nyoshul Khen Rinpoche, with additional details from Khenpo Ngawang Palzang, *Wondrous Dance of Illusion,* p. 29.

First Teaching of the 3rd Dodrupchen: Oral account of Tulku Thondup Rinpoche.

Flowers Magically Appear: Oral account of Nyoshul Khen Rinpoche; Dodrup Tenpai Nyima, *Dewdrop of Amrita.*

Food for a Day Is Plenty: Khenpo Kunpel, *Elixir of Faith.*

The Gift from Lungtok's Mother: Oral account of Nyoshul Khen Rinpoche, with additional details from Khenpo Ngawang Palzang, *Wondrous Dance of Illusion,* p. 29.

The Great Master Patrul: Oral account of Nyoshul Khen Rinpoche.

Gyalwa Changchup's Prediction: Oral account of Nyoshul Khen Rinpoche.

The Haunted Fortress: Oral account of Dilgo Khyentse Rinpoche.

How Patrul Taught at the Willow Hermitage: Oral account of Khenpo Könchog Mönlam, who was told the story by Kunu Rinpoche.

Infant Patrul: Dodrup Tenpai Nyima, *Dewdrop of Amrita;* Khenpo Kunpel, *Elixir of Faith.*

An Insight into Patrul's Mind: Dodrup Tenpai Nyima, *Dewdrop of Amrita.*

Introduction: Biographical details adapted from Dilgo Khyentse Rinpoche, *Heart Treasure of the Enlightened Ones,* trans. Padmakara Translation Group (Boston: Shambhala Publications, 1992).

Jamyang Khyentse Wangpo Countermands Patrul's Advice: Adapted from Tulku Urgyen Rinpoche, *Blazing Splendor,* pp. 253–54; additional details from Chökyi Nyima, *The Union of Mahamudra and Dzogchen,* p. 158.

Jigme Gyalwai Nyugu and the Harmful Spirit: Oral account of Dilgo Khyentse Rinpoche.

Just Sitting on His Bed: Oral account of Khenpo Jampel Dorje.

Karmai Khenpo Rinchen Dargye Requests Teachings: Oral account of Nyoshul Khen Rinpoche.

The Key to Practice: Adapted from Khenpo Ngawang Palzang, *Wondrous Dance of Illusion,* p. 28.

Khenchen Tashi Özer Tries to See Patrul: Oral account of Dilgo Khentse Rinpoche; Khenpo Kunpel, *Elixir of Faith;* and Tulku Urgyen's *Blazing Splendor.*

Khenpo Könchog Drönme Tries to See Patrul: Adapted from Tulku Thondup, *Masters of Meditation and Miracles,* pp. 231–2.

The Land of the Insect-Eaters: Translated from the Tibetan text of Nyoshul Khyen Rinpoche, *rang bzhin rdzogs pa chen po'i chos 'byung rig 'dzin brgyud pa'i rnam thar ngo mtshar nor bu'i bedurya'i phreng ba* (A Marvelous Garland of Rare Gems), vol. 2, folio 153a. Kathmandu: Samye Memorial Institute, 1996.

Last Days and Hours: Dodrup Tenpai Nyima, *Dewdrop of Amrita;* Khenpo Kunpel, *Elixir of Faith.*

Little Monk: Oral account of Nyoshul Khen Rinpoche.

Lo-nga Tulku and Patrul's Carpet: Oral account of Nyoshul Khen Rinpoche.

Longing for Solitudes: *Collected Works of Patrul Rinpoche* (2003), vol. 8, p. 275.

The Lotus-Grove Play: Oral account of Dilgo Khyentse Rinpoche and verses translated from Patrul Rinpoche's *gtam pad ma tshal gyi zlos gar, Collected Works of Patrul Rinpoche* (2003), vol. 1, pp. 301–55.

Lungtok and the Bandit Chief: Oral account of Garchen Rinpoche.

Lungtok Learns Backward: Oral account of Nyoshul Khen Rinpoche.

Lungtok Leaves His Lama: Adapted from Khenpo Ngawang Palzang, *Wondrous Dance of Illusion,* p. 198, with additional details from Tulku Urgyen Chemchog.

Lungtok Meets His Root Master: Oral account of Nyoshul Khen Rinpoche.

Lungtok Practices in the Glacier Wilderness: Adapted from Khenpo Ngawang Palzang, *Wondrous Dance of Illusion,* pp. 27–28.

Lungtok's Dream: Adapted from Khenpo Ngawang Palzang, *Wondrous Dance of Illusion,* p. 82; oral account of Nyoshul Khen Rinpoche.

Lungtok's Mother: Oral account of Nyoshul Khen Rinpoche.

Meeting the 3rd Dodrupchen: Khenpo Kunpel, *Elixir of Faith.*

A Meeting of Two Minds: Dodrup Tenpai Nyima, *Dewdrop of Amrita;* Khenpo Kunpel, *Elixir of Faith.*

Meeting with a Yogi: Tulku Urgyen, *Blazing Splendor,* p. 256.

A Monk Makes a Full Confession: Oral account of Khenpo Könchog Mönlam, who was told the story by Kunu Rinpoche.

Nine Brothers Delight Patrul: Oral account of Dilgo Khyentse Rinpoche.

An Offering of Silver: Oral account of Dilgo Khyentse Rinpoche.

On the Nature of Mind: Excerpt from *theg mchog ati'i man ngag gnas lugs gsal ston, Collected Works of Patrul Rinpoche* (2003), vol. 5, pp. 179–81, 193.

One Taste: *Collected Works of Patrul Rinpoche* (2003), vol. 8, p. 286.

The Palge Lineage: Dodrup Tenpai Nyima, *Dewdrop of Amrita;* Khenpo Kunpel, *Elixir of Faith.*

The Palge Tulku Goes His Own Way: Dodrup Tenpai Nyima, *Dewdrop of Amrita.*

Patrul Accepts What He Is Given: Oral accounts of Dilgo Khyentse Rinpoche and Nyoshul Khen Rinpoche; Dodrup Tenpai Nyima, *Dewdrop of Amrita;* Khenpo Kunpel, *Elixir of Faith.*

Patrul and Chokgyur Lingpa: *Blazing Splendor,* pp. 83–84, with additional details from the oral account of Nyoshul Khen Rinpoche.

Patrul and Chokgyur Lingpa's Yellow Parchment: Oral account of Dilgo Khyentse Rinpoche.

Patrul and Jamyang Khyentse Wangpo: Oral account of Nyoshul Khen Rinpoche.

Patrul and Lama Mipham: Oral account of Dilgo Khyentse Rinpoche.

Patrul and the Learned Geshe: I am no longer certain of who told me this story, but it could be from Changsar Gönpo Tulku Khyenrap Gyatso.

Patrul and the Paramita of Patience: Oral account of Nyoshul Khen Rinpoche.

Patrul and the Prescient Monk: Oral account of Yantang Rinpoche.

Patrul and the Three Dargye Monks: Oral account of Nyoshul Khen Rinpoche.

Patrul and the Tossed Louse: Oral account of Khenpo Jampel Dorje.

Patrul and the Venue of Vultures: Oral account of Tulku Urgyen Chemchog.

Patrul and the Widow: Oral account of Nyoshul Khen Rinpoche.

Patrul Asks the Great Kathok Situ for a Favor: Oral accounts of Dilgo Khyentse Rinpoche and Nyoshul Khen Rinpoche.

Patrul Begs for More Beggars: Khenpo Kunpel, *Elixir of Faith.*

Patrul Expresses Confidence in Chokgyur Lingpa: Oral account of Nyoshul Khen Rinpoche; Dodrup Tenpai Nyima, *Dewdrop of Amrita;* Khenpo Kunpel, *Elixir of Faith;* Tulku Urgyen, *Blazing Splendor,* p. 84.

Patrul Finds His Limit: Adapted from Khenpo Ngawang Palzang, *Wondrous Dance of Illusion,* p. 77.

Patrul Gives Away a Fine Mandala: Oral account of Dilgo Khyentse Rinpoche, who was told the story by Khenpo Thubga (mkhan po thub dga', 1886–1956).

Patrul Gives Teachings in the Forest: Oral account of Nyoshul Khen Rinpoche; additional details from Khenpo Ngawang Palzang, *Wondrous Dance of Illusion,* p. 30.

Patrul Goes Begging for Food: Oral account of Dilgo Khyentse Rinpoche and several others.

Patrul in Awe: Oral account of Khenpo Shönri.

Patrul Introduces Lungtok to the Nature of Mind: Adapted from Khenpo Ngawang Palzang, *Wondrous Dance of Illusion,* p. 82, and oral account of Nyoshul Khen Rinpoche.

Patrul Is Asked to Bestow Special Teachings: Oral account of Khenpo Pema Wangyal; additional details from Adzom Gyalse Gyurme Dorje, Biography of Adzom Drukpa.

Patrul Is Distraught: Oral account of Khenpo Tsering Gonpo.

Patrul Is Taught His Own Teachings: Oral account of Nyoshul Khen Rinpoche.

Patrul Is Tricked by a Nomad Family: Oral account of Khenpo Könchog Mönlam, who was told the story by Kunu Rinpoche.

Patrul Is Tricked by Another Nomad Family: Oral account of Khenpo Könchog Mönlam, who was told the story by Kunu Rinpoche.

Patrul Is Upset and Disappears: Oral account of Nyoshul Khen Rinpoche.

Patrul Judges a Great Debate: Oral account of Dilgo Khyentse Rinpoche.

Patrul Laughs Over an Old Man's Corpse: Oral account of Nyoshul Khen Rinpoche; Khenpo Kunpel, *Elixir of Faith.*

Patrul Leaves Dzogchen Monastery: Oral account of Dilgo Khyentse Rinpoche.

Patrul Lectures Himself on His Practice: Oral account of Trogawa Rinpoche.

Patrul Meets an Exemplary Monk: Oral account of Nyoshul Khen Rinpoche, with details about Patrul's visit to Dzamthang from Dodrup Tenpai Nyima, *Dewdrop of Amrita.*

Patrul Meets Two Murderers: Oral account of Dilgo Khyentse Rinpoche, with some details from Khenpo Pema Wangyal of Gemang Monastery.

Patrul Mentions His Past Lives: Dodrup Tenpai Nyima, *Dewdrop of Amrita;* Khenpo Kunpel, *Elixir of Faith.*

Patrul on Having Things: Oral account of Dilgo Khyentse Rinpoche.

Patrul Pacifies a Blood Feud: Oral account of Nyoshul Khen Rinpoche; additional details about Patrul's teaching in that area from Dodrup Tenpai Nyima, *Dewdrop of Amrita.*

Patrul Paints Some Tormas: Oral account of Nyoshul Khen Rinpoche.

Patrul Passes Dargye Monastery Again: Oral account of Khenpo Jampel Dorje.

Patrul Practices in a Haunted Charnel Ground: Oral account of Nyoshul Khen Rinpoche.

Patrul Practices in the Ari Forest Wilderness: Oral account of Nyoshul Khen Rinpoche.

Patrul Practices Tummo in a Blizzard: Oral account of Tulku Urgyen Chemchog.

Patrul Practices Yoga: Khenpo Kunpel, *Elixir of Faith.*

Patrul Reads Tertön Sogyal's Mind: Oral account of Nyoshul Khen.

Patrul Receives a Special Transmission: Dodrup Tenpai Nyima, *Dewdrop of Amrita;* Khenpo Kunpel, *Elixir of Faith;* and oral account of Dilgo Khyentse Rinpoche.

Patrul Receives an Extraordinary Guest: Oral account of Garchen Rinpoche.

Patrul Receives Lo-nga Tulku: Oral account of Dilgo Khyentse Rinpoche.

Patrul Receives Teachings from an Old Lama: Oral account of Khenpo Könchog Mönlam, who was told the story by Kunu Rinpoche.

Patrul Receives Teachings from the Mahasiddha of Trom: Oral account of Nyoshul Khen Rinpoche.

Patrul Takes On a Powerful Adversary: Khenpo Kunpel, *Elixir of Faith.*

Patrul Takes Tea with a Little Girl: Oral account of Dilgo Khyentse Rinpoche.

Patrul Teaches Khenpo Yönten Gyatso: Oral account of Dilgo Khyentse Rinpoche, passed on by Khenpo Thubga; additional details from Khenpo Pema Wangyal of Gemang Monastery.

Patrul Teaches the Great Perfection at Trama Lung: Dodrup Tenpai Nyima, *Dewdrop of Amrita.*

Patrul the Scholar: Tulku Urgyen Rinpoche, *Blazing Splendor,* p. 253; additional details from Chökyi Nyima, *The Union of Mahamudra and Dzogchen,* p. 157.

Patrul Travels in an Unusual Way: Oral account of Khenpo Palga.

Patrul Tries to Meet Shabkar: Oral accounts of Dilgo Khyentse Rinpoche and Nyoshul Khen Rinpoche. The Shabkar verse translation is by Matthieu Ricard. The first stanza is from pp. 102–3 of *The Life of Shabkar: The Autobiography of a Tibetan Yogin* (Albany: State University of New York Press, 1994, reprinted 2001 by Snow Lion), and the second stanza from p. 535.

Patrul Tries to Offer Prostrations: Oral account of Dilgo Khyentse Rinpoche.

Patrul Waits in Line to Receive a Blessing: Oral accounts of Nyoshul Khen Rinpoche and Tulku Pema Wangyal (Taklung Tsetrul Pema Wangyal Rinpoche).

Patrul's Dedication to Practice: Adapted, with material from the original Tibetan text, from Khenpo Ngawang Palzang, *Wondrous Dance of Illusion,* p. 77.

Patrul's Encampment: Based on Tsoknyi Rinpoche, *Fearless Simplicity: The Dzogchen Way of Living Freely in a Complex World,* trans. Erik Pema Kunsang, p. 29, with a quotation from *Words of My Perfect Teacher,* p. 130.

Patrul's Gift of Tea: Oral account of Dilgo Khyentse Rinpoche.

Patrul's Last Great Public Ganachakra: Khenpo Kunpel, *Elixir of Faith.*

Patrul's Miraculous Recovery: Dodrup Tenpai Nyima, *Dewdrop of Amrita.*

Patrul's Offering to the Horseflies: Khenpo Kunpel, *Elixir of Faith;* oral account of Nyoshul Khen Rinpoche.

Patrul's Pain: Oral account of Nyoshul Khen Rinpoche.

Patrul's Patrician Manners: Oral account of Tulku Thondup Rinpoche.

Patrul's Pointing-Out Instruction for an Old Nomad: Oral account of Nyoshul Khen Rinpoche.

Patrul's Respect for the Natural Course of the Elements: Khenpo Kunpel, *Elixir of Faith,* and *Collected Works of Patrul Rinpoche* (2003), vol. 1, pp. 520–21.

Patrul's Root Guru: Dodrup Tenpai Nyima, *Dewdrop of Amrita;* Khenpo Kunpel, *Elixir of Faith.*

Patrul's Rude Manners: Oral account of Yangtang Rinpoche.

Patrul's Teacher Demonstrates Clairvoyance: Oral account of Dilgo Khyentse Rinpoche.

Patrul's Teachings Inspire All Beings: Dodrup Tenpai Nyima, *Dewdrop of Amrita.*

Patrul's Unique Qualities: Dodrup Tenpai Nyima, *Dewdrop of Amrita;* Khenpo Kunpel, *Elixir of Faith.*

A Piece of Advice: *Collected Works of Patrul Rinpoche* (2003), vol. 8, pp. 358–59.

The Quick-Thinking Lama: Oral account of Khenpo Palga.

The Return of Wangchok Dorje: Pema Trinley, who lived until ninety, told this story to Tulku Urgyen Rinpoche when he was a child. See Tulku Urgyen Rinpoche, *Blazing Splendor,* p. 69. Additional details from the oral account of Orgyen Tobgyal Rinpoche.

A Robber Sets His Sights on an Offering of Silver: Oral account of Nyoshul Khen Rinpoche.

Second Visit of the 3rd Dodrupchen: Oral account of Tulku Thondup Rinpoche.

Seeking an Audience with a Very Important Lama: Oral account of Nyoshul Khen Rinpoche.

Seeking an Audience with Another Very Important Lama: Oral account of Nyoshul Khen Rinpoche.

Some Love Him, Some Fear Him: Oral account of Khenpo Jampel Dorje.

"That's It!": Based on Khenpo Ngawang Palzang, *Wondrous Dance of Illusion,* p. 29.

Trama Tulku Receives Instructions: Khenpo Kunpel, *Elixir of Faith.*

A Tulku Has a Change of Name: Oral account of Khenpo Palga.

Two of a Kind: Oral account of Dilgo Khyentse Rinpoche.

Visible Effects of Yoga: Adapted from Dilgo Khyentse, *Brilliant Moon,* p. 87.

Wangchok Dorje's Renunciation: Adapted from Tulku Urgyen Rinpoche, *Blazing Splendor,* pp. 67–69; Orgyen Tobgyal Rinpoche, *The Life of Chokgyur Lingpa,* p. 26; oral account of Orgyen Tobgyal Rinpoche.

Words of Warning: *Collected Works of Patrul Rinpoche* (2003), vol. 8, p. 143.

"You've Ruined It!" Based on Tulku Thondup, *Masters of Meditation and Miracles,* pp. 209–10.

Sources for Biographical Notes

The sources below have not been quoted verbatim but were used to summarize and adapt information about the masters, disciples, and other figures in the Biographical Notes section.

ADZOM DRUKPA: Based on Alexander Gardner and Samten Chhosphel, "The First Adzom Drukpa, Drodul Pawo Dorje" (2009), http://treasuryoflives.org/biographies/view/Adzom-Drukpa-Pawo-Dorje/8574 (accessed October 2016).

ALAK DO-NGAK GYATSO: Based on Adam Pearcey, "Japa Dongak Gyatso" (2014), http://treasuryoflives.org/biographies/view/Japa-Dongak-Gyatso/12785 (accessed October 2016).

CHOKGYUR DECHEN LINGPA: Summarized and adapted with permission from *The Life of Chokgyur Lingpa,* told by Orgyen Tobgyal Rinpoche and translated by Tulku Jigmey Khyentse and Erik Pema Kunsang. Rangjung Yeshe Publications e-book available at http://padmasambhavagururinpoche.com/wp-content/uploads/2015/11/Chokgyur_Lingpa_Life-1.pdf (accessed October 2016).

CHÖYING RANGDRÖL: Biography of Chöying Rangdröl: *rgyal ba kah thog pa'i snyan brgyud 'dzin pa kun gyi gtsug rgyan mtsho phu sgrub chen 'gyur med chos dbyings rang grol gyi rnam thar snying bsdus dad pa'i chu gter,* written by Kyungtrul Tsewang Dorje (khyung sprul tshe dbang rdo rje), published by the Nyakrong Tsozig Monastery Publishing House (nyag rong mtsho gzigs dgon pa'i dpe tshogs), ca. 2013.

DO KHYENTSE YESHE DORJE: Based on Tulku Thondup, *Masters of Meditation and Miracles,* with some material added. See also the autobiography of Do Khyentse, *rig 'dzin 'jigs med gling p'ai yang srid sngags 'chang 'ja lus rdo rje'i rnam thar mkha' 'gro'i zhal lung* (Sichuan Minorities Press, 1997).

DOLA JIGME KALZANG: Oral tradition from Kyala Khenpo, based on Tulku Thondup, *Masters of Meditation and Miracles,* pp. 172–73; oral account of Dilgo Khyentse Rinpoche.

GYALSE SHENPHEN THAYE: Khetsun Zangpo, Biographical Dictionary of Tibet and Tibetan Buddhism; Karma Delek, Biography of Gyalse Shenphen Thaye: *rgyal sras gzhan phan mtha' yas kyi mdzad rnam mdor bsdus in rgyud sgyu 'phrul drwa ba rtsa rgyud gsang ba snying po'i 'grel pa kun bzang thigs kyi ti ka* (Tibetan People's Publishing House, bod ljongs mi dmangs dpe skrun khang, 2008); Khenpo Shenga, Biography of Önpo Tendzin Norbu: *dpal ldan dam pa'i thun mong phy'i rnam par thar pa mdor bsdus su bkod pa dad pa'i 'jug ngogs* (Gemang Monastery, 2007); and Rigpa Shedra Wiki, www.rigpawiki.org/ (accessed October 2016).

GYURME PEMA NAMGYAL: Matthieu Ricard, Preface to *Collected Works of Shechen Gyaltsap Pema Gyurme Namgyal* (Delhi: Shechen Publications, 1997).

JAMGÖN KONGTRUL: Oral teachings from Dilgo Khyentse Rinpoche; E. Gene Smith, *Among Tibetan Texts: History and Literature of the Himalayan Plateau* (Somerville, Mass.: Wisdom Publications, 2001); *The Autobiography of Jamgön Kongtrul: A Gem of Many Colors,* trans. Richard Barron (Ithaca, N.Y.: Snow Lion, 2003); Alexander Gardner, "Jamgon Kongtrul Lodro Taye" (2015), http://treasuryoflives.org/biographies/view/Jamgon-Kongtrul-Lodro-Taye/4358 (accessed October 2016).

JAMYANG KHYENTSE WANGPO: Jamgön Kongtrul, *The Life of Jamyang Khyentse Wangpo,* trans. M. Akester (New Delhi: Shechen Publications, 2012); Alexander Gardner, "Jamyang Khyentse Wangpo" (2010), http://treasuryoflives.org/biographies/view/Jamyang-Khyentse-Wangpo/4291 (accessed October 2016); Nyoshul Khenpo Jamyang Dorje, *A Marvelous Garland of Rare Gems: Biographies of Masters of Awareness in the Dzogchen Lineage,* trans. Richard Barron (Padma Publishing, 2005); and oral tradition from Dilgo Khyentse Rinpoche.

JIGME GYALWAI NYUGU: Based on Gyalwai Nyugu website, http://www.gyalwai-nyugu.com/jigme-gyalwai-nyugu/, as well as on the Tibetan biography of Jigme Gyalwai Nyugu: *'gro mgon bla ma rje'i gsang gsum rnam thar rgya mtsho las thun mong phyi'i mngon rtogs rgyal sras lam bzang* (New Delhi: Shechen Publications, 2004).

JIGME LINGPA: Based on various Tibetan sources and oral teachings by Dilgo Khyentse Rinpoche.

JIGME NGOTSAR GYATSO: Summarized from "The Story of Kilung Monastery," www.kilung.org/the-story-of-kilung-monastery/ (accessed October 2016); and oral sources.

JIGME PHUNTSOK JUNGNE: Based on Tulku Thondup, *Masters of Meditation and Miracles,* pp. 211–14; and oral traditions.

JIGME TENPAI NYIMA: Based on Tulku Thondup, *Masters of Meditation and Miracles,* pp. 237–50, and *rang bzhin rdzogs pa chen po'i chos 'byung rig 'dzin brgyud pa'i rnam thar ngo mtshar nor bu'i bedurya'i phreng ba* (published in English as *A Marvelous Garland of Rare Gems*) by Nyoshul Khen Rinpoche.

JIGME TRINLEY ÖZER: Summarized from Ron Garry, "The First Dodrubchen, Jigme Trinle Ozer" (2007), https://treasuryoflives.org/biographies/view/Jigme-Trinle-Ozer/P293 (accessed October 2016), and other sources.

KARMAI KHENPO RINCHEN DARGYE: Based on "Karmey Khenpo Rinchen Dargye," http://rywiki.tsadra.org/index.php/Karmey_Khenpo_Rinchen_Dargye (accessed October 2016).

KATHOK SITU: "Petit compendium chronologique de maîtres spirituels et grands érudits du bouddhisme tibétain" (Small Chronological Compendium of Indian and Tibetan Buddhist Masters), www.matthieuricard.org/articles/petit-compendium-chronologique-de-maitres-spirituels-et-grands-erudits-du-bouddhisme-tibetain. For the Zi story, oral account of Nyoshul Khen Rinpoche.

Khenchen Tashi Özer: Based on "Khenchen Tashi Ozer" (from *dus 'khor chos 'byung indra ni la'i phra tshom* [History of Kalachakra], by Khenpo Lodrö Dönyö, pp. 555–58), Rangjung Yeshe Wiki, http://rywiki.tsadra.org/index.php/Khenchen_Tashi_Ozer (accessed October 2016).

Khenpo Kunzang Palden: Based on "Kunzang Pelden" by Samten Chhosphel (2012) at www.treasuryoflives.org/biographies/view/Kunzang-Pelden/9593 (accessed October 2016), with additional material from the author.

Khenpo Pema Dorje: Based on Adam Pearcey, "Pema Vajra" (2012), http://treasuryoflives.org/biographies/view/Pema-Vajra/9355 (accessed October 2016).

Khenpo Shenphen Chökyi Nangwa: Matthieu Ricard, Preface to the commentaries by Khenpo Shenphen Chökyi Nangwa on the *Thirteen Great Treatises* (*gzhung chen bcu gsum*) (Delhi: Könchog Lhadrepa, 1993).

Khenpo Yönten Gyatso: Written by Matthieu Ricard from various notes.

Lama Mipham Rinpoche: Based on numerous written and oral sources, including the biography of Lama Mipham Jamyang Namgyal Gyatso written in Tibetan by Dilgo Khyentse Rinpoche (see Written Sources, below).

Longchen Rabjam: *The Life of Longchenpa*, compiled and edited by Jampa Mackenzie Stewart (Boston: Shambhala Publications, 2014); Stephane Arguillère, *Profusion de la vaste sphère: La vie et l'oeuvre de Klong-chen rab 'byams* (Leuven, Belgium: Peeters Publishers, 2007).

Mingyur Namkhai Dorje: Based on Samten Chhosphel, "The Fourth Dzogchen Drubwang, Mingyur Namkhai Dorje" (2011), http://treasuryoflives.org/biographies/view/Dzogchen-Drubwang-04-Mingyur-Namkai-Dorje/3020 (accessed October 2016); Tulku Thondup, *Masters of Meditation and Miracles*, pp. 175–78; and an oral story heard from Dilgo Khyentse Rinpoche.

Minyak Kunzang Sönam: Written by Matthieu Ricard from various notes.

Nyoshul Lungtok: Based on "Nyoshul Lungtok Tenpé Nyima," www.rigpawiki.org/index.php?title=Nyoshul_Lungtok_Tenpé_Nyima (accessed October 2016), slightly modified and completed with additional details.

Önpo Orgyen Tendzin Norbu: Excerpts and summary of the biography of Önpo Tenga written at the request of Mipham Rinpoche by Khenpo Shenphen Nangwa (Shenga), who accompanied Önpo Tenga for thirteen years. Translated by Matthieu Ricard.

Pema Dechen Zangpo: Based on "Mura Rinpoche," http://rywiki.tsadra.org/index.php/Mura_Rinpoche (accessed October 2016), and oral accounts told to Matthieu Ricard by Dilgo Khyentse Rinpoche.

Rogza Sönam Palge, Drupwang: Summarized from Tulku Dakpa, "The Biography of Drubwang Rogza Palge Rinpoche" (http://tdr.bio/previous-life/), and oral sources.

Shabkar Tsogdruk Rangdröl: Matthieu Ricard, trans., *The Life of Shabkar: The Autobiography of a Tibetan Yogin* (Albany: State University of New York Press, 1994, reprinted 2001 by Snow Lion).

Shechen Öntrul Gyurme Thutop Namgyal: Dorje Rabten, Biography of Shechen Öntrul: *mkhas shing dngos grub brnyes pa'i rdo rje slob dpon 'jam dbyangs dgyes pa'i blo gros mtsho skyes bshad pa'i sgra dbyangs kyi rtogs brjod mdor bsdus pa skal bzang mgul rgyan* (New Delhi: Shechen Publications, 2000); as well as Tendzin Kunzang Lungtok Tenpai Nyima (bstan 'dzin kun bzang lung rtogs bstan pa'i nyi ma), *snga 'gyur rdzogs chen chos 'byung chen mo snga 'gyur grub dbang rgyal ba rdzogs chen pa'i gdan rabs chos brgyud dang bcas pa'i byung ba brjod pa'i gtam yid bzhin dbang gi rgyal po'i phreng ba* (Beijing: khang krung go'i bod rig pa dpe skrun khang, 2004).

Written Sources

Works in Tibetan

Adzom Gyalse Gyurme Dorje. Biography of Adzom Drukpa: *rje btsun grub pa'i dbang phyug rig 'dzin 'gro 'dul dpa' bo rdo rje'i rnam thar skal bzang yid kyi gdung sel*. Written by his son Adzom Gyalse Rigdzin Gyurme Dorje (a 'dzoms rgyal sras rig 'dzin 'gyur me rdo rje, 1895–ca. 1959), at the behest of Dzongsar Khyentse Chökyi Lodrö and others, at Adzom Chöjor, Tashi Gopher Ling (bkra shis dge 'phel gling) in the wood bird year (1945).

Dilgo Khyentse Rinpoche. Biography of Lama Mipham Jamyang Namgyal Gyatso: *gsang chen chos kyi shing rta 'jigs med smra ba'i seng ge kun mkhyen bla ma mi pham 'jam dbyangs rnam rgyal rgya mtsho'i rnam thar snying po bsdus pa ngo mtshar bdud rtsi'i snang ba. 144 pages*. New Delhi: Shechen Publications, 2014.

Dodrup Tenpai Nyima (Dodrupchen Jigme Tenpai Nyima, 3rd Dodrupchen). Dewdrop of Amrita (biography of Patrul Rinpoche): *mtshungs bral rgyal ba'i myu gu o rgyan 'jigs med chos kyi dbang po'i rtogs brjod phyogs tsam gleng ba bdud rtsi'i zil thigs*. In the Collected Works (*gsung 'bum*) of Dodrupchen Jigme Tenpai Nyima, vol. 4, pp. 115–46. Gangtok, Sikkim: Dodrupchen Rinpoche, 1974–1975.

Jigme Lingpa. Adzom Chögar (a 'dzom chos sgar) redaction of the Collected Works of Kunkhyen Jigme Lingpa Rangjung Dorje Khyentse Özer (kun mkhyen 'jigs med gling pa ran byung rdo rje mkhyen brtse'i 'od zer). 14 vols. Paro, Bhutan: Lama Ngodrup and Sherab Demy, 1985 (now under the umbrella of Shechen Publications).

Karma Delek. Biography of Gyalse Shenphen Thaye: *rgyal sras gzhan phan mtha' yas kyi mdzad rnam mdor bsdus in rgyud sgyu 'phrul drwa ba rtsa rgyud gsang ba snying po'i 'grel pa kun bzang thigs kyi ti ka*. Lhasa: Tibetan People's Publishing House (bod ljongs mi dmangs dpe skrun khang), 2008.

Khenpo Kunpel (Kunzang Palden, mkhan po kun bzang dpal ldan). Elixir of Faith (biography of Patrul Rinpoche): *rdza dpal sprul gyi rnam thar dad pa'i gsos sman bdud rtsi'i bum bcud*. New Delhi: Konchhog Lhadrepa, 1997.

Khenpo Ngawang Palzang (mkhan po ngag dbang dpal bzang). Autobiography of Khenpo Ngawang Palzang: *ngag dbang dpal bzang gi rnam thar: 'od gsal snying po padma las 'brel rtsal gyi rtogs brjod ngo mtshar sgyu ma'i rol gar*. Bir, India: Tsondu Senghe, 1983. (Published in English as *Wondrous Dance of Illusion*.)

Khenpo Shenga (Khenpo Shenphen Chökyi Nangwa). Biography of Önpo Orgyen Tendzin Norbu: *dpal ldan dam pa'i thun mong phy'i rnam par thar pa mdor bsdus su bkod pa dad pa'i 'jug ngogs*. Published by Khenpo Dönnyi at Gemang Monastery, 2007.

Khetsun Sangpo, comp. Biographical Dictionary of Tibet and Tibetan Buddhism: *bod du sgrub brgyad shing rta mched brgyad las*. 13 vols. Library of Tibetan Works and Archives, 1973–1981.

Nyoshul Khenpo (Nyoshul Khen Rinpoche, Jamyang Dorje). A Marvelous Garland of Rare Gems: *rang bzhin rdzogs pa chen po'i chos 'byung rig 'dzin brgyud pa'i rnam thar ngo mtshar nor bu'i bedurya'i phreng ba*. 2 vols. Kathmandu: Samye Memorial Institute, 1996. English translation by Richard Barron: *A Marvelous Garland of Rare Gems: Biographies of Masters of Awareness in the Dzogchen Lineage*. Junction City, Calif.: Padma Publishing, 2005. French translation by Christian Bruyat: *L'Avènement de la Grande Perfection naturelle, ou La Merveilleuse Guirlande de joyaux des lignées des vidyadharas*. Plazac, France: Éditions Padmakara, 2016.

Patrul Rinpoche. Collected Works of Patrul Rinpoche: *dpal sprul o rgyan 'jigs med chos kyi dbang po'i gsung 'bum*. 8 vols. Chengdu, China: Si khron mi rigs dpe skrun khang, 2003, 2009.

Works in English

Chökyi Nyima. *The Union of Mahamudra and Dzogchen: A Commentary on "The Quintessence of Spiritual Practice: The Direct Instructions of the Great Compassionate One"* by Karma Chagme Rinpoche. Translated by Erik Pema Kunsang. Edited by Marcia B. Schmidt. Hong Kong: North Atlantic Books, 2004. (Root text is a translation of *'phags pa thugs rje chen po'i dmar khrid phyag rdzogs zung 'jug gi nyams len snying po bsdus pa bzhugs so*.)

Dilgo Khyentse Rinpoche. *Brilliant Moon: The Autobiography of Dilgo Khyentse*. Supplemented with testimonies from his students. Translated by Ani Jinpa Palmo. Boston: Shambhala Publications, 2008.

Dudjom Rinpoche. *The Nyingma School of Tibetan Buddhism: Its Fundamentals and History*. Translated by Gyurme Dorje. Somerville, Mass.: Wisdom Publications, 2005. (Translation of the *snga 'gyur rdo rje theg pa'i bstan pa rin po che'i ji ltar byung ba'i tshul*.)

Jampa Mackenzie Stewart (ed.). *The Life of Longchenpa: The Omniscient Dharma King of the Vast Expanse*. Boston: Shambhala Publications, 2014.

Khenpo Kunzang Palden (Khenpo Kunpel). *The Nectar of Manjushri's Speech: A Detailed Commentary on Shantideva's Way of the Bodhisattva*. 1st ed. Translated by the Padmakara Translation Group. Boston: Shambhala Publications, 2010.

Khenpo Ngawang Palzang. *Wondrous Dance of Illusion: The Autobiography of Khenpo Ngawang Palzang*. Translated from the Tibetan by Heidi L. Nevin and J. Jakob Leschly.

Edited by Gyurme Dorje. Ithaca, N.Y.: Snow Lion, 2013. (See listing for Tibetan edition above.)

Longchenpa. *Trilogy of Rest.* Vol. 1: *Finding Rest in the Nature of the Mind.* Translated by the Padmakara Translation Group. Boulder: Shambhala Publications, 2017.

______. *Trilogy of Rest.* Vol. 2: *Finding Rest in Meditative Absorption.* Translated by the Padmakara Translation Group. Boulder: Shambhala Publications, forthcoming.

Orgyen Tobgyal Rinpoche. *The Life of Chokgyur Lingpa* (1983). Translated by Tulku Jigmey Khyentse and Erik Pema Kunsang. 47 pages. Rangjung Yeshe Publications, 2000. http://padmasambhavagururinpoche.com/wp-content/uploads/2015/11/Chokgyur_Lingpa_Life-1.pdf (accessed October 2016).

Rigpa ShedraWiki. www.rigpawiki.org.

Shantideva. *The Way of the Bodhisattva:* A Translation of the *Bodhicharyavatara.* Rev. ed. Translated by the Padmakara Translation Group. Boston: Shambhala Publications (Shambhala Classics), 2006.

The Treasury of Lives. A biographical encyclopedia of Tibet, Inner Asia, and the Himalaya. http://treasuryoflives.org. Biographies by Alexander Gardner, Samten Chhosphel, Adam Pearcey, and Ron Gary.

Tsoknyi Rinpoche. *Fearless Simplicity: The Dzogchen Way of Living Freely in a Complex World.* Translated by Erik Pema Kunsang. Boudhanath and Hong Kong: North Atlantic Books, 2003.

Tulku Thondup. *Enlightened Living: Teachings of the Tibetan Buddhist Masters.* Boston: Shambhala Publications, 1990.

———. *Masters of Meditation and Miracles: Lives of the Great Buddhist Masters of India and Tibet.* Boston: Shambhala Publications, 1999.

Tulku Urgyen Rinpoche. *Blazing Splendor: The Memoirs of Tulku Urgyen Rinpoche.* Kathmandu: North Atlantic Books, 2005.

ACKNOWLEDGMENTS

MATTHIEU RICARD

I am immensely grateful to my root teachers, Kyabje Kangyur Rinpoche, Kyabje Dilgo Khyentse Rinpoche, and Taklung Tsetrul Pema Wangyal Rinpoche, and to many other great teachers, learned scholars, and practitioners, thanks to whom I came to learn of Patrul Rinpoche's life and teachings. It is indeed due to their kindness that I was able to conceive great devotion and confidence in this very unique master and aspired to know more about his life story and to read his teachings.

I was very fortunate to receive the reading transmission (lung) of Patrul Rinpoche's collected works from my root teacher, Kyabje Dilgo Khyentse Rinpoche, in 1987, at Drupwang Penor Rinpoche's monastery, Namdroling, in South India. (Dilgo Khyentse Rinpoche received the transmission of Patrul Rinpoche's collected works from Khenpo Söpa Tharching of Benchen Monastery.) From Khyentse Rinpoche I also heard many of the stories found in this book.

I am particularly grateful to Nyoshul Khen Rinpoche, Jamyang Dorje, who, while we were staying at Punakha in Bhutan, in the presence of Dilgo Khyentse Rinpoche, kindly spent several evenings telling me in great detail many of the oral stories that are found in this book. I was able to record these stories and translate them.

I am also thankful to Khenpo Orgyen, who later transcribed these recordings in Tibetan and published them in 2011, in a small booklet in Nepal, adding excerpts form Patrul Rinpoche's biography by Khenpo Kunpel. Thanks to these transcripts, I was able to correct a few points of the translation with precision.

I am also much indebted to the many masters, khenpos, lamas, and old practitioners whom I endlessly questioned about Patrul Rinpoche's life, especially in Kham.

Thank you, too, to my friends in Tibet with whom I traveled many times through Kham and Amdo, since 1985, visiting along the way the many places where Patrul Rinpoche and his teachers and disciples had lived. In this way, I was also able to meet a number of direct students of some of Patrul Rinpoche's direct disciples, as well as fourth-generation descendants of Patrul Rinpoche's sister Chungne (chung nas).

Dagpo Tulku Rinpoche, Sönam Gyaltsen, one of the most learned contemporary scholars, patiently answered the numerous questions I put to him in order to clarify many points of the stories and some difficult points of the teachings as well, giving me a bit more confidence in the reliability of the final version.

My thanks to Tulku Thondup Rinpoche for kindly reading through the manuscript and giving us some most useful suggestions.

I am very grateful to the Gere Foundation for their support, many years ago, in the preliminary editing of this work, and more recently to Eric Colombel and the Tsadra Foundation for their support to the final editing.

Thanks to the following for their generosity in allowing us to consult and adapt details from their work: Erik Pema Kunsang and Marcia Schmidt for material from Tulku Urgyen Rinpoche's *Blazing Splendor;* Heidi Nevin and Jakob Leschly for material from Khenpo Ngawang Palzang's *Wondrous Dance of Illusion;* Tulku Thondup Rinpoche for material from *Masters of Meditation and Miracles* and *Enlightened Living;* Chökyi Nyima Rinpoche and his translator, Erik Pema Kunsang, for material from *The Union of Mahamudra and Dzogchen;* the team and contributors of the remarkable website The Treasury of Lives (http://treasuryoflives.org/), in particular, Alexander Gardner, Samten Chhosphel, Adam Pearcey, and Ron Garry.

The Tibetan Buddhist Resource Center (http://tbrc.org/), founded by our late invaluable and irreplaceable friend E. G. Smith, has always been a most precious resource.

Countless thanks to Luciana Chiaravalli for so graciously, skillfully, and patiently creating the very intricate chart of Patrul Rinpoche's spiritual lineage as well as the chart of his family line.

Many thanks to Gyurme Dorje, Mike Farmer, and Kevin Feeney for allowing us to use, as a basis for our map of the places related to Patrul Rinpoche, the very fine maps included in Gyurme Dorje's *Footprint Tibet Handbook: The Travel Guide,* and for granting permission to modify and simplify these maps for our purpose.

Above all, I must offer my deep gratitude to Constance Wilkinson. While living in Nepal, she worked for four years as editor-in-chief of the complex 700-page translation of *The Life of Shabkar: The Autobiography of a Tibetan Yogin.* She and her family left Nepal in 1993; we had not been in touch since then. In 2012, I happened to call a friend, Susan, in New York. I heard Susan call out the name Constance in the background, and I said, "Constance Wilkinson?" Susan gave her the phone and we spoke, for the first time in decades. Somehow the subject of Patrul came up, all the many stories I had collected and teachings I had translated, and out of the blue she offered to help me finish this project that, although so dear to my heart, had lain unfinished for decades.

Following this auspicious coincidence, I sent her the rough transcription and translation of stories just as I'd heard them. She toiled over the years on reworking these original stories and on editing my translations of some poems and pieces of advice. Later, we added other stories, found in other sources. Once there was a rough manuscript, though we were on opposite sides of the world, we worked to bring the project together. Over the next year and a half we've been exchanging files over the Internet countless times, sending drafts back and forth over the continents, Skyping now and again, as we continued to refine the text, polish the translations, arrange the stories and teachings in a suitable order, check other available sources in Tibetan and English, and clarify as much of the chronology as possible in order to bring the text to its present shape.

Without her skills and perseverance, these stories might have continued to languish, unfinished. After having worked together on *The Life of Shabkar,* it was a joy to collaborate again on this inspiring collection, which we hope may bring benefit for all.

We are both grateful to Shambhala Publications, especially to Nikko Odiseos, for enthusiastically taking up this project and bringing it to publication.

A final and heartfelt thank-you to Kendra Crossen Burroughs for going through the whole manuscript with great care and competence; for meticulously checking the consistency of countless names of people, places, and texts; for making sure that anything that needed explanation or clarification would be taken care of; and for significantly improving the presentation of the text.

CONSTANCE WILKINSON

To my teachers, my deep gratitude.

To family and friends, my appreciative thanks.

I am very grateful to Eric Colombel of the Tsadra Foundation for his timely and generous support.

My thanks to Erik Pema Kunsang for his absolutely indispensable Rangjung Yeshe/Nitartha online Tibetan-English dictionary, featuring the work of so many fine translators, including Jim Valby, Ives Waldo, and Richard Barron. My thanks as well to Tony Duff for his indeed illuminating *Illuminator Tibetan-English Dictionary* (www.tibetanlanguage.org/PDF/illuminator.pdf) and his PKTC online dictionary (www.pktc.org/dictionary/).

Greg Moscatt, my patient and humorous husband, has been instrumental in creating the auspicious conditions for undertaking this work.

My thanks to Matthieu Ricard, patient and compassionate, for allowing me the privilege to work on this project, recounting the words and deeds of this extraordinary master.

In this collection of true stories, we have the possibility to encounter Patrul in all his many aspects: unpretentious Patrul, the wise and gentle; irreverent, mischievous trickster Patrul, acute and uncompromising; determined, diligent Patrul, who won't waste an instant, whose compassionate actions benefit beings however possible—teaching, writing, scolding, teasing, always inspiring—by whatever means a situation demands.

Relaxed and open, brave and aware, Dzogchen Patrul, relaxed yet alert, meets the challenge of any moment, whether skillfully outsmarting bullies, or hurling insults at himself, or feeding horseflies with his own blood, or graciously emptying bedpans.

Whoever's here—perfect!
Whatever happens—fine!
The Dzogchen yogi.

As long as space lasts,
And as long as beings exist,
May I, too, remain
To dissipate the suffering of the world!

SHANTIDEVA

INDEX

Owing to the many alternative names for Tibetan lamas, some names in the index have been alphabetized beginning with a title (e.g., Khenpo) in cases where such titles have been consistently used for particular individuals in the book. For the sake of brevity, we have not indexed the Biographical Notes or Glossary in the back matter.